Digital Hesitation

Why B2B Companies Aren't Reaching Their Full Potential

J.B. Wood
Thomas Lah
The TSIA Research Team

Table of Contents

1 | Digital Hesitation

By J.B. Wood and Thomas Lah

The predominant business model in an industry can change quickly. The rise of Netflix meant not only the death of Blockbuster, but it also constitutes a real threat to the future of movie theaters. The emergence of Uber didn't just hurt the taxi business, it contributed to the temporary bankruptcy of Hertz. And Amazon didn't just doom Barnes & Noble bookstores, it is threatening brick-and-mortar retail giants all over the world.

But we've always wondered...what was going through the minds of the executives at Hertz or Blockbuster at that time? Did they know their end was nigh? Did they realize their business model was being completely disrupted? Or did they just think they were losing a few orders?

Today almost every company is a tech company. And they are all riding a digital transformation (DT) wave that is disrupting the business and operating models of their industry. When DT marches through an industry, the results can be devastating to companies that are complacent. Digital capabilities upend the way customers buy and consume your products and services. Can you imagine being a bank without a mobile app today? A large retailer without an e-commerce site? And it's not just business-to-consumer (B2C) companies. Will there be enterprise tech providers of tomorrow with which a customer can't scope, price, and place a complex order online? Or industrial equipment providers that don't use predictive analytics to completely eliminate customer outages?

One of the reasons that the term "digital transformation" has become so popular is because it is so vague. You can stuff just about any kind of digital project or investment under its purview, and it sounds progressive. But the reality is that *meaningful* DT usually shows up differently in each industry. The nature of the pivotal projects and the outcomes they deliver are based on how disruptive certain technology products and projects can be to the status quo of a particular marketplace. In consumer retail, DT has been synonymous with e-commerce and supply chain; not a different type of business, a different way of going to market. But, in other B2C industries, like transportation and hospitality, DT has brought entirely new forms of competition in the form of breakthrough ridesharing or home-sharing business models.

So, to be valuable, this book must be targeted. It is aimed at technology and industrial product companies that serve business customers, commonly referred to as business-to-business (B2B) companies. While there are certainly lessons here for companies in other industries, the B2B sectors will be our focus.

Wait! Yet Another Book About Digital Transformation?

Before we go further, let us address a fair question: There is already a lot of literature about DT. So why are the perspectives in this book any better or more important?

Our company name, TSIA, stands for the Technology & Services Industry Association. We are an industry research firm that is under nondisclosure with hundreds of the world's leading public companies in hardware and software technology, as well as industrial, healthcare, and B2B/B2C professional service markets.

Each of these member companies agrees to provide non-public data to TSIA about its business practices and operating results. We have industry experts and data scientists who then compile and analyze that data. We are trying to answer a specific question: What business practices are working better than others *in the real world?* Then, we look at the actual financial and operating results being generated, and how much better they are than other practices that might not be considered best practices. Once we know there is a best practice that is actually worth pursuing, we identify the specific corporate capabilities that any one of our member companies would need to execute it. Armed with that insight, we can work with a specific company, tell it where it is today on the journey, what's missing, what's already good, what can be adapted, and what tactics, timelines, and returns it can expect along the way.

In short, TSIA has a unique perch. We have seen just about everything that is good, bad, and missing from the DT of hundreds of the globe's most important companies. That includes the new companies that are trying to disrupt the old ones, the old ones that are fighting off the new ones, and all the companies that see opportunity in software and the cloud. In short, we have unparalleled facts and insights that are derived from this amazing business community—probably more facts and more insight than any other source. And, most importantly, it's real-world stuff. We don't share a member company's data with the public, which includes customers, analysts, or the media. If a TSIA member company is exaggerating its performance to TSIA, then it is just wasting its money. It's how our model works; it's a clean, safe place to tell the truth about the challenges of business evolutions big and small, and then learn how the best companies in the world accelerate them. We are also obligated to connect dots that form patterns. If we combine what we see at one company with what we see at others, we can spot trends or possibilities, both productive and counterproductive, very early. Think of it as on-demand management insight.

Finally, TSIA is looking at DT from an executive leadership perspective, not an information technology (IT) perspective. While deciding, developing, and managing architectures, data models, applications, development operations, security, and so forth—are all critical to effective DT—we are assuming companies can get that job done. What we want executives to do with this book is to think big, and then effectively set the conditions for success.

The Migration We Predicted

Before we move ahead, we must first go back a few years. In 2013, we published a best-selling tech book titled *B4B: How Technology and Big Data Are Reinventing the Customer-Supplier Relationship.*[1] This book correctly predicted the (then) forthcoming evolution of B2B business models. Figure 1.1 shares a quick review.

The B4B Model

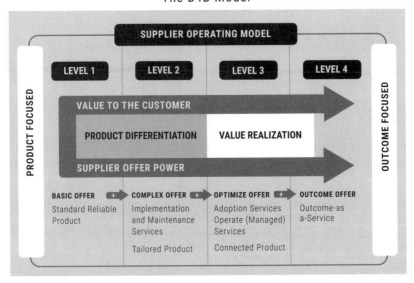

FIGURE 1.1 The B4B Model

The B4B model allows companies to place part or all their portfolio into one of four levels. The level then clarifies the key value premise to the customer and how it should compete against rival offers at the same level. Offers that are designed to compete at higher levels require more advanced product capabilities and services. Most B2B companies and their channel partners traditionally operated as Level 1 or Level 2 suppliers. The hallmark of offers that compete at Level 1 and Level 2 is that they are products (hardware, software, systems) that are sold to and operated by the customer. While the supplier may offer services to get or keep the product operational, the customer assumes all the risk of turning its big capital-expenditure (CapEx) purchase into business outcome return on investment (ROI). In layman's terms, the customer paid for it, and it works. Whether the customer uses it very much or extracts value from it is up to them.

Most technology and industrial companies today are well on their way to moving their portfolio away from Level 1 and Level 2. In most B2B industries, it's just not good enough anymore. Most companies are moving completely or partially to being a Level 3 supplier that effectively rents its technology as a subscription and whose services actively manage and optimize the customer's use of the technology to increase adoption and ROI success. Some are even experimenting with Level 4 sales discussions based on improving specific customer business outcomes. Level 3 and Level 4 suppliers are learning that there are a few characteristic pillars of these transformations:

- Their revenues shift from up-front transactions to recurring subscriptions (over a multiyear life cycle). That, according to the stock market, is a good thing.
- If the customer does not get the promised outcomes, they can stop subscribing. That is a bad thing.
- The supplier MUST be digitally connected to the customer via the product. That is a minimum requirement.

Digital Transformation: Wave One

These objectives—moving to recurring revenue and connected products, combined with classic IT activities, like moving workloads to the cloud and automating daily activities via new apps—constituted what we are calling Wave One of DT for most B2B tech and industrial companies. So, in the first wave of DT, technology providers started selling their technology as a service and got their technology more connected so that they had better visibility into what the customer was actually doing with the technology.

And the truth is, even after a decade, most companies are still navigating the Wave One journey. That was primarily a journey for legacy incumbents. They have spent many millions of dollars to migrate their business models, and they still have lots of work to do. They are amazed at how long it is taking. But the good news is this Wave One of DT is now well understood. As a result, we now have case studies to examine and healthy patterns to follow for Wave One transformation.

However, this book is called *Digital Hesitation*. In it we will spend time examining why most companies in Wave One of DT are under-performing. More importantly, we want to focus on what's coming next—about considering what "all the way" will look like on the journey to digitally transform your B2B company. So, if you are still struggling through the first wave of DT, you need to accept that a second wave is coming, and it's going to be more challenging than the first. This book will help born-in-the-cloud B2B companies to exploit their "clean slate" operating models. And, to be fair to everyone, it will also help large incumbents to defend their future.

Digital Transformation: Wave Two

As we watch these leading companies navigate the digital transformations of their industry, we can observe a few central themes. The first, as we mentioned, is that most are still actively on the Wave One journey. They are migrating their product portfolio to some form of subscription or consumption-based, recurring revenue model. They are also fully connected to (at least) their newer products. Some have done a better job than others about going back and connecting to older on-premises products in the field. In addition, they have implemented new cloud-based solutions for many of their main business applications and are moving some or all workloads to the cloud. Finally, they are beginning to pilot new service capabilities designed to accelerate customers through the land-adopt-expand-renew (APLAER) customer life cycle in order to improve adoption, stimulate expansion, and optimize renewals. (Note: APLAER is an update to TSIA's well known LAER model. Please refer to Chapter 6 for an explanation of APLAER.)

All good so far? (By the way, if your company is not already well along in all these journeys, we politely suggest that you are behind the curve.)

But, as this is happening in industry sector after industry sector, we are seeing the pattern shown in Figure 1.2 emerge—and it applies to companies both old and new.

Moving from Level 2 to Level 3

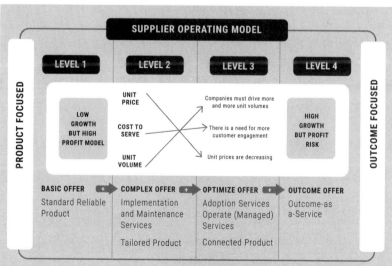

FIGURE 1.2 Moving from Level 2 to Level 3

As markets, even traditionally hardware-centric segments, become software and subscription-dominant, companies are getting caught in a vicious cycle:

- Unit prices begin to drop over time because of software's high margins and new entrants' willingness to buy market share with lower prices.

- To maintain even flat revenues, incumbent companies must therefore sell and deliver more and more units every quarter.

- That increases the need for sales, marketing, and service/success resources.

- The total cost to serve customers threatens to trend upward.

- This growth-versus-profit trade-off throws a wrench into the transformation engine. Incumbent executives hesitate to fund those higher costs at scale. As a result, both unit sales and the customer experience suffer.

- Entrants eat at the market share of the incumbents through lower customer costs and a simpler, better customer experience.

Have you ever seen the Salesforce advertisement shown in Figure 1.3 on the front page of *The Wall Street Journal?*

You could draw a similar picture for hundreds of specific B2B market segments as new entrants disrupt the old hierarchy. It's hard to attribute this cycle to just one thing. Instead, we will settle for two:

- Born-in-the cloud companies struggle far less with the growth-versus-profit trade-off. For them and their investors, growth clearly trumps profits. If spending more money on serving customers means more growth, little, including losses, will hold them back.

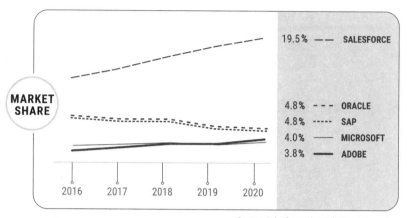

FIGURE 1.3 Salesforce CRM Ranking Advertisement

- Large incumbents have legacy organizations and processes they are loath to transform or disrupt. But the new entrants aren't held back by this weight.

So, what is Wave Two of DT? It's about reimagining the customer's path to value.

With very few exceptions, you should relate to Figure 1.4. Piece by piece, decision by decision, department by department, you have built a maze around your core value proposition. Your customers must navigate that maze, and it usually is extremely arduous.

There are many layers of complexity on that customer's journey to value. There is the sales layer, the configuration and pricing layers, the implementation layer, the training layer, the maintenance layer, the upgrade layer, the administrative layer, and on and on. So, ask yourself: Do my buyers spend more time and treasure navigating our maze or enjoying the value of our offers? That is a fair question not just for the legacy incumbents, but for

The Value Maze

FIGURE 1.4 The Value Maze

the born-in-the-cloud companies, too! Most NewCos, or proposed corporate spin-off, startup, or subsidiary companies, may
not have needed to worry about Wave One DT since they were
founded with a cloud-based solution and a subscription-based
offer; but let's face it, they still sell and service like they are
Oracle or GE.

We all need to clear a path through the maze. That is the essence of Wave Two DT. Below are a few examples of the goals of
Wave Two DT for both new and old companies:

- Remove friction from your growth engine.
- Develop offers that deliver measurable value.
- Reduce cost to serve.
- Defend profitable price points by linking to business outcomes.

Wave Two Is Already Happening: The Haves and the Have Nots

Most people could probably agree that a reasonable definition of a "successful" company today would be that they have:

1. Healthy top-line growth.
2. Market capitalization value that exceeds annual company revenues.

Over time in the technology industry, successful companies like Cisco, Oracle, Microsoft, and Salesforce have demonstrated double-digit annual revenue growth and market caps that are five times, 10 times, or more, than their annual revenues. This is why tech has been such an exciting industry in which to both work and invest. But it is clear, even the tech industry is not exempt from digital transformation. Its impact is creating "haves" and "have nots," even among the most technically advanced companies in the world. As an example, since 2008, TSIA has tracked the quarterly financial performance of 50 of the world's largest technology companies in an index called the Technology & Services 50 (T&S 50).[3] Did you know that in the first calendar quarter of 2021, only eight of the 50 companies have their top line growing 10% or greater and a market cap at least four times annual revenue? Historically, this has not been a high bar for a high-flying technology company. Now, less than 20% of incumbents pass this test, yet hundreds of born-in-the-cloud companies do. The bifurcation of companies into "haves" or "have nots" is truly happening.

Is Wave Two DT a Choice?

To get a bit more specific, TSIA analyzed the growing capability gaps between fast-growing tech providers and struggling tech providers. What is creating the gap? You guessed it: Wave Two digital offers and capabilities. In addition to digital XaaS offers and the other elements of Wave One DT, the fast-growing tech companies with very high valuations have more of the following four capabilities in place:

- **Low-friction land and product-led growth (PLG).** This capability allows customers to start using the technology for free, or with minimal up-front commitments, and then have the product platform itself unlock more revenue. Freemium offers, in-use product offers, and automated renewals are all examples of PLG.

- **Transform data into insights.** This capability involves gathering meaningful telemetry on how the customer is actually using the technology, how to apply analytics to that telemetry, and then play back business insights to the customers to help them climb the value ladder.

- **A fully digital customer experience (DCX).** DCX is defined as the ability for customers to engage with a company across the entire APLAER life cycle on some or all their solutions.

- **Clear links between product and service capabilities and customer business outcomes.** This can be described as the ability to draw the connections and collect the data that clearly prove the industry-specific (or customer-specific) business impact of your offers.

These are all digitally enabled, Wave Two capabilities. Armed with broader data sets and better analytics, we are not only going to be able to optimize adoption and customer value, but we are also going to improve the entire customer life cycle from pre-sales to renewal. These capabilities will not only deliver superior customer experience and improved customer business outcomes, but they will also make your company's growth more frictionless. If companies cannot perform these functions, they will fall onto the pile of highly commoditized "tools"—the same pile of "tools" that are exhausting internal IT organizations, frustrating CFOs, and overwhelming users. Put simply, the more of these capabilities you have, the brighter your future looks.

Wave Two of DT is here, and it's going to move faster and leave more carnage in its wake than Wave One. This time it's about truly attacking the automation of the entire customer experience (CX). It's about upending the way customers buy and consume your complex products and services. It's about being able to confidently assume the financial risk of your customer's use of your solution because you can track value and tie pricing to it. And perhaps one of the most important single concepts in this book is about your company bringing your product features and your digital customer experience together into a single platform.

Wave Two is your company building a simple, wonderful digital customer experience that leads customers to enjoy the journey to specific business outcomes...and then...to want a lot more of that same experience.

Why Wave Two Will Be Harder Than Wave One: The Human Problem

Most aspects of transformation management are about balancing hard evidence with human realities. Leading a large, established company through digital transformation is absolutely that kind of challenge. There are hard facts and figures, like your market share declining or your cost of sales increasing. And then there is managing and protecting the organization you and your team have built. That organization is full of employees and partners. They all have familiar names, faces, and families. You love and care about them. It is in your DNA to keep them safe from danger. You also want them to be optimistic about their future with the firm so they can deliver short-term performance. But sometimes the facts and figures tell you it's time for a radical change to that organization.

And there are other names and faces in your ecosystem: your shareholders. Theirs are the names of institutional investors, private equity firms, venture capitalists, analysts, and retail investors.

They, too, have wants and needs that you care about. They, too, want to believe they are safe from danger. They, too, want to feel optimistic.

And therein lies the problem with most DTs. As executives navigate the Wave One and Wave Two DT journey, they must coldly balance the empirical case for change in their business with the desire not to disrupt the human side of the equation. Sometimes the human side takes over, and executives either subconsciously or knowingly underestimate the acute criticality of their market situation. Maybe it is because the radical change will be in the organization you grew up in or in the one that "made" your company. And the human problem scales up and down. It could also be changing a small team or a small process. In a May 2021 TSIA poll of over 1,000 corporate managers and executives, more than 90% rated their company as a "have" versus a "have not" when it came to the corporate capabilities they needed for the future. But when those same respondents weighed in on whether they *actually* had the specific, critical capabilities identified by TSIA, the yes votes dropped into the 20% range. So, how could they have been so overly optimistic and under-self-critical? It's simple: they are humans. Just like the good people at Hertz and Blockbuster, they will hesitate until enough customers jump ship to a "have" company. By then it's too late.

And we empathize. It is exceedingly difficult for most technology and industrial company executives to consider going "all the way" with DT. It truly carries the potential of upsetting a lot of the names and faces—the employees, partners, and shareholders you care about—along the way. We often see even the best, most famous companies stop short of their full DT potential. Some of the voices are telling them what they've already done in Wave One is enough. Maybe some of their leaders feel it will be the job of their successor to navigate these tough transformations. But, for whatever reasons, as we will examine throughout this book, there is *so* much more potential that is being left on the table.

In *Digital Hesitation,* we will address many real-world concerns that executive leadership teams have. For those of you who are familiar with our literature, you may remember our infamous "fish" model. Well, we are here to say that the "fish" is still alive and well, unfortunately. What's the fish model? Think about it like this: Any new capabilities that suppliers need to add in order to play at another supplier's level are going to add to short-term costs. But that is not the worst of it. There is a second, often simultaneous problem, especially in moving to Level 3 or Level 4 (using our B4B terminology again). That second problem is a revenue problem; specifically, the timing of those revenues. As we said, most Level 1 and Level 2 suppliers are used to getting paid up front. Once they deliver their technology, they can recognize the revenue and collect the cash. But, starting at Level 3, suppliers usually offer operating-expense (OpEx) pricing models, such as subscriptions or pay-for-consumption. So far, the evidence that many customers prefer that model is overwhelming. Many of the traditional software companies that made the brave move to OpEx pricing alternatives have been surprised by how many customers have switched. When they do, instead of getting a huge chunk of revenue up front, suppliers must wait and defer those revenues over an extended period of months or years. The contract amount may be the same, but the timing of the revenue recognition is not. If enough customers switch from the CapEx pricing model to OpEx, the supplier's short-term revenues dip compared to previous periods.

We drew these two transitions on a piece of paper using a status-quo starting point. Then we drew one timeline that represents the short-term investment ramp-up period needed to create new organizational capabilities, and a second timeline that represents the short-term revenue trough brought on by the shift to OpEx pricing models. Our drawing took on the unmistakable shape of a fish, as seen in Figure 1.5.

On the far left, you see the status quo portrayed, which is fairly flat revenue with fairly stable costs. The space between those lines

The Financial Fish of Transformation

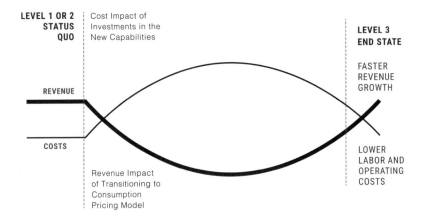

FIGURE 1.5 The TSIA Fish Model

represents the profits of the supplier. The whole reason to embark on the journey is because of how those same two lines look on the far right (the "tail"). Revenues are now growing strongly, thanks to the supplier's new Level 3 or Level 4 offers. At the same time, new technology-fueled and data-driven operating models are driving down labor and operating costs.

We don't know of anyone who has started at Level 1 or Level 2 and successfully transformed their primary supplier operating model to Level 3 or Level 4 without experiencing the fish. It is the fish that has most Level 1 and Level 2 CEOs hesitating. At the same time, they frustratingly watch as many new entrants get to launch their company starting at the far right. They get the benefits of the new model without having to worry about their time spent in the belly of the fish.

But there is an overwhelming pattern when it comes to how most every company has attacked the multiyear fish period. And we can easily apply Wave One and Wave Two DTs to it, as shown in Figure 1.6.

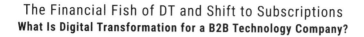

The Financial Fish of DT and Shift to Subscriptions
What Is Digital Transformation for a B2B Technology Company?

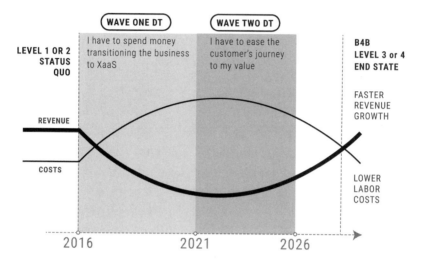

FIGURE 1.6 Wave One and Wave Two DT in the Fish Model

Most companies have thought about the transformation journey primarily in terms of the pivot to XaaS and recurring revenue. As we have repeatedly said in this chapter, it was their Wave One DT. But your leadership team must accept that there is a Wave Two.

So *Digital Hesitation* will tackle subjects with which your company must come to terms, such as:

- The difficulty incumbent CEOs, CFOs, and directors face in accepting and managing through the incongruous valuation models of their value investors versus their new competition's growth investors. We will examine the winning plays to message and successfully deliver your company's stock price through your DT.

- How to think about and manage the costs of Wave One and Wave Two DT, and how to keep everyone in the organization working toward common goals. This is important whether your company is five years old or 50 years old.

- Becoming totally convinced of this thought, we can have a more profitable and faster-growing business at the end of Wave Two DT. And any of you who have read our other books know that we believe a good business is growing *and* profitable.

In short, what we have observed in the real world is no surprise to you: True digital transformation for technology and industrial companies—meaning going *all the way*—takes guts, resolve, and commitment. But not doing it? There is no such possibility for tomorrow's "have" companies. The "have nots" who hesitate will slowly wither away, their share of markets replaced.

Why is Wave Two so important to becoming a profitable XaaS company? It's because Wave Two generates the inflection point in both curves in the belly of the fish. It's where your volumes start heading up and your costs start heading down, as seen in Figure 1.7.

The Financial Fish of DT and Shift to Subscriptions
Why Is This So Critical?

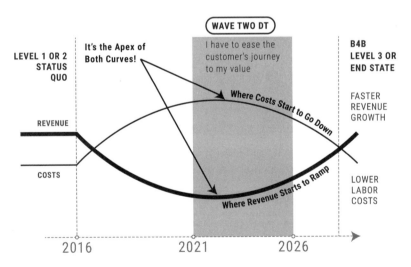

FIGURE 1.7 The Critical Wave Two Inflection Point

That's why this book is important to every B2B company that provides a technology deliverable to its customers. Your future growth and profits will depend on being able to sell and deliver more units at a lower cost per unit than you do right now. Only by easing the customer's journey to value can that be accomplished. Before we delve into the forward-looking tactics we are recommending for your consideration, we want to outline a few overarching constructs to guide your team's thinking.

2 | Complexity Kills

By J.B. Wood

As Amazon's Jeff Bezos taught us, there has to be alignment between the complexity of a task and the power of a digital toolset to automate it. If the task is too complex, the toolset might not be able to handle it (Figure 2.1). That's why the company started with something simple like selling books. But for many companies, especially in B2B, that's been the perfect excuse not to fully digitally transform. "What we do is just too complex," goes the logic.

In fact, for decades, the most successful tech and industrial companies embraced complexity as their friend; and, by and large, customers let them get away with it. Customers needed massive help to navigate complexity across the entire solution life cycle. Large companies required their customers to choose from among thousands of products that all had to be configured, priced, sold, installed, integrated, operated, maintained, and upgraded. But it was OK because customers were willing to put up with long purchase cycles...and long implementation cycles...and large-scale employee-training classes...and ongoing upgrade tasks...and needed maintenance. They were willing to purchase services from the company or its channel partners to help operationalize the complex solutions. The suppliers made

The Digital Business Shift

- High Price, Big Land
- Thousands of SKUs
- Complex Configurations
- Labor-Based CX
- Slow Time-to-Value
- Engineering and Sales Led

FIGURE 2.1 The Digital Business Shift

huge revenue and profit on the services, and the customers got something they needed. Think of it: Trillions of dollars spent by customers to manage the complex offers that the enterprise tech companies themselves created!

But that wasn't the only source of complexity. Doing business with these companies was like doing business with the federal government. There were departments inside departments inside departments. Specialists on top of specialists. Systems that didn't talk to systems. Product salespeople who didn't talk to service salespeople. And neither of whom talked to their own channel partners. Customers needed a phonebook the size of that of a small city to know whom to call for what.

None of these complexities are going to survive the next decade. Offers will be simplified. The experience of doing business will be simplified. The two things (the offers and the operations of the company) will unite into a single digital customer experience.

That's why digital transformation really begins with business process transformation. Companies must "lean out" their customer experience and the organizations that support them. And product managers have to end the practice of saying a product is ready for market when it's still full of complexity and not integrated into the operations (marketing, sales, service) of the company.

We were talking about this topic with Bill McDermott, CEO of ServiceNow, and he said it right: "Simplicity is the ultimate compliment."

We respectfully request that you and your team etch this thought into your minds: *The next killer feature is simplicity*. But, as Figure 2.2 shows, it's going to require a massive rethinking of your business. And the human problem is going to get in your way.

This book is going to unpack many of the subjects you see listed in Figure 2.2. Right now, you and many other technology and industrial company executives may say this view is a bridge too far. We can say, because we were there, that virtually no executives leading the dominant enterprise tech companies of the early 2000s saw something like Amazon Web Services coming. But it did, and it (along with its successors) are disrupting everything about the data center business (and more!). Now companies like HPE and Dell are discovering that, while it's hard work, a robust DCX is possible. As software eats the world in your industry sector, we can predictably say some version of this disruption is in the future; it could be an incumbent, it could be a challenger.

The Digital Business Shift: Complexity versus Simplicity

FIGURE 2.2 The Digital Business Shift: Complexity versus Simplicity

What Is DT *Really* About? The North Star

As we said in Chapter 1, the reason that the term digital transformation has become so popular is because it is so vague.

If you look up the term "digital transformation," you get definitions like the one in Figure 2.3. While this definition is all true, it's not really that instructive. It simply says to "think different," as Apple used to say, and then automate it. But we think there is a more useful thought, a sort of North Star of digital transformation—one that can help a company's employees approach the daunting task of unraveling complexity and engineering simplicity, as illustrated in Figure 2.4.

Digital Transformation Defined

Digital Transformation

dig·i·tal / *adjective* | trans·for·ma·tion / *noun*

1. The novel use of digital technology to solve traditional problems. These digital solutions enable inherently new types of innovation and creativity, rather than simply enhance and support traditional methods.

Source: Wikipedia

FIGURE 2.3 Digital Transformation Defined

TSIA's North Star of Digital Transformation

FIGURE 2.4 TSIA's North Star of Digital Transformation

Let's take a moment to think about the nature of business complexity. We would say that experiencing complexity is about navigating choices, disconnects, and information vacuums. It doesn't matter if it's a person or a system. Someone or something needs a task completed in the pursuit of a goal but can't figure out how to do it. So, the someone or something reaches out for help. Let's call that Course A. If it gets the help, it reaches its goal. It's happy and productive. If it doesn't, its need goes unmet. Often the someone or something gets only some help and gets only a portion of its needs met. In either case, it seeks Course B. And then Course C, and so on. As the someone or something carries on, it becomes increasingly inefficient. It may fatigue or run out of time. It may quit its pursuit. It may seek an alternative. That is the experience of complexity.

Think of a customer who wants a price for a product or service. If you're a consumer, you can usually visit a website and get a price. If it's a more complex offer, you have to go through a bit of a configuration process first. Take shopping for a car online as an example. It's fun! You can change the color of the car you like. You can add the "sport package." You build the car of your dreams in five minutes. And then you get your price.

But if you are an enterprise buyer looking for a price on a complex business solution, you don't often have that fun buying experience. What you get instead goes something like this:

1. Go to the company website.
2. Fill out a contact form.
3. Get an auto-generated email response saying someone will contact you soon.
4. Wait.
5. Get an email from someone who wants to schedule a time to talk.
6. Go back and forth by email until a date is agreed.
7. Wait.

8. The meeting finally takes place. The buyer states what they want and asks what the price will be.

9. "It depends," the seller says.

10. "On what?" the buyer says.

11. "Well, we need more information first," the seller replies.

12. "Like what?" the buyer recoils.

13. "Well, let me ask you a few questions…" and the interrogation begins.

14. "OK, thanks for that!" (The interrogation might mercifully be ending.)

15. "So, now I can connect you with the right salesperson." Momentary silence.

16. "But I thought *you* were a salesperson," the buyer finally says, as it dawns on them that this is not going to be a simple process to answer their simple question about price.

17. "I will have them contact you soon," the seller says.

18. Wait.

19. Go to Step 5 and repeat the process again with your account executive.

20. Then, go one more time to Step 5 through Step 14 with their technical expert(s).

21. Wait.

22. Get an email saying they have a price and are ready to tell you what it is.

23. Repeat Step 5 through Step 8.

24. Attend a meeting with everyone you met along the way and their manager. Finally get the price.

25. Also learn that the price is assuming some things and may be different based on further clarification.

26. And…that the price could be better (or worse) if the buyer could (or could not) commit this month.

There are lots of disconnects in that sequence. They are caused by information vacuums between the buyer's situation and the seller's offers. Days, weeks, months go by while sales teams try to discover the detailed information required to configure and price the appropriate solution. Technical experts, consultants, and channel partners all must be brought to bear on the vacuum. They must perform tasks. The buyer must perform tasks. They have to turn disconnects into connects.

Why? Because it's complicated.

Now, let's back up a second. You know the car-shopping experience we just mentioned? If you had wanted to buy a car 20 years ago, you would have gone to a dealership to speak with a salesperson. The discussion would have been only slightly shorter than our enterprise solution shopping experience. Did you want the heated seats? What about the special rims? The car you want in the color you want with the special rims is not in stock. The seller will call some other dealerships. The price? The seller needs to talk with their manager. But, before they tell you the price, you need to call your spouse so they can come down to the dealership...and bring the title to the car you are trading.

We guarantee you that most automotive companies did not believe then that a DCX could replace the dealership selling process. Buying a car was simply too complex. There were too many disconnects. Too big of an information vacuum between the consumer and the car company. Tasks needed to be performed. Visits and test drives needed to be made. They needed dealers with salespeople to perform those tasks.

Then they started to get better data. They realized that the buyers who bought the heated seats also bought the special rims. They created the "sport package." They cut the number of packages down to two or three instead of offering 28 a la carte options. They discovered that video could minimize or even eliminate the need to actually sit in the driver's seat. They knew the exact car you wanted was somewhere in the supply or distribution chain, and their computers could locate it and route it to the dealership closest to you.

Then Elon Musk came along and decided that you should be able to configure, price, and buy a Tesla on your smartphone...and get it delivered to your door. He started closing Tesla dealerships that had just opened. Carvana then proved you can even remove the risk from the highly risky business of buying a used car. They simplified and "de-risked" a complex task. That allowed technology to master the remaining complexity. If you're thinking of buying a Tesla, you should know that they now have a DCX for the entire ownership life cycle. You can get trained on the navigation system, order service visits, even trade in your old model for a new one...all on your phone.

Lots of experts and analysts agree that the selling process is changing to the buying process. Do you really think that a DCX isn't coming to your market segment in the next few years?

But first you have to transform your complexity into simplicity. You must have everyone in your company asking themselves the North Star question:

If we had that data, we could do X and no longer have to do Y?

Hopefully, the person who no longer needs to do Y is your customer. As an example, if we knew what features customers usually bought together, we could package up our stock-keeping units (SKU). Customers wouldn't have to make as many choices, and our sales teams would no longer have to create detailed, custom configurations for every deal. If we then had the data on what customer segments preferred which package, we could create a recommendation engine so that our salespeople didn't have to involve a technical specialist on every deal. If we then had data that said that most customers who chose Package A later needed to add Product 3 to ultimately succeed, and that the customers who chose Package C instead of package A and B had lower rates of adoption, expansion, and renewal, then we could include Product 3 into Package A and eliminate Package C. That would mean we wouldn't have to provide as much service to generate customer success. It also means we could confidently automate the installation and integration of the products in Package A and Package B, and we would no longer need to ask customers to spend so much money and time on implementation. That would give the customer faster time to value, and they would be ready to upsell and cross-sell sooner. Consequently, we would increase the total lifetime spending of each customer.

In short, it's about transforming your customer's journey to your value from a maze to a garden path, as seen in Figure 2.5.

Wave Two of Digital Transformation

FIGURE 2.5 Wave Two DT: From Maze to Garden Path

Wave Two DT Is a Neural Network

A neural network is a series of algorithms that endeavors to recognize underlying relationships in a set of data through a process that mimics the way the human brain operates. Neural networks can adapt to changing input so that the network generates the best possible result without needing to redesign the output criteria.[1] In short, a neural network consists of inputs and outputs—data in, insight out—with a hidden layer of analytics in the middle.

In Chapter 1, we suggested that your Wave Two strategy should focus on these goals:

- Remove friction from your growth engine.
- Develop offers that deliver measurable value.
- Reduce cost to serve.
- Defend profitable price points by linking to business outcomes.

And to do it by employing tactics like these:

- Low-friction land and product-led growth.
- Signal liquidity and analytics-driven insights.
- A fully digital customer experience.
- Clear links between product and service capabilities and customer business outcomes.

To accomplish Wave Two of DT, it is not executing one project, and it is not executing a bunch of independent projects. It's managing a neural network of projects, as illustrated in Figure 2.6.

One project enables the next one. And that enables two more. They get progressively more powerful as they build new business capabilities and eliminate previous complexity. This is the beauty of DT North Star thinking.

These results are great when they happen inside a single department or function of the company. Figure 2.7 shows a real-world example of a neural network of projects that TSIA recommended to a large tech company; the example was designed to help it think about and justify digitally transforming the customer service experience.

As you can see, even within one department, it isn't a single project. It's an integrated network of projects. Designs like this are great. They can really transform how a department operates and interacts with customers. But it's far better when this happens across departments in the company, as seen in Figure 2.8 (page 33).

Neural Network of Projects

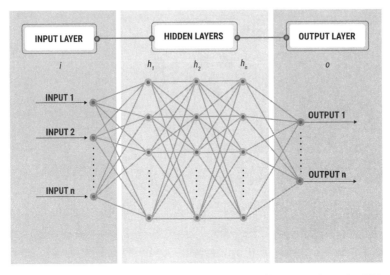

Source: Shukla, Lavanya. September 2019.
"Designing Your Neural Networks." Towards Data Science.

FIGURE 2.6 Neural Network of Projects

A Customer Service R&D Budget Justification

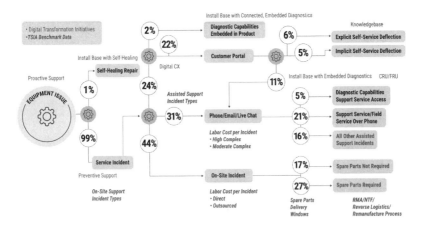

FIGURE 2.7 Example: Neural Network of Projects

Neural Network of Projects Across One and Multiple Departments

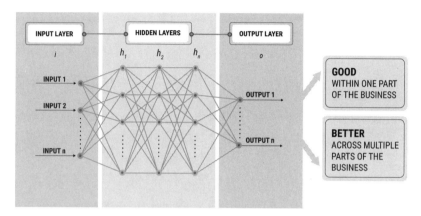

FIGURE 2.8 Neural Network of Projects Across One and Multiple Departments

That's when it starts to get cool. When sales organizations get new operational capabilities, service organizations no longer need to perform as many tasks. When service organizations collect better data about their customers, sales organizations can upsell more easily and more often. That means companies can increase quotas and no longer need to add more salespeople to grow. You get the picture.

Synchronization among departments is becoming more critical because we often see companies that have different departments transforming at shockingly different speeds. Out-of-synch departments cripple the DCX, as seen in Figure 2.9.

When this happens, customers are experiencing the company more like several different companies. Doing business with some parts of the company is a highly automated experience. Other parts are agonizingly labor-based. Some things happen instantly, and other things take weeks or even months to get processed. Why do things often unfold like this? It's usually for

Out-of-Sync Departments Cripple the DCX

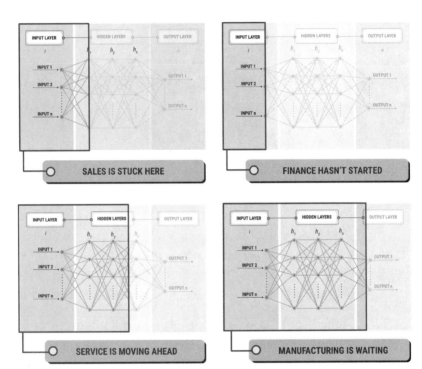

FIGURE 2.9 What Happens When DT Is Out of Sync

two reasons. The first is that the path to automation or transformation for some departments is pretty well known, while others are truly pioneering. Customer support self-service, for example, has many known best practices on which a company can call. But configure-price-quote (CPQ) is usually a complex series of steps kept far away from the customer's eyes, at least in B2B. The second challenge is that the leadership of different departments may have more or less commitment to DT. One may be aggressively carving out OpEx dollars to use for innovation, while others prefer to use every dollar available for headcount.

Coordinating all these activities is critical but, as we will cover in a minute, we have also seen companies go too far. Their effort to control departments leads to stifling the company's entire DT momentum.

But even successfully coordinating projects is not the "all-the-way" dream of the second wave of digital transformation. The end state vision is *when the operational capabilities of your company (marketing, sales, service) are integrated into the features and functions of your technology products solution*, as seen in Figure 2.10.

Talk about a different spin on the definition of a finished product! It might boggle the mind of many complex B2B companies, especially ones with a big hardware component in their portfolio. But it is possible if you think big about the goal, simplify the process, and draw your own version of this picture.

Integrating Product Features with Operational Capabilities to Form a DCX

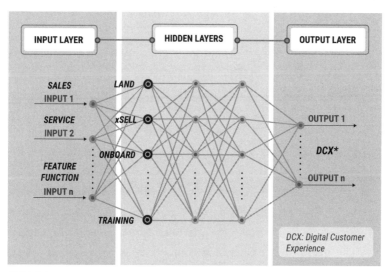

FIGURE 2.10 Integrating Product Features with Operational Capabilities to Form a DCX

Think Macromanagement

As a team, your company leadership culture could drive you to a couple of different methods of attack on DT. Some companies try to micromanage every aspect of DT. Usually it's an epic failure for the whole company. It would be like a single project to end global poverty. It may be well-intentioned, but it's not going to happen.

Others basically distribute DT to the individual departments: "Hey, Sales, transform!" "Hey, Finance, transform!" Our observation is that this actually is a better strategy than micromanagement of the entire company's DT. Why? Because at least some good stuff gets done. Individual departments move the needle for their business function.

But you know who loses in this fail? The customer. At TSIA, we like this analogy: You know what happens if you wax one fender of your car? It makes the rest of your car look bad. That is how many companies' DTs are experienced by the customer. For example, the "My Digital Customer Service Portal" is awesome. But when the customer needs to talk with someone about an accounting question, they need to dig out a small-city phonebook to find the right person to contact. It's a frustrating and confusing customer experience.

Funding the Digital Transformation

That brings us to one final thought about where many digital transformations fail: money. We actually believe that the funding for your DT journey is based on two principals: visibility and amount. We think more visibility will increase the amount. Getting enough funding may require not just the support of senior management, but also the support of shareholders. A real Wave Two DT journey can force companies through the belly of the fish. It can be a mistake to try to make that invisible because your overall expense levels could visibly increase and profits could visibly decrease. You have to get shareholders to go with you on that journey. We will discuss best practices for navigating that in Chapter 10.

This also begs another interesting question: Do we need to revisit the public parameters of R&D spending? Every tech and industrial company has an R&D budget. Simply put, it's the percentage of total revenue that is being earmarked for specific product development activities. The qualifying R&D spend was a subset of the total product development department budget. And if you're a public company, it's probably public data. Many companies pick a number based on benchmarks or promote their commitment to innovation by setting a number that's slightly higher than the competition. That well-understood concept has worked for decades. Some companies believe spending more on R&D can actually have a positive effect on their stock price.

But what happens when the features of the product are embedded within the operating capabilities platform of the company? Where does the investment in product R&D stop and the investment in OpEx marketing, sales, service, and finance begin? It's increasingly becoming a moot point. Every department needs an R&D budget. They all must innovate. They all have to integrate into the neural network of DCX and the features of products. Product managers need to figure out how to execute in-use onboarding and training, success and support, next-feature or upgrade marketing, and in-app payments. Individual departments like education, services, marketing, and finance have to spend to integrate and interoperate with the new product or service features. Isn't that R&D? The product and the operations of the company are becoming one.

Imagine if each department of the company—not just product development—had a visible DT R&D budget allocation. That budget would be earmarked for projects tied to the neural network of the DCX. It would be more for some departments, like services, and less for others, like HR. But it would be visible and could be added up. You would promote it to analysts as your commitment to innovation and outstanding customer experience. The CIO would know not only the total amount the company was spending, but also what the projects are and how they fit into the neural network. Then, the DCX leadership and their two-pizza teams could facilitate the integration among departments needed to achieve the company's overall goals. Just food for thought…

Ready, Set, Go!

So, it's almost time to get started on your Wave Two DT journey. But, before we go, there are some precautions: You have to be READY to rethink everything. With the exception of start-ups with a narrow product focus, B2B companies were always thought to be inherently complex with no realistic path to a simple, digital customer experience. That's not only going to prove untrue, but becoming super-easy to work with and offering instant time to value are going to become major market share determinants in almost every sector of the economy. What's at stake you ask? Born-in-the cloud companies have a fairly digitally enabled business but, with a few exceptions, they lack the scale (employees, partners, and portfolio) of their legacy rivals. The legacy companies have plenty of scale, but they're often not as digitally enabled. That gives us a simple way to describe the race for tomorrow's dominance of B2B market segments. Will the cloud-native companies get to scale first? Or will the legacy companies digitally transform first? Whoever is the first to achieve both, probably wins. Are you ready for that? Because it's likely to be *that* critical in the end.

Next, you have to be SET to succeed. In this book, we have asserted that Wave One of DT was pretty limited in scope—even if it didn't feel that way when you were going through it. We have suggested that Wave Two is about going all the way. So, it's fair to ask us what "all the way" means.

As you most certainly agree, DT is not (just) about applying technology. Oh, if it were only that simple! Assuming your company's leadership agrees on its business model(s), we would summarize the challenges we see companies trying to master into the four groups listed below and charted in Figure 2.11.

- Workflows
- Users
- Data and Analytics
- Digital Operations and Customer Experience Technology Platform(s)

You could argue that this is not new news, and we would agree. What matters is how you stitch the components together. We believe there is an order and a life cycle to successful W2DT.

TSIA's All the Way DT Model

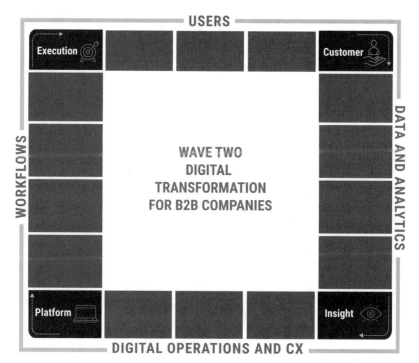

FIGURE 2.11 TSIA's All the Way DT Model

There are certain essential, digitally powered workflows that are typically different than most B2B companies' current workflows. Workflow changes are tough because they challenge the human factor. But these new workflows help the users be more successful because they are powered by a digital operations and customer experience (DOCX) that contains the data and analytics that make the workflows easier. You have to sell the team on that single sentence.

We say that because once we fill in the All the Way DT Model another level, as shown in Figure 2.12, you may say, "It's too complex," which we just said is a no-no. So, stay calm and we will walk you through it in this book.

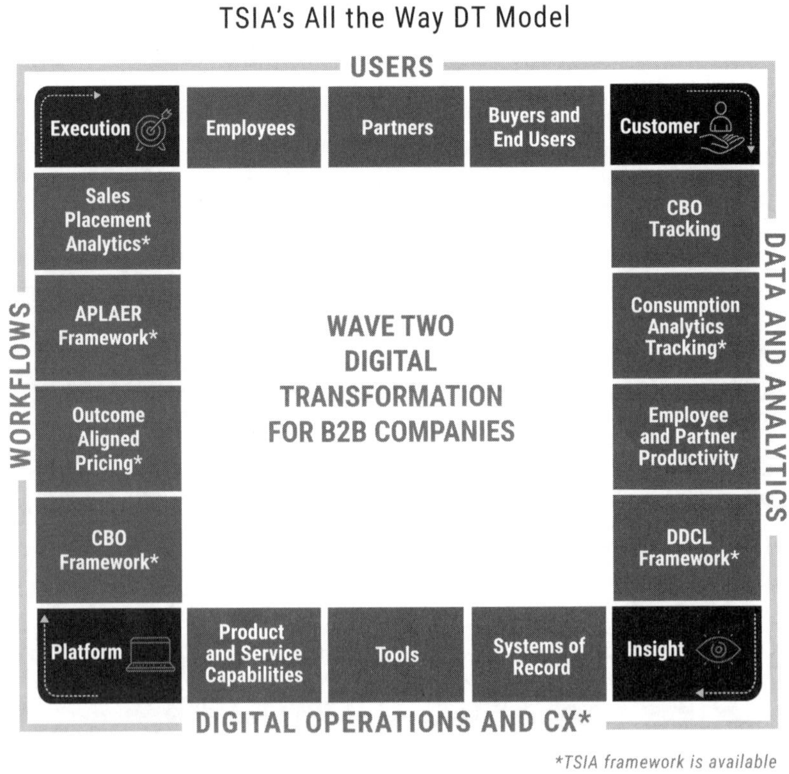

TSIA's All the Way DT Model

USERS				
Execution	Employees	Partners	Buyers and End Users	Customer
Sales Placement Analytics*				CBO Tracking
APLAER Framework*		WAVE TWO DIGITAL TRANSFORMATION FOR B2B COMPANIES		Consumption Analytics Tracking*
Outcome Aligned Pricing*				Employee and Partner Productivity
CBO Framework*				DDCL Framework*
Platform	Product and Service Capabilities	Tools	Systems of Record	Insight

WORKFLOWS (left side) · **DATA AND ANALYTICS** (right side)

DIGITAL OPERATIONS AND CX*

TSIA framework is available

FIGURE 2.12 TSIA's All the Way DT Model Workflows

We are going to focus primarily on workflows. That's because workflows tell you what the process is, what data and analytics you need, what technical capabilities you need, and what your users will be doing. There are five key workflows that make up the essence of W2DT:

- Discover, Design, Create, Launch (DDCL): A best-practice framework for how new XaaS offers are designed, built, and launched.

- Place, Land, Expand, Adopt, Renew (PLAER): A best-practice framework for how to escort customers through the entire solution life cycle.

- Product-Led Growth (PLG): A go-to-market strategy that builds the methods of acquisition, adoption, retention, and expansion directly into the product experience.

- Digital Customer Experience (DCX): A best-practice framework for user and non-enterprise buyers to self-service across the entire solution life cycle.

- Customer Business Outcomes (CBO): A best-practice framework for how to link your products and services to the business results your customers can achieve.

These five workflows, we believe, make up the core of W2DT. If you have great product experiences and a fair price, along with excellence in these five workflows, you will be hugely successful. Throughout the course of this book, we will unfold and explain these. Each chapter will unpack or tie into one or more workflows. It will then discuss the data and analytics requirements and who the users are. Taken together, the workflows, data, and users define the functional requirements of the DOCX platform that is outlined in Appendix B.

So, let's GO and explore what full digital transformation looks like for enterprise tech and industrial companies. Along the way, let's not forget these three tenets of good DT management:

- You must relentlessly seek to master your customer and operational complexity.

- The operational capabilities of your company (marketing, sales, and service) must be integrated into the experience of your technology products solution.

- Every department needs an R&D budget since every department is now integrated with your product experience.

3 | Confronting the Unique Challenges of B2B Digital Customer Experience

By Vele Galovski

The assertion that DCX is of growing importance to all companies is hardly new. But most of the literature and examples that are regularly cited are about B2C companies. In this book, we will examine six critical goals for Wave Two DT that we think could have a huge impact on successful B2B companies of the future. They all revolve, in whole or in part, around the idea of lowering your operating costs while simultaneously improving your customers' journey to value. And obviously we are encouraging you to accomplish as many of these goals as possible through your company's digital customer experience. We will examine:

- Products that Climb the Value Ladder
- Value-Aligned Pricing

- The Lean Digital Sales Force
- Customer Success at Scale
- Digitally Enabled Partners
- Managed Services: The Business of "Your Mess for More"

But we also know it won't be easy. We will be dedicating an entire chapter to each of these focus areas. Each chapter is written by TSIA's top experts in that domain. Each of these experts leads a global research practice that focuses on industry best practices in critical capabilities, like next-generation sales, customer success, renewal and expansion, field and support services, product and service portfolio offer management, channel management, and several more. We gave each expert the freedom to zoom in on the topic that they see as the highest potential, frequently under-performing aspect of DT in that business function. They analyze the challenges and propose solutions. It's up to your company to choose to act. TSIA can advise you, as it does daily with hundreds of other leading companies. But, ultimately, these digital challenges cause hesitation for a reason: they're tough, especially when your job is to solve them digitally wherever possible.

Let's begin this chapter by asking a few honest questions. In your private, personal opinion, how good is your company's current digital customer experience? Then ask yourself a follow-up question: In your personal opinion, is your company currently putting enough time and resources toward that goal? Now, finally, why is that?

For many (or most) employees of B2B companies, the answers we hear are "inadequate," "not enough," and "lack of true executive prioritization." OK, fair enough. Like many of you, we think that needs to change. So here is a statement that may be strong enough to cause people to think twice: What if we told you that as much as 40% of your company's current expenses are spent compensating for a weak DCX and that in the next five years your market share could be doubled (or halved) based on how effective your DCX is. And, as we pointed out in Chapter 1, as unit prices for enterprise technology are pressured downward and unit volumes must increase to compensate, getting more digital efficiency and scalability into your business is do or die.

That is why it deserves maniacal executive focus...it's where your future lies. While there may be some companies with a great DCX that fail, there will be precious few successful companies that lack a great DCX.

In the previous chapters, we noted that the end-state vision of the second wave of digital transformation is when the offers and operations of the company unite into a single digital customer experience across the entire ownership life cycle. Implied in this end state is that the DCX must be consistent and integrated across multiple channels.

Taken in this light, an enterprise-grade DCX is much more than a customer's experience on a digital platform.

To level-set the discussion, we propose the following DCX definition:

"The right experience, in the right channel; from first touch, through sale, onboarding, value realization, and expansion that enables the achievement of targeted customer business outcomes over and over again."

Figure 3.1 illustrates the end-to-end enterprise DCX journey.

End-to-End Enterprise DCX Journey

Go-to-Market — Learn / Try / Buy

Onboarding — Configure / Implement

Value Realization — Monitor / Operate / Adopt

Expansion — Optimize / Expand / Renew

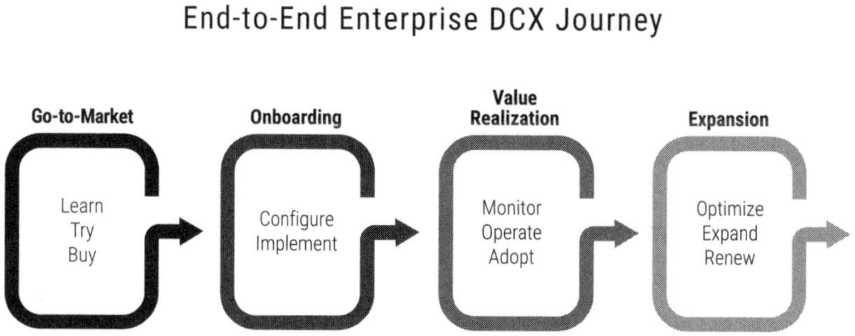

FIGURE 3.1 End-to-End Enterprise DCX Journey

With this definition of enterprise-grade DCX, how is the industry really doing in terms of delivering end-to-end integration across the customer life cycle? The short answer is, not so good, even among many born-in-the-cloud companies. Why? TSIA asserts that an effective DCX is being prevented by the following three factors:

1. The overwhelming complexity of technical product features (what TSIA calls the consumption gap).

2. A stovepiped, lumpy, department-first approach rather than a user-led approach to creating digital experiences.

3. The inability to identify and build the capabilities that customers want most.

The Consumption Gap

One major problem with today's DCX is rooted in the way every tech company historically developed its products. Most companies got their start by building a better mousetrap, a product that differentiated them from anything else in the marketplace. Over time, these companies added additional features and complexity to their product in an effort to stay one step ahead of the competition.

Unfortunately, all these add-ons far outpaced a customer's ability to consume and effectively use the new and improved product. The result is not only technical bloat, but what TSIA calls the consumption gap, seen in Figure 3.2. And the gap frequently gets larger over time for most B2B companies.

Far from a theoretical example, the consumption-gap problem has become such a huge issue in the industry that it has led to the creation of entire internal departments or organizations, both at the tech company and its customers, to minimize the impact throughout the customer life cycle. Here are five examples of large departments within tech companies that have been created or have grown larger to shield the customer from complexity:

The Consumption Gap

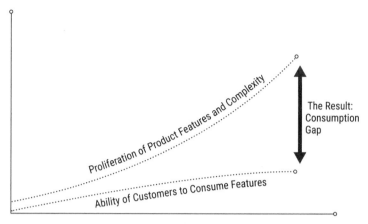

FIGURE 3.2 The Consumption Gap

1. **Land Sales.** The products and services are not easily discovered, configurable, or purchased. They require a salesperson to translate and assist the customer with the purchase.

2. **Customer Success.** Achieving full value realization requires a team to help the customer use the product they just purchased, including adoption and success plays.

3. **Customer Support.** High product complexity and high failure rates require contacting a live support agent to get the customer performing again, even for simple incidents such as logging in or how-to questions.

4. **Field Service.** The lack of telemetry from on-premise equipment requires the preventable dispatch of a field service engineer and spare parts to resolve incidents.

5. **Renew and Expand Sales.** Since customers are unaware of all the "value-added" features and upgrades recently added to the product, an account salesperson is required to recommend upgrades and secure the renewal.

That's why we make the argument that closing the consumption gap costs could save B2B companies as much as 40% of selling, services, general, and administrative expenses (SG&A). These and other huge departments ran like businesses within the business, each with its own P&L. They were so huge that most not only had their own budgets, they also had their own business process design functions, their own IT and development resources, and their own customer experience objectives. So, while they couldn't control what the company did, they could control what THEY did. And so many acted in the only way possible—they built their own DCX.

Figure 3.3 illustrates the fundamental challenge of B2B DCX.

The Fundamental Challenge of B2B DCX

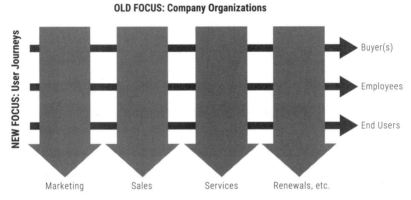

FIGURE 3.3 Focus Is the Fundamental Challenge of B2B DCX

Stovepiped and Underinvested Efforts

We now know that this siloed, departmental approach may be great for command and control of a global enterprise, but it isn't the right design construct for a DCX. We now know that USERS are the primary design focus. And it's not a single, conglomerated user. Your proliferation of product and operational complexity usually means it is impossible to design a single experience that meets the needs of every user persona at a customer. So there seems to be growing consensus that modeling your DCX journey starts by understanding all of your high-importance personas, as seen in Figure 3.4.

Each persona should get a seamless experience on their part of the customer journey. That might start and end somewhere from first touch, through sale, onboarding, value realization, and expansion; whatever it takes to enable them to achieve their targeted business outcome.

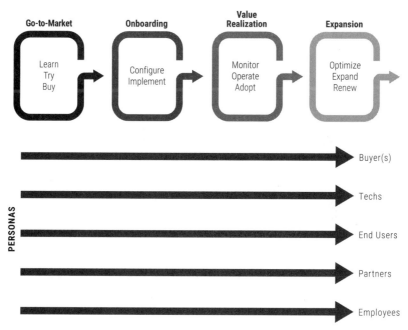

FIGURE 3.4 Modeling Your Enterprise DCX Journey for All Important Personas

However, as we just mentioned, most B2B companies are not even close to the end-state vision, including many born-in-the-cloud companies. Even those companies still too often tackle the DCX modeling problem in their organizational silos, as shown in Figure 3.5. Each persona can end up with multiple, disconnected

Too Many Companies Tackle
the Problem Organizationally

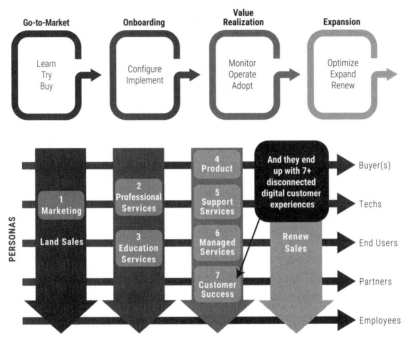

FIGURE 3.5 Too Many Companies Tackle the Problem Organizationally

digital customer experiences as they move through the end-to-end life cycle.

And even that happens only if each organization has the funding to attempt a digital customer experience for their part of the journey. As noted in Chapter 2, the lack of a visible digital transformation R&D budget allocation for each department can lead to huge gaps in the DCX life-cycle journey, where some departments have a DCX and others don't, as seen in Figure 3.6.

Ultimately, every department will have to integrate into the neural network of DCX and the features of products.

Huge Gaps with No DCX

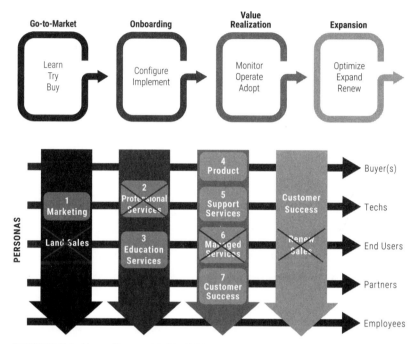

FIGURE 3.6 Huge Gaps with No DCX

What Do Your Customers Want the Experience to Be?

Although no enterprise company has achieved the end state of digital transformation, there are many outstanding customer-experience examples worth calling out. Listed below is a summary of capabilities that various TSIA member companies have incorporated into each segment of their DCX journey that will become foundational requirements for most companies sometime in the future. We are building a growing list of actual examples that we can share with you. These are becoming common capabilities sprouting up at company after company.

Go-to-Market and Onboarding

Your DCX begins before the customer buys the product and, ideally, never ends. And, like most things, what happens early in the journey is a huge determinant of success or failure in the rest of the life cycle. The first impression created and the data that is collected when a customer is interested in your solution is a lasting impression and a key to future value creation.

Figure 3.7 emphasizes the beginning of the DCX journey.

The objective of "learn, try, and buy" is to reduce friction, make it easy to purchase your solution, and set the conditions for long-term success both for the customer and for you.

- Go-to-Market
  - o Learn
    - ← Automated marketing campaigns
    - ← Education on offers/features
    - ← Auto-discovery (marketplaces, Google search)
    - ← Capture the customer's desired business outcomes
  - o Try
    - ← Free trials
    - ← Freemium offers
    - ← Pilot programs

Journey to Value Realization DCX Capabilities

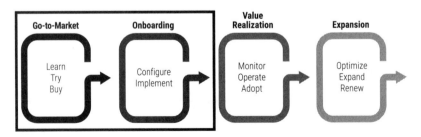

FIGURE 3.7 Journey to Value Realization DCX Capabilities

    o   Buy

- In-trial offers
- Easy CPQ
- Order from website or offsite marketplaces
- Analytics-driven prescriptions
- Simple/standard service catalog
- Partner portal for reselling

Ideally, some basic value has been realized during the learn-and-try segments. Once the solution is purchased, it is absolutely imperative that customers realize value as quickly as possible. TSIA's research correlates fast-time-to-initial-value with higher renewal rates and annual recurring revenue (ARR) growth. Therefore, reducing the time-to-value is a key objective of the on-boarding segment of the customer journey.

- Onboarding
  - o Automated onboarding
  - o Automated provisioning
  - o Auto-configuration management database (CMDB) population
  - o Auto-configuration management

Value Realization

The goal of DCX capabilities in the value realization segment (Figure 3.8) is to earn the right to cross-sell, upsell, and renew by delivering customer business outcomes via a pleasing, unique customer experience. Future business models are very dependent on ARR and you cannot cross-sell, upsell, or renew a dissatisfied customer. The objective of monitor, operate, and adopt capabilities is to deliver the promise of your solution.

Value Realization DCX Capabilities

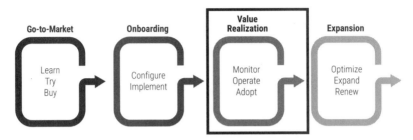

FIGURE 3.8 Value Realization DCX Capabilities

- Monitor
    - Telemetry
    - Predictive algorithms
    - Automated support interventions
    - Auto-notification to supplier (OEM) of technical issues (modification requests)
    - Partner information technology service management (ITSM) e-bonding for support status
- Operate
    - Automated discovery
    - Event correlation
    - Data analytics
    - Proactive incident resolution
    - Software development and IT operations (DevOps) loop with product development
    - Delivery application integration and orchestration
    - Partner-enabled platform with operations analytics and insights
    - Partner-enabled e-bonding to integrate with their ITSM and data analytics systems

- Adopt
  - o Adoption analytics
  - o Automated adoption scoring
  - o Automated adoption plays
  - o Peer/user benchmarking
  - o Automated health scores

Expansion

The general theme of DCX capabilities in the expansion segment (Figure 3.9) enables you to tell the customer what outcomes you have delivered and why they are ready for even more. And, it makes it easy for them to continue the relationship with you because you earned it in the value-creation segment.

- Optimize
  - o Automated notification when value event is realized
  - o Automated business impact analysis (positive/negative)
  - o Simple ROI savings
  - o While-you-were-sleeping reports (actions taken to eliminate/prevent incidents from occurring)
  - o Automated predictable outcomes

Expansion DCX Capabilities

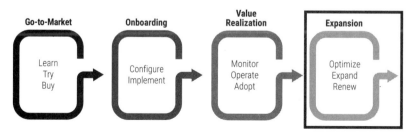

FIGURE 3.9 Expansion DCX Capabilities

- Expand
  - In-product offers
  - Automated CS recommendations for offer features
  - Automated CS/sales recommendations for new offers
  - Partner portal for guided expansion
  - Automated predictable expansions
- Renew
  - Automated renewal
  - Partner portal
  - Automated predictable renewals
  - Automated quoting (CPQ)
  - Self-serve transaction processing (shopping cart)

The DCX capabilities listed above are areas of excellence within the organizational silos. However, the end state requires a seamless integration across these capabilities as the different personas move through their journey. This requires documented, omnichannel experience standards. Here are a few examples:

- **Persistent.** Customers expect, at every touchpoint, the employee to know their conversation history and be able to pick up where they left off, regardless of the topic and regardless of where they are in the DCX journey.
- **Personalized.** All interactions with customers, across all communication and support channels, should be written into the contact history in the customer relationship management (CRM) system. One of the core values of CRM is that it represents a personalized "360-degree view" of the customer, but this only works if cross-channel integration exists.
- **Intelligent.** With a complete customer interaction history, the screen-pop received with a customer phone call, email, or chat session can include recent cross-channel interactions

for reference. Proactively prompting your employee with this information is key—you can't expect them to go hunting for it once the conversation has begun. Consolidating all interaction records in a single place and putting this history front and center for employees is a major step toward reducing customer effort and improving the customer experience by never forcing a customer to reiterate problems or previous conversations.

Realistic and Reasonable Minimal Viable Experiences (MVE)

We have sensitized you to the patterns of failure caused by most B2B companies' ingrained complexity and siloed approaches to tackling DCX. As you seek to overcome them, it is important (and freeing!) to realize you aren't going to solve all your business' problems overnight. As you no doubt know, you will be embracing all the classic learnings of new-wave software development in your DCX journey. You will think about building MVEs. You will test them for market fit. If not, you will fail fast and come back at it again. You will embrace agile, fast development cycles for adding to your MVEs. You will accept up front that NOT everything needs to be digital at first. You are going to have systems that don't talk to each other for a while. You are going to have some bad or missing data for a while. So, during those periods, it's OK to ask a user to launch an activity in your DCX, then your company performs the task manually perform the task manually, and then post the results back into the DCX. These next six chapters are journeys, not single projects. Be patient, persistent, and realistic. So, armed with this mindset, let's explore what Wave Two digital transformation could look like.

4 | Products that Climb the Value Ladder

By Laura Fay

The practices that fueled growth and captured market share in transactional CapEx models are not those that fuel growth in consumption-based OpEx models. Traditionally, with the focus on perpetual licenses and units shipped, growth and market share calculations were a function of the number of logos on the suppliers' books. With customers paying "by the drink" or paying ahead for cloud-delivered subscriptions, company growth is hugely dependent on solution adoption and customer-value realization, as seen in Figure 4.1.

Supplier Growth Dependency: CapEx versus OpEx

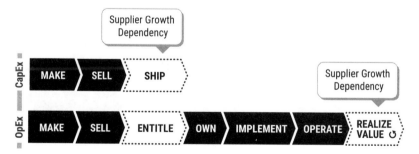

FIGURE 4.1 Supplier Growth Dependency: CapEx versus OpEx

This model difference profoundly changes the roles that the supplier and customer play in the choreography of the relationship. To succeed and grow, suppliers now must lead this dance with the customer as their engaged partner. Regardless of the reason, if the customer is unable to adopt the solution (as in the customer gets measurable business value from using the solution), the supplier's business does not grow.

Knowing how to respond to this tempo change begins with understanding the responsibilities, cost, complexity, and risk shifts and adapting accordingly.

Let's first acknowledge the responsibility shift. In the CapEx model, seen in Figure 4.2, the supplier was responsible for creating a technically differentiated product and selling that asset to the customer. The sale was based on an assertion by the supplier that the technology would contribute to a customer's desired outcome (e.g., increase revenue, reduce cost of operations, mitigate risk). The customer, upon taking possession of the asset, was responsible for rendering it operable in their environment, running it, and training their team how to use it. Many technology products went a good distance in helping the customer achieve their intended

CapEx Model: Supplier Responsibility versus Customer Responsibility

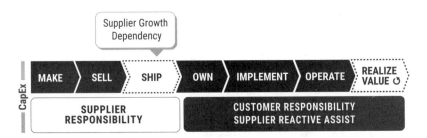

FIGURE 4.2 CapEx Model: Supplier Responsibility versus Customer Responsibility

goals; however, very few actually attached financial calculations to prove that the promise of the technology delivered on the original stated value proposition. Pretty nice position for the supplier, don't you think?

Attributes of Successful Traditional Offers

For success in this traditional business environment, the technology products needed the baseline capabilities of differentiated feature/function. Once deployed on premise, they needed to exhibit the attributes of reliability, security, performance, and typically single-instance scale; essentially, just enough to *promise* the value proposition and to compete sufficiently in the market to get the customer to buy the technology in the first place. Market growth was all but ensured upon continual successful execution of this step.

Successful Traditional Technology Attributes: Product Differentiation

Traditionally, successful technology products offered a collection of competitively viable features and use cases along with the table stakes of quality and adherence to applicable compliance and security standards.

Successful Traditional Service Attributes: Value Realization

After the technology purchase, it was up to the customer to do everything necessary to ultimately realize the value of their purchase. Suppliers and their partners provided portfolios of monetized services to assist the customer with that value realization process. The annual technical support contracts proved to be a highly profitable franchise for technology vendors and their reseller partners.

Traditionally, suppliers differentiated their technical support service offerings primarily based on response service level agreements (SLA), with emphasis on remote versus on-site technical support. Maintenance and support offerings, in particular, have emphasized reactive assistance, with pockets of proactive services and technical account management provided to a small number of key customers for premium fees. In this traditional model, technical assistance has typically been limited to specific categories of product issues (e.g., installation, configuration, product updates) and the coverage of specific languages or geographies within limited hours of operation. Online self-paced training has increasingly been included in standard support offerings because the complexity of technology has grown. When customers needed "operate services," partners often stepped in to fill that role. Vendors were happy to outsource it. They preferred not to take on the incremental cost of operating their own complex technology. This is often referred to in the industry as "your mess for less." We'll cover more on this in Chapter 9.

The above model has been alive and well for decades; however, its decline is accelerating, fueled by cloud technologies and the ability for the line of business to purchase a service with its operating budget. This puts the customer in the driver's seat of demanding simplicity, with the supplier absorbing what was once the remit of IT. Technology providers now own the technology and have the responsibility to uptime, performance, scale, and adoption SLAs of that technology (Figure 4.3). The customer's main role became engaging with the product and ultimately benefiting from the value of its use. If the customer didn't realize tangible value from Supplier A's solution, they would simply find a new dance partner in Supplier B.

In absorbing this complexity, suppliers take on significantly more revenue risk, while seeing their gross margins drop as a result of the increase in cost of goods sold (COGS). In sum, the model differences demand that suppliers reevaluate their value

OpEx Model: Supplier Responsibility versus Customer Responsibility

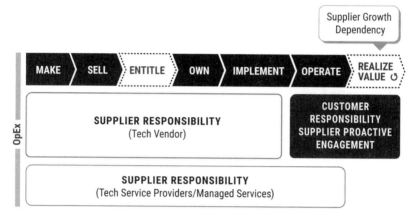

FIGURE 4.3 OpEx Model: Supplier Responsibility versus Customer Responsibility

creation, value delivery, and pricing models to factor for the changes to:

- Customer expectation.
- Value proposition.
- Cost of customer acquisition.
- Cost of driving customer adoption.
- Ongoing delivery obligations.
- Hosting costs.
- Consumption measurements.
- Cash flow.

The technology provider now has the responsibility for delivering exceptionally differentiated experiences that tangibly improve customer business metrics. Done well, this can result in a continually expanding relationship while absorbing complexity and related expenses.

Specifically for managed services, in Chapter 9 we double-click into the evolution of the your-mess-for-less concept referred to above and consider "your mess for more" that addresses this changed customer relationship and how suppliers are positioning for growth.

The different attributes of the traditional and XaaS model are summarized in Figure 4.4.

Traditional versus XaaS Model Attribute

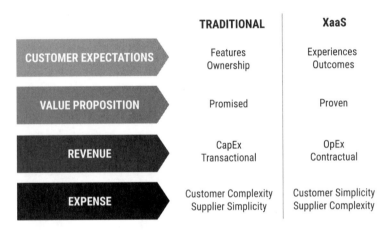

	TRADITIONAL	XaaS
CUSTOMER EXPECTATIONS	Features Ownership	Experiences Outcomes
VALUE PROPOSITION	Promised	Proven
REVENUE	CapEx Transactional	OpEx Contractual
EXPENSE	Customer Complexity Supplier Simplicity	Customer Simplicity Supplier Complexity

FIGURE 4.4 Traditional versus XaaS Model Attributes

The Value Gap

Both XaaS and traditional tech offers can result in a gap between the value that customers want to realize and what the supplier has to offer. Let's call this the "value and outcomes gap," as illustrated in Figure 4.5.

As previously emphasized, the tech providers' business grows when its customer realizes the value and outcomes from the offers. Imagine the ideal world where all technology providers are completely in tune with the needs and wants of their target

The Value and Outcomes Gap

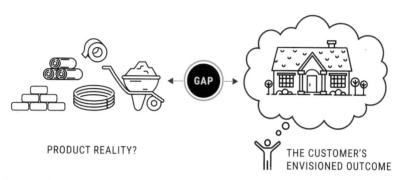

PRODUCT REALITY?   THE CUSTOMER'S
                                   ENVISIONED OUTCOME

FIGURE 4.5 The Value and Outcomes Gap

customers. In this world, these suppliers intentionally go about creating value propositions that meet those needs. The suppliers design offers to deliver on that value proposition, align their pricing to that value, and measure the customer's realization of that value. This ideal scenario is depicted in the hypothetical graph seen in Figure 4.6. It represents the perfect alignment between the desire of the customer, the intention of the supplier, and the capability of the supplier to design, price, deliver, and measure the value. This is a perfect representation of ideal offer-market fit.

Is this idealistic? Certainly. However, businesses that expect to grow consumption offers dependent on adoption need to strive for this necessary value alignment.

Now, let's see what the TSIA data actually tells us. This data, as seen in Figure 4.7, quantifies the value and outcomes gap. With only 30% of suppliers offering value-based offers and barely a few more engaging in the practice of measuring outcomes means that, across the industry, 70% of the rungs on the value ladder are missing! This reinforces our assertion in Chapter 1 that the majority of companies have yet to crack the Wave Two nut when it comes to developing offers that deliver measurable value.

Ideal Offer-Market Fit

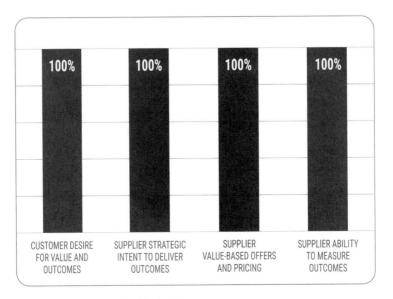

FIGURE 4.6 Ideal Offer-Market Fit

The Values and Outcomes Gap: What the Data Tells Us

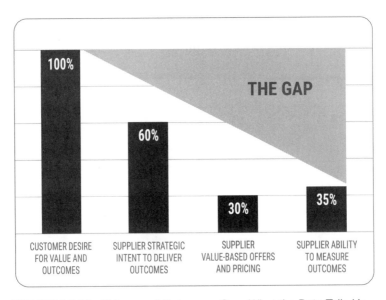

FIGURE 4.7 The Values and Outcomes Gap: What the Data Tells Us

A 70% gap is large, to say the least. In the face of such a large value gap, customer-facing teams are performing heroics in this gap zone to close it. Let's look at some of the practices that are simply harder when significant gaps exist on the value ladder.

Sales

Software subscription win rates are 39% better by proactively selling outcomes[1] versus responding to requests for proposal (RFP). Outcome-based selling is therefore on the rise. A full 82% of B2B technology companies surveyed[2] either have a "value management" function for all offers, some offers, or are planning to offer it. This is a function that attempts to close the value gap. They do this by mapping the technology provider's offer impact on the customers' business.

The guidance that many sales executives give to their teams is, "start by understanding the value you deliver today." That's sound advice, because the job they have undertaken, whether they realize it or not, is trying to identify the value gap.

In the face of the value gap, sales require more effort and depend on more "salesmanship" to assess the offer-customer fit. Further, more leaps of faith on the part of the customer in the purchase decision are required. In sum, this all amounts to potentially more risk to both the technology provider and the customer.

Customer Success

The customer success team's primary role is to ensure the customer realizes the value they were promised at the time of sale. As outlined above, the sales team is exercising its strengths to close the gap on the perceived versus the actual value proposition. Now, it's the customer success team's job to make that a reality for the customer. Often a tough job, and arguably the customer success function's *raison d'etre*, is to fill the value and outcomes gap qualified in Figure 4.7.

Human effort is expended on manual systems to monitor adoption and customer health, validate the customer experiences, build business outcome success plans, identify customer growth opportunities, and more. It has become an accepted, often large cost of business in recurring revenue models. Today, just 45% of companies with recurring revenue models are attempting to monetize this cost.[3] These businesses have varying degrees of success in covering that cost through monetization efforts. What's even more impressive is that 55% of these companies are consciously, or unconsciously, accepting the fact that value and outcomes gaps exist and are assuming the associated cost of the value gap. While automation of the mundane tasks helps with scale, we see later in this chapter that there are bigger levers to pull to make an impact on the value gap.

Expansion and Renewal

Research tells us that a growing number of businesses engage in a formal value-management process for all accounts, at least their largest accounts, or they are starting to introduce it. This value-management process is an attempt to provide validation to the customer that value has been delivered and make the case to continue using and perhaps expanding use of the solution. Given that renewal sales is a prescriptive process in which volumes of known renewal opportunities are transacted, efficiency dominates all operational factors. Slowing enough to engage in a formal value management process adds friction in the renewal gears and correspondingly creates headwinds in expansion.

In sum, the symptoms of the value and outcomes gap are:

- Less effective, more costly sales that often are dependent on heroic salesmanship.
- Costly customer success efforts.

- Friction in the renewal gears.
- Headwinds in expansion.

Customer-facing teams are working hard to keep customers on-side, engaged, and moving toward full value realization, but at an unsustainable operational cost! To make the high customer-engagement costs real, look at the net operating income (NOI) trend of TSIA's Cloud 40 Index between 2015 and 2021, seen in Figure 4.8. While improving, collective profit has never been in positive territory.

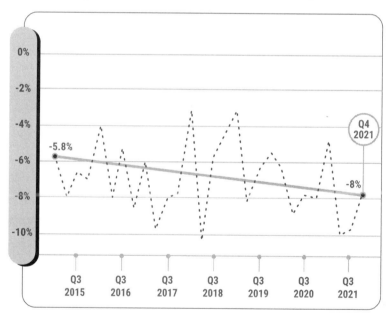

FIGURE 4.8 NOI Trends per TSIA's Cloud 40 Index

Is the Industry Closing the Value Gap Fast Enough?

What could take a bite out of the high-cost structure of XaaS business models? What if core products were inherently designed to drive and measure the outcomes customers desire? What if the outcome was embedded in the core design just waiting to be unlocked?

This looks like the Innovator's Dilemma,[4] but what TSIA's research exposes is that even in the face of increased customer demand for consumption models and despite the correlation of key practices with adoption, retention, and ARR, the majority in the industry (born-in-the cloud SaaS, incumbent hardware, industrial, health tech, and software companies) is not deviating much from traditional operating practices for creating offers and designing user experiences.

TSIA continually benchmarks these product organizations' practices. Below are just a few data points that illustrate these behaviors:

- Just 30% of companies are creating value- and outcome-based offers and pricing.
- 75% are not documenting the trial usage patterns that generate product qualified leads (PQL).
- Virtually no product teams are prompting users with feature or new-offer suggestions within the product experience.
- Just a third of companies have a well-defined and measurable formula for customer "stickiness."
- Less than 25% of product development teams are defining product experiences with knowledge of the customers' business processes.
- Just 19% are leveraging viral network effect features.
- Less than 40% are embedding help, (micro) learning, or education into the user experience.
- Less than half of products are capturing product NPS feedback.
- A mere 14% are measuring customer effort in the form of customer effort scores (CES).

Based on TSIA benchmark data, we could continue to add to the above list, but no doubt you get the point. This is why we stress the power of merging the operating capabilities of the business with the features of the product.

The Value Ladder Challenge

The presence of a large value gap is like being at the bottom rungs of a value ladder. As technology companies climb the ladder, more and more capabilities are integrated into their offers to ensure that the customer realizes the most value possible. But technology-provider businesses can face many challenges when confronted with the challenge of climbing the ladder.

We've established that what has made the products successful in the past will not result in success over the long term. Climbing the XaaS value ladder requires different strengths, skills, and capabilities. Climbing the ladder requires performing deeper discovery into the customer's business processes and a large dependency on data and analytics to design, create, launch, and tangibly prove the value proposition shown in Figure 4.9.

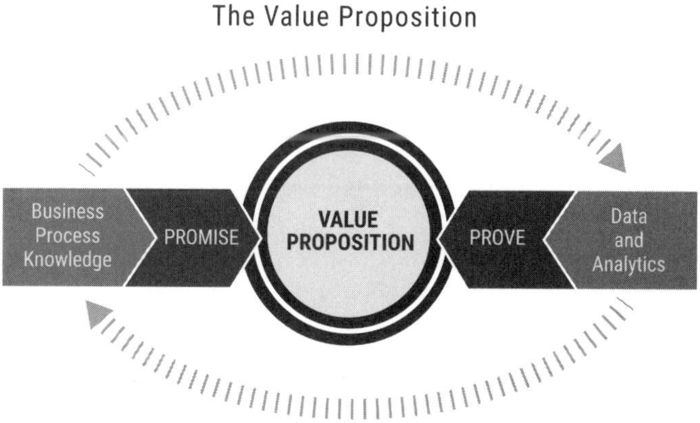

The Value Proposition

FIGURE 4.9 The Value Proposition

The prospect of taking that journey can be daunting. Evidence indicates that there's a range of reasons that technology businesses are not taking on the challenge with enough intent and haste in the face of customer and investor demand. These include:

- Lack of awareness of the rapidly changing market dynamics.
- Denial that the traditional offers are rapidly commoditizing.
- Complacency about learning what it takes to build scalable XaaS revenue streams.
- Inertia due to being comfortable with the status quo.
- The "build it and they will come" mentality, where once the XaaS offers are defined, it is assumed they will just sell themselves and adoption will be automatic.
- Fear of the unknown, which includes not knowing where to start nor how to anticipate challenges.
- Overconfidence, which results in blind spots to the operational differences in the XaaS model.

As businesses navigate the challenges of climbing the value ladder, they often face operational headwinds that require investment and bold leadership to overcome. These headwinds include:

- Complexity.
- Lack of data.
- Lack of operational capability.
- Skills gap.
- "Not invented here" cultures.

These challenges must be quickly overcome if businesses are to prevail. While companies are focused on the climb, competitors are not standing still.

As Jack Welch, the former CEO of General Electric, once famously said, "If the rate of change on the outside is greater than the rate of change on the inside, the end is near." If the end is not immediately apparent, you can be sure your company is headed for decline over the long term. TSIA's T&S 50 Index tells this story very well, with its 1.6% CAGR between 2015 and 2020 and declining margin performance.

We must take this voyage with business and human awareness, fearlessness, compassion, intention, and an open mind to internalize the industry's lessons.

So far in this chapter we've identified the following:

- Changing customer relationships in XaaS recurring revenue business models.
- The value gap of the majority of technology companies.
- The efforts and costs involved in the face of the value gap.

Hopefully, by now you are convinced that something has to give. This value gap has to be addressed if technology suppliers are to grow the business. They must have customers continually realize value, capture a continuous and fair exchange for delivering the value, and they must accomplish both these things at scale (that is, profitably).

When we think about products that climb the value ladder in the context of the Wave Two Digital Transformation, we note the relevance in the following areas:

- **Users.** Suppliers must create compelling and tangible value propositions for both buyers and the end users of their target customer segments and create viable partner value propositions. The ecosystem of partners actively contributes to the value exchange with the supplier and the value consumption of the buyer and end user.
- **Customer business outcomes (CBO).** Discovering the business outcomes that the customer is after is job one in the process of creating products that climb the value ladder.

- **Discover, design, create, launch (DDCL).** This is the process where the value-based products are conceived and brought to market.
- **APLAER.** It's during this process phase that value is actually realized by the customer.

Customer journey analytics help us actually measure if the customer is realizing the intended value as they navigate their journey with the supplier and related partners. Figure 4.10 highlights the areas in the W2DT framework impacted when building capabilities to have products that climb the value ladder.

TSIA's W2DT Model

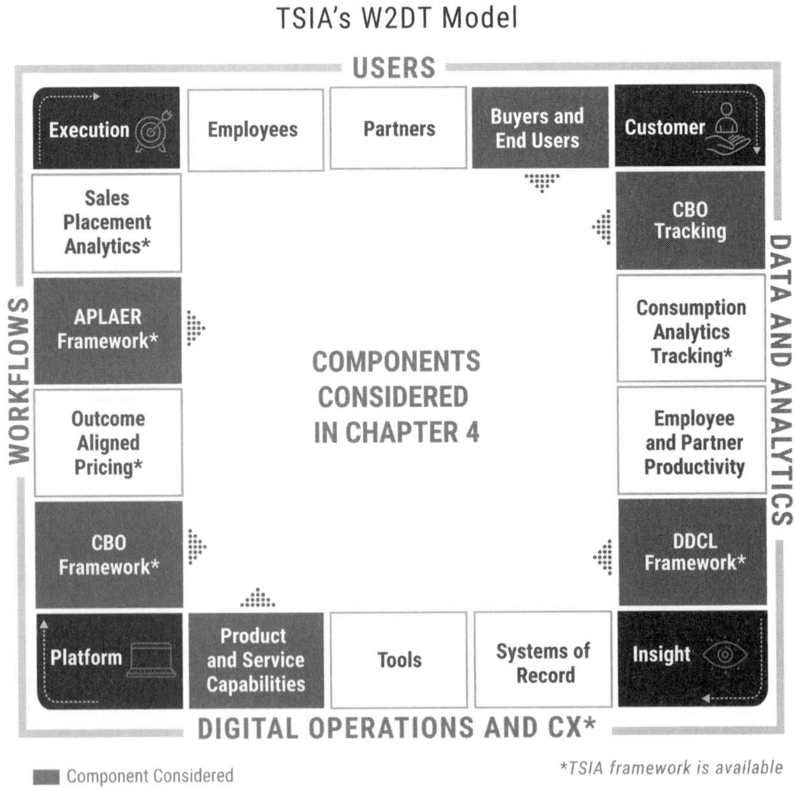

FIGURE 4.10 W2DT Framework and Products that Climb the Value Ladder

What follows is a series of five workstreams that help XaaS businesses close the value and outcomes gap with products that climb the value ladder. Here we will examine how to:

1. Set the organization up for value management success.
2. Discover what the customer values.
3. Design offers that climb the value ladder.
4. Integrate operational capabilities into the digital customer experience.
5. Measure the value.

1. Set the Organization Up for Value Management Success

TSIA research has established, through numerous cross-organizational studies, that siloed, unaligned, and inwardly focused functions create significant drag and add friction to the operational gears of business growth. To give true consideration to the organizational implications of effectively managing value, let's start by looking at the interdependencies along the XaaS Value Stream seen in Figure 4.11.

The XaaS Value Stream

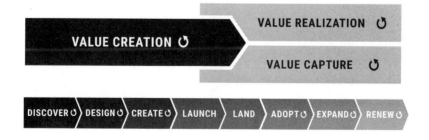

FIGURE 4.11 The XaaS Value Stream

The work product of the value creation phase has outsized influence on the effectiveness and efficiency of the customer value realization and the sales function's to capture that value in the form of revenue. However, a value gap exists.

The reality is that the majority of technology vendor businesses continue to organize as if they are operating in a make-sell-ship business model, with the business of value mapping predominantly conducted by the sales and services organizations or the customer themselves.

These teams are working hard to understand the customer's goals and prove the value propositions with the presence of a business value mapping function, often known as the value management office (VMO). Today's VMOs mainly exist to close the value gap with their largest customers so they are happy.

The value gap cannot be closed by today's VMO construct. Why? Because the value gap is large; VMO activities are highly manual and focused on only the largest large customers. The value gap must be solved at scale and reach all customers.

In this operating model, it's also not difficult to see the chasm that exists in the majority of B2B technology organizations between the value creation activities and the customer value capture and realization activities, as seen in Figure 4.12.

So, who in the company owns solving this value and outcomes gap? In a recent TSIA poll,[5] the industry weighed in on that very question, and the results can be seen in Figure 4.13.

Clearly, every department plays a contributing role in the end-to-end management of value from the discovery of what that means to the target customer, to the sale, delivery, adoption, expansion, renewal, and, ultimately, customer lifetime value (CLTV) growth.

In an effort to align to the concept of value management across the entire company, the concepts associated with value mapping conducted by a sales-focused VMO must shift left, all the way up the value stream to the very beginning of the XaaS offer life, illustrated in Figure 4.14 (page 78).

The Value and Outcomes Gap

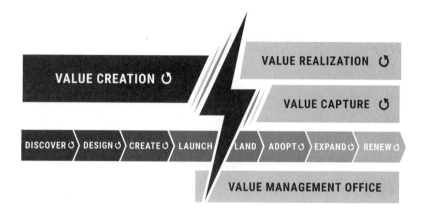

FIGURE 4.12 The Value and Outcomes Gap

Who Owns Closing the Value and Outcomes Gap?

FIGURE 4:13 Who Owns Closing the Value and Outcomes Gap?

From Product Management to Value Management

Everyone knows that the reason a business exists is to create value, monetize that value, and make a profit. This is true, whether you are an ice-cream store, a car rental company, or an established technology company. If we accept this premise, then arguably, as

Aligning Value Management across the Entire Company

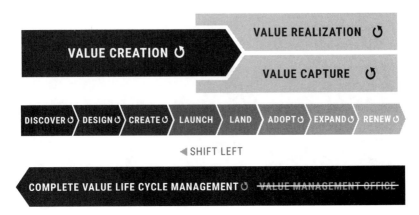

FIGURE 4.14 Aligning Value Management across the Entire Company

a technology industry, our focus should be on value and actively creating, monetizing, and managing that value.

So why is the team that's responsible for creating and monetizing the core value proposition referred to as *product* management? Let's take a moment to understand that evolution.

Hewlett Packard was one of the very first tech companies to recognize the need for product management. The company leveraged the earlier Proctor & Gamble "brand man" model to create sustained, year-on-year growth of 20% between 1943 and 1993. The HP interpretation of the brand-man ethos was all about ensuring that its product was anticipating the market trends and was responsive to the market and the customer needs throughout the product development cycle. Anyone related to product management will recognize this concept because it underpins the role of modern product management to this day.

As far back as the 1980s, Harvard Business School's Theodore Levitt coined the term "whole product"[6] to describe the additional elements that were often required to round out customer offers to ensure that the value was realized.

But it's time for another seismic shift in recognizing that with the business model shift to XaaS, it's no longer about just the product; it's about continuous delivery of value within service-intensive economic engines.

To drive a cultural shift of the product team away from feeds and speeds, features and functions, or anything that associates with the latest shiny tech objects, and toward an organization that consciously creates, delivers, and life-cycle manages the VALUE, businesses could do well to:

1. Rename product management to value management to drive home the expectation of where the ownership lies for creating tangible value offers that customers expect and will adopt.

2. Formally establish a value management life-cycle process to ensure holistic contribution from all relevant stakeholders, as defined below and illustrated in Figure 4.15:

    a. Product management is responsible for managing the full value life cycle.

    b. The process has engagement and collaboration from the sales, service, and product functions.

    c. The process is led by the value management organization.

Ensure the value management function reports centrally to the CEO/business unit general manager to leave no doubt of its importance to the scalable growth of the business.

The industry is increasingly recognizing the outsized impact of product management in recurring revenue models, which are highly dependent on effective outcome selling, effective adoption, scalable renewal processes, and customer outcome realization. Further, the industry shows strong signs of understanding that these business outcomes are only possible with offers that are intentionally designed to deliver value and outcomes with no gaps in the value chain.

Customer Value Management

FIGURE 4.15 Value Management Life Cycle

The manifestation of that recognition is illustrated by the central reporting of the function to the C-suite. SaaS businesses are leading the charge in this central product management reporting trend, as seen in the research data shown in Figure 4.16,[7] but even the hardware companies with aspirations to grow their XaaS revenues are taking note.

This increasing rate of the central reporting relationship is a recognition that the goal of double-digit, as-a-service revenue growth is never to be realized with siloed organizations that are reflective of a make-sell-ship-only culture. Further, this growth can't be realized without the operational capabilities of marketing, sales, and service being integrated into the technology product experience, as outlined in Chapter 2. Given that the digital experience is the only scalability differentiator in a technology business, there is an increasing expectation that product management

Central Reporting of Product Management
to CEO or Business Unit GM

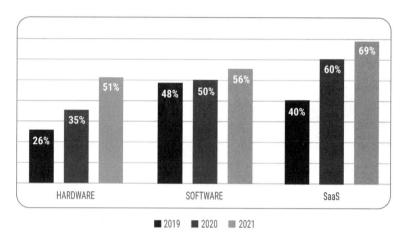

FIGURE 4.16 Central Reporting of Product Management to CEO or Business Unit GM

is uniquely positioned as a proxy for the business to lead and engage across the company to drive the engine of growth.

Product management teams reporting to the CEO or a business unit GM are under a bigger spotlight and more pressure to address these essential questions:

1. How do you define the customer value and outcomes?
2. How do you build offers to realize value and outcomes?
3. Can the sales team be trained and enabled to sell the value and outcomes?
4. Can customer success scale by gaining insights into customer value realization?
5. Can value and outcomes be proven at the time of renewal and expansion?
6. What expansion opportunities are possible when customers achieve the intended outcomes?

7. Is the product designed and built effectively to empower partners to drive adoption of your core offers and deliver customer outcomes?

8. Does the platform have telemetry to provide customer, internal, and partner stakeholders the visibility they need to realize their outcomes?

9. Does the platform have the ability to lower APLAER costs and improve results across the customer life cycle?

Many product management teams, and in particular the product management teams that are tucked in under the engineering function, face some real capability gaps when it comes to addressing these essential questions.

These product management knowledge gaps include:

- The gap in the XaaS foundational business model knowledge.
- The gap between the ability to define, measure, and price the value proposition.
- Understanding the changing nature and needs of the partner ecosystem to drive adoption, renewal, expansion, and business scale.
- The gap between current offers and the needs of the customer. With the VMO residing in sales, how can businesses "shift left" that process for use in defining the value propositions?
- The gap between what it takes to effectively operationalize the technology, particularly when it's on premise. With managed services teams operationalizing previously created technology, how can businesses "shift left" that knowledge to inherently design and embed the non-functional requirements (NFR)[8] for operating the technology?

These knowledge gaps are addressable, and in some cases with resources that reside within their own companies.

Now think about what different perceptions could be created with the renaming of product management to value management. Below are a few:

- What about the conversation between a customer value manager (CVM) and the customer? Would the customer be more likely to appreciate that the business is uniquely focused on designing solutions that help them realize tangible value and business outcomes? Absolutely.

- Imagine the conversions between the CVM and the engineering, sales, services, or finance functions. Might there be an implicit alignment around customer value? You bet.

- What about a value life-cycle management process rather than the term product life cycle or new product introduction (NPI), the favored term for shipping new products to market in tech? Very likely.

- Context is everything and perception has a way of becoming reality. Names matter.

Three big questions remain when it comes to making a move like the one suggested above.

1. Charter: Does your organization have the clear responsibility from senior leadership to focus on actual customer value realized?

2. Knowledge: Does your current product management team have the knowledge required to understand all the elements in the recurring revenue engine to be effective?

3. Funding: With the "shift left" of responsibility to lead the value management life cycle, the increasingly vertical market focus of successful XaaS businesses, the new added complexity of value over features, not to mention the superior customer insights required, must the current product management structures absorb more work?

On this first question of XaaS knowledge, the reader might be surprised to learn that fewer than 40% of surveyed product managers[9] in tech could whiteboard the calculation for ARR if asked. This statistic includes product management from cloud-native companies. The knowledge gap must be addressed for product management to lead the customer value life cycle for their products.

An analogy is worthwhile to help us understand the importance of this point. Would you as a business leader accept that a product manager for an iOS mobile app does not need to completely understand everything about the platform, including the iOS operating environment, tools available, Apple App Store distribution methods, or Apple revenue sharing model? Of course not. So why do leaders accept that product managers developing products and offers for success in the XaaS business model may not understand everything about the model and how every decision, from architecture to features to portfolio design to pricing to analytics, have a material impact on the viability of the offers and the scalability of the business as a whole? Interestingly, while many product managers come to the role with an MBA, few learned anything about recurring revenue service-intensive business models.

Can you and your product management team pass the simple XaaS knowledge test in Figure 4.17?

If not, they are operating with material blind spots when it comes to designing products that climb the value ladder.

On the question of funding the product management team to take on more work to lead the value life cycle, from where are these funds likely to come? Let's put a few considerations on the table:

- If offers are intentionally designed to deliver value and outcome for each vertical served, will that help reduce the cost of sales?

- If the operational capabilities of the company (marketing, sales, service) are designed into the digital experience, will that drive down the cost of related operations?

XaaS Knowledge Test

CAN YOU AND YOUR PRODUCT MANAGEMENT TEAM PASS THIS SIMPLE XaaS KNOWLEDGE TEST?

XaaS BUSINESS MODE	ANSWER
Name at least four elements that positively or negatively impact the ARR calculation:	
Define the relationship between onboarding and subscription renewal rates:	
Explain the impact of non-monetized customer success on the business P&L:	
Outline the difference that price discounting makes when shipping units versus subscription licenses:	
Describe the role of products designed for vertical segmentation on profitability:	

FIGURE 4.17 XaaS Knowledge Test

Should funds be reinvested from reduced human expenditures that comes with the digital customer experience? Absolutely. This is arguably part of Wave Two of digital transformation.

In the end, your digital experience is your only scalable differentiator. Product management funding must be right-sized for the job.

To summarize this section on setting up the organization for success, it's no longer only about delivering cool features on schedule, but it *is* about discovering what the customer values in each targeted vertical subsegment, designing offers that deliver the targeted value and outcomes, and creating products that deliver immersive experiences that drive up value for the customer with use and drive up value capture for the supplier. Setting up the organization for success includes the following considerations:

1. Establish the value management office with a cross-functional team of product, marketing, sales, service, and partners.
2. Ensure that value life-cycle management is led by an outbound, vertically focused product management role.
3. Rename the product management function to value management.
4. Ensure that the value management function reports directly to the C-suite.
5. Invest in team education on value life-cycle management and the XaaS business model.
6. Inspect and realign budgets to address shifted responsibilities.

2. Discover What the Customer Values

Designing products that deliver value and outcomes on a recurring basis starts with understanding the customer's problem. Customer discovery is a foundational step to get right. Discovery is the process of identification and analysis of a market segment including personas and their use cases in the "problem space." Discovery in this context is similar to the kind of customer-specific discovery that a smart sales team would do to ensure the proper fit of a proposed solution to a prospect's business outcome objectives. But in this case, it's discovery at the level of an entire market segment. Figure 4.18 highlights this phase in the customer value management model.

Research reveals that verticalization is trending with XaaS businesses in search of profits. Even Salesforce and ServiceNow are pursuing vertical solutions to improve this profit profile after 19 and 16 years, respectively, to demonstrate their first positive NOI.

Figure 4.19 illustrates how to get from problem to solution via vertical markets and target segments.

The Process of Discovery in Customer Value Management

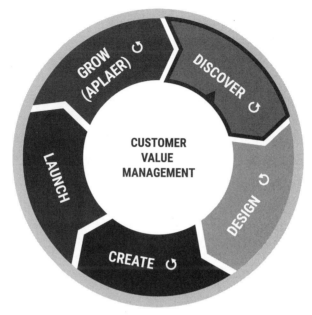

FIGURE 4.18 The Process of Discovery in Customer Value Management

Verticalization as a Means to Improve the Profit Profile

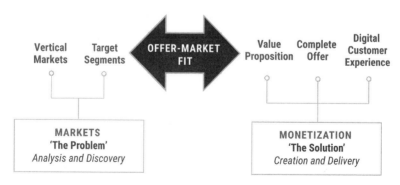

FIGURE 4.19 Verticalization as a Means to Improve the Profit Profile

A vertical market is a market in which suppliers offer products and services specific to an industry, trade, profession, or other group of customers with specialized needs. Healthcare or financial services are such vertical examples. A single vertical market can have multiple market subsegments. Collectively, this is what we call the problem space.

Examples of vertical markets and their segments are listed in Figure 4.20.

It's critical to get as granular as possible in the business-process discovery process. As we'll see later in this chapter, the closer the value proposition gets to solving for particular use cases, the higher the offer-market fit. High offer-market fit delivers a myriad of benefits, not the least of which is customer satisfaction, revenue growth, and, when combined with other practices, scalable supplier operations.

Example: Vertical Markets and Their Segments

VERTICAL MARKETS	SEGMENT EXAMPLES
FINANCIAL SERVICES	Wealth Management, Institutional Banking, Consumer Banking, Stock Trading, Insurance
HEALTHCARE	Regional Hospitals, Large Hospital Networks, Doctors' Offices
AUTOMOTIVE	Auto Parts Suppliers, Auto Manufacturers, Auto Dealers
TECHNOLOGY PROVIDERS	Security, Healthcare, Industrial Equipment, Ad Tech, Artificial Intelligence, Large Global Enterprises, Startups
US GOVERNMENT	Department of Defense (DoD), State, Local, and Education Government Agencies (SLED), Department of Housing and Urban Development (HUD), Federal Emergency Management Agency (FEMA), Internal Revenue Service (IRS)

FIGURE 4.20 Example: Vertical Markets and Their Segments

Within each subsegment, there are personas who are engaged in a series of workflows to do their jobs. What are the business outcomes that these groups (segments) of customers are seeking? As we put ourselves in the customers' shoes, Figure 4.21 examines their likely narrative.

Desired Outcomes Segmented by Customer Persona

	CUSTOMER LENS
BUSINESS OUTCOMES	• What business outcome am I seeking?
FINANCIAL RESULTS	• What financial results will I realize for the business upon achieving this business outcome?
KPIs	• What are the KPIs I must monitor to ensure I am on track to achieve my business outcome? • Can my supplier and/or their partner provide the KPI monitoring for me?
PRACTICES	• What practices and capabilities do I need to master to achieve my business outcomes with this technology provider's solution? • What can I expect from my technology provider and their partner(s)?
ROLES	• What role do I and the technology provider play in achieving the outcome?
TECHNOLOGIES	• How do the supplier's technology, services, data, processes, people, and partners help to improve my KPIs, financial results, and targeted business outcome?

FIGURE 4.21 Desired Outcomes Segmented by Customer Persona

Let's use Hubspot as an example of deeply understanding the workflows and business outcome objectives of a user persona. To keep it simple we will use a horizontal (multi-vertical) persona. HubSpot is a provider of software products for inbound marketing, sales, and customer service. Hubspot's target audience for its marketing hub products is marketing departments.

Within many of these marketing departments are demand-generation teams. The *business outcome* these customers seek is the generation of marketing qualified leads (MQL) that can be passed along to their sales teams, many of which will generate *financial results* as they convert into paying customers. Figure 4.22 illustrates this process.

The Business Development Funnel

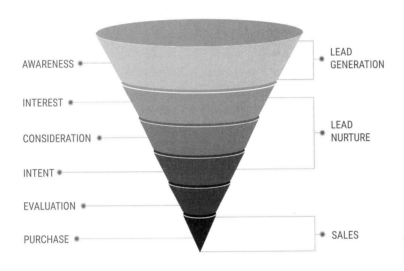

Source: HubSpot

FIGURE 4.22 The Business Development Funnel

These demand-generation teams monitor the entire funnel of activities. They are the KPIs associated with awareness campaigns, the growth of the contact database, the contacts' pre-sales engagement scores, the conversion rates, and the number of MQLs generated.

On the quest to generate the outcome of MQL volume, demand-generation teams engage in various practices to develop their contact database via marketing campaigns (in the form of paid and organic digital search, product placement, email, social media, direct mail, public relations, affiliate marketing, and content marketing) to drive the numbers to the highest possible level. These contacts are what HubSpot's marketing platform customers value highly. The customers' demand-generation teams (roles) engage in creating awareness and nurture campaigns, and HubSpot provides the software to empower those activities.

With this business process knowledge, the HubSpot product teams are now in a position to think about how the features of their product might best help the users achieve their goals and the data that's needed to tangibly demonstrate to the user how the technology, services, and analytics actually contribute to that.

In sum, the essential elements of customer discovery on the path to creating products that climb the value ladder are:

1. Identify the business outcomes the customer is trying to achieve.
2. Determine what it values toward achieving those goals.
3. Deeply understand all the activities and workflow steps in which the customer engages to achieve its goals.

3. Design Offers that Climb the Value Ladder

With a deep understanding of customers' desired business outcomes and their methods to measure success, we can now begin the process of engineering the outcome, identifying value metrics, and creating the solutions that are inherently designed for the highest level of offer-market fit.

Figure 4.23 highlights this phase in the customer value management model.

The key question with which to start is: How does your offer portfolio become highly compelling in the eyes of the customer to improve their target business outcomes?

The Process of Discovery in Customer Value Management

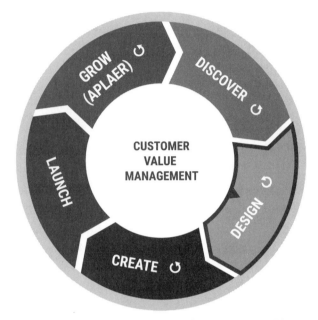

FIGURE 4.23 The Process of Design in Customer Value Management

Defining Value

It involves deep consideration of technologies, roles, practices, and KPIs to achieve the business results upon delivering the expected business outcomes for the customer on a continual basis.

Four supplier types were first introduced in the book *B4B*[10] and are seen in Figure 4.24. As suppliers move from Level 1 to Level 4, they are reducing the value gap discussed above and increasing the customer value realization.

In each of these stages, the relationship between the supplier and the customer becomes increasingly effective, transitioning from a transactional relationship to one that is contractual that evolves from delivery of a service with an SLA to delivery of value with a value level agreement (VLA) or delivery of a business outcome with an outcome level agreement (OLA).

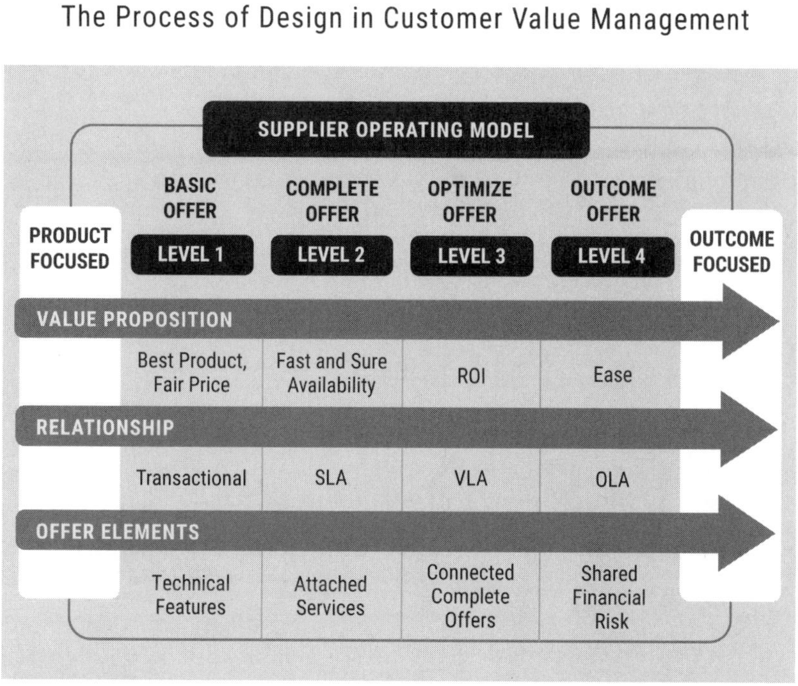

The Process of Design in Customer Value Management

SUPPLIER OPERATING MODEL				
	BASIC OFFER	COMPLETE OFFER	OPTIMIZE OFFER	OUTCOME OFFER
PRODUCT FOCUSED	LEVEL 1	LEVEL 2	LEVEL 3	LEVEL 4	OUTCOME FOCUSED
VALUE PROPOSITION	Best Product, Fair Price	Fast and Sure Availability	ROI	Ease
RELATIONSHIP	Transactional	SLA	VLA	OLA
OFFER ELEMENTS	Technical Features	Attached Services	Connected Complete Offers	Shared Financial Risk

FIGURE 4.24 The Supplier Operating Model: The Four Supplier Types

VLAs may not be contractual in nature, although they are implied in that the supplier-customer relationship is put at churn risk if they are not continuously achieved.

Likewise, the value propositions become increasingly effective in delivering value and reducing complexity for the customer.

The development of "complete" offers with highly tangible value propositions is necessary for climbing the value ladder. Complete offers are defined as a set of technology, services, data, and analytics advised by the customer journey and designed to continually unlock value and deliver a desired business outcome via an immersive digital experience.

This definition is the next generation of the "whole product" idea mentioned earlier, but taken to the next level with data and the digital customer experience.

Optimize (Level 3) and outcome (Level 4) offers are not possible without data. Data provides the insights to the customer journey, consumption patterns, and the trends enabling technology providers to deliver value back to customers in the form of productivity analysis, workflow efficiencies, risks mitigated, cost savings, revenue generated, and value realized.

An example of a complete offer is Cubic's NextBus,[11] outlined below:

- Vertical market: Municipal departments of transportation
- User personas: Passengers, drivers, transport operations management
- Offer: Optimized bus schedule management
- Offer attributes: Cloud-based digital platform serving all user personas:
  - Hardware:
    - Energy-conscious digital displays for transit stations, bus stops, and passenger vehicles
    - Driver control unit: A GPS-enabled intelligent management and communications device that delivers real-time analytics and provides two-way operator messaging to empower driver decision making
  - Software:
    - GPS and advanced computer modeling: Automated passenger counter, vehicle location, turn-by-turn navigation
    - Digital platform supporting open data APIs
    - Passenger mobile apps
    - Passenger payment validator
  - Data and analytics: Real-time passenger transit information, bus schedule adherence status, real-time arrival predictions

- o Services: Technology support and managed services, data analytics, and visualization services
- Immersive digital experience: Cubic uses data gathered from sensor data to enable:
  - o Announcement of bus arrival times to electronic billboards at bus stops
  - o Passenger journey planning via the mobile app, including changing bus ETA, route information, delay alerts, and fare collection
  - o Effective transportation operations management, including delays or congestions, with the ability to reroute to serve the biggest ridership needs
- o Tangible value metrics: Increased bus ridership
- o Tangible business outcome: Reduced personal vehicle miles traveled per person
- o Expansion opportunities: Building on NextBus as the backbone, Cubic can expand engagement under the NextCity umbrella
  - o Expansion offers:
    - □ Revenue management for fare collection, road-user charging, and more
    - □ Surface transport management: Monitoring and control of urban and inter-urban road networks
    - □ Cubic Interactive as a service: Integrated advertising and loyalty as a service connecting transit agencies with brands seeking to reach riders

Additional examples of complete offers can also be found in Chapter 9, specifically:

- Kaeser's Compressed Air as a Service
- Michelin's Transportation Solutions

- Philips Healthcare's Enterprise Monitoring as a Service
- Diebold ATM as a Service
- Dell Technologies Data Center as a Service

Engineering the Business Outcome

Once the customer segment's value and outcome metrics are understood, the key question becomes: How does the supplier's offer portfolio evolve to become highly compelling in the eyes of the customer while achieving the technology provider's business objectives of optimized revenue capture and operational scale?

This begins the creative process of transforming a XaaS offer from its traditional configuration into an offer that includes the necessary attributes to succeed in a XaaS world. Ultimately, the journey is one of forming tighter, mutually beneficial, sticky relationships that improve critical value metrics for the customer. It involves deep consideration of technologies, roles, practices, and KPIs to achieve the business results upon delivering the expected business outcomes for the customer on a continual basis.

The key questions every supplier must answer when engineering that outcome are depicted in Figure 4.25.

How can suppliers assess the degree of offer-market fit they have established? The framework outlines four levels. Each of these XaaS offer levels comes with a set of essential and incremental attributes critical to meeting the customer expectation, differentiating in the market, and achieving an acceptable level of supplier financial performance.

For optimal value alignment with the customer and to realize strong financial performance at scale, there are essential and compelling attributes on this Level 1 through Level 4 continuum that enables these states. Achieving scale and profit with the XaaS offer portfolio requires mastery of a set of attributes. The next section outlines these attributes.

Considerations When Engineering Customer Outcomes

	SUPPLIER/PARTNER LENS
BUSINESS OUTCOMES	Are our offers (and those of our partners) optimally aligned to the customer's target business outcomes?
FINANCIAL RESULTS	How is the customer's financial performance affected upon achieving the target outcomes? How does this affect our financial performance?
KPIs	What KPIs should I monitor... • To ensure the customer is on track to achieve their targeted business outcome? • To ensure cost-effective sale and delivery of the outcome?
PRACTICES	What practices and capabilities do I need to improve... • The customer's target business outcomes? • Our ability to deliver the targeted value at reasonable cost? • (Optional) The partner's ability to service and grow the customer?
ROLES	What are the combined set of roles across the customer, (the partners) and our business play in achieving the outcome?
TECHNOLOGIES	How do our technology, services, data, people, processes, and partners, help to improve the customer KPIs, financial results, and targeted business outcome?

FIGURE 4.25 Considerations When Engineering Customer Outcomes

Attributes of Compelling XaaS Offers

When developing compelling XaaS offers, this shift in customer expectations must be considered. Otherwise, a technology provider defaults to simply port technical feature functionality to the cloud and slap a subscription-based pricing model on this new offer. This can be done, but it does not result in a compelling XaaS offer. The "eight great attributes" listed below are necessary to make a XaaS offering compelling to enterprise customers:

1. **Operational simplicity.** The XaaS offer is not hard to technically implement or run. Any operational complexity is assumed by the vendor.

2. **Pay as you need.** The customer does not pay for capacity or features that are not being utilized.

3. **Enhanced insights.** Leveraging new telemetry generated by a XaaS platform, the technology provider can apply analytics and AI to provide new valuable insights to the customer.

4. **Accelerated adoption.** The vendor is adept at helping key roles within the customer's organization effectively utilize the capabilities of the technology, often via a combination of product- and customer success-led engagements.

5. **Process optimization.** The technology helps optimize and digitize key employee or customer-facing processes.

6. **Specific KPI improvements.** The adoption of the technology can be linked to the improvement of KPIs within the customer's environment.

7. **Quantified financial gains.** The adoption of the technology can be linked to specific financial improvements that are tracked and quantified.

8. **Accelerated business outcomes.** The adoption of the technology can directly be linked to helping the customer achieve strategic business objectives.

In sum, the essential elements of designing offers that intentionally deliver value and outcome realization include:

1. Perform outcome engineering for each vertical subsegment (to advise your offer design).

2. Assemble complete-offer portfolios that improve the value metrics.

3. Price the tangible customer value (covered in Chapter 5).

4. Integrate Operational Capabilities into the Digital Customer Experience

The process by which a prospect becomes a customer, and every engagement the company has with that customer, has the opportunity to be digitized. This includes many touchpoints with the sales, marketing, and services teams, as detailed in Chapter 3. This aligns well with the concept of product-led growth (PLG).[12]

PLG is a strategy centered on applying a digital product to the marketing, sale, and successful growth of a supplier's value proposition. The PLG go-to-market strategy is realized by building the methods of discovery, acquisition, adoption, renewal, and expansion into the digital product experience itself. The product is not only creating the promise of value, but it also plays a starring role in actually delivering the value and expanding the customer's usage (and spending!).

In a fully realized digital customer experience, tasks and roles that were traditionally labelled front- and back-office functions are now blended to provide an optimal customer experience. The most obvious of these traditionally back-office activities is billing and payments processing. An example is e-commerce capabilities for purchasing initial subscriptions and automatically renewing them. B2B buyers have begun to take this for granted and can expect technology providers to dramatically increase the degree to which they are engaging in this. A great example is Autodesk's store,[13] enabling the initial purchase and automatic renewal processing of a variety of architectural, design, simulation, and manufacturing software products.

In sum, designing and automating *all* operational capabilities necessary to deliver the complete customer experience will drive up the value metrics while measuring the performance of each step. This is ultimately bringing the product to bear on the problem. As we stated earlier, your technology is your only scalable differentiator. B2B technology suppliers are strongly encouraged to take a digital product-led approach to every experience.

5. Measure the Value

The visibility to customer usage patterns and practice behaviors provides vendors with a unique opportunity to truly understand how the customers are using their solutions. Now more than ever, there's an opportunity for technology providers to leverage that visibility to not just talk about value propositions, but also to truly align the creation and delivery of value with the customer realization of value; and further, actually have that reflected in the pricing models. More on pricing new value propositions will be discussed in the next chapter.

Tangible value comes in the form of measuring value and outcomes. Establishing this during the offer-design phase greases the skids for new customer sales and removes friction from the renewal and expansion process. There's nothing like providing objective data to customers, taking all subjective arguments off the table and actually proving the original product promise. This process shifts some level of empowerment back to the supplier and significantly increases the supplier's pricing power. More on this will also be shared in the next chapter.

Further, the power of establishing customer value and outcome metrics is also seen in the internal focus it creates. The product design discussion must ask this question: "How does driving up a well-identified customer value metric contribute to the customer's desired business outcome?" Answering that class of question ensures that product teams remain laser focused on what matters to the customer and orient all customer experiences to achieve that goal. Cultural shift, anyone?

Chapter 4 Takeaways

This book makes the case that high-growth, high-profit technology business models will be anchored in simplicity and value realization. Executive teams and product leaders must internalize and act upon the key assertions of this chapter, at least within technology companies that plan to remain relevant. They are:

- The practices that fueled growth and captured market share in transactional CapEx models are not the ones that will fuel growth in consumption-based OpEx models.

- Success depends on value, not products.
- Growth and scale depend on exceptionally differentiated experiences that tangibly improve customer business metrics.
- Product management organizations are at the epicenter of a company's ability to build offers that accelerate value realization for customers.
- The value-creation team must deeply understand the business model for which they are designing.
- Assemble complete-offer portfolios that improve value metrics.
- Your digital experience is your only scalable differentiator.
- Organizational focus can be achieved by aligning actions to value metrics.

Do you have what it takes to climb the next rungs of the value ladder? The future of your business may depend on it.

5 | Outcome-Aligned Pricing

By Laura Fay

"Pricing is what you pay for the value received.
If you've got the power to raise prices without losing business to
a competitor, you've got a very good business.
And if you have to have a prayer session before raising the price
by 10%, then you've got a terrible business."

— *Warren Buffett*

The Impact

Pricing has one of the biggest impacts on the bottom line, often even more than customer acquisition costs and customer retention. It is the fastest and most effective way for businesses to increase profits or make funds available for other investments. As far back as 1992, *Harvard Business Review* research revealed that a 1% improvement in pricing leads to an 11.1% hike in operating profit![1] Consistently, in an article titled "The Power of Pricing,"[2] McKinsey reported that on the average income statement of an S&P 1500 company, a price rise of 1%, if volumes remained stable, would generate an 8% increase in operating profits. That's an impact of nearly 50% greater than a 1% drop in variable costs (such as materials and labor) and more than 300% greater than the impact of a 1% sales volume increase.

Why does pricing make such a relatively bigger difference to the bottom line? Unlike new-customer acquisition and customer retention, there's little-to-no ongoing operational cost associated with pricing changes. The price-point lever can therefore have an outsized influence on the gross and operating margin of the business.

Beyond the short-term impact on profitability, pricing also affects brand perception. There is a famous story told by the founders of the eyeglass frame upstart Warby Parker. Based on the cost to manufacture its frames, the initial business plan set a price of $25 per frame. It could be a profitable company at that price point. Yet, when it tested that price point with advisors, the feedback was ubiquitous: "No one will buy your frames. They will assume they are cheap and poor quality." They raised the list price to $99, still well below the price others were charging. This pricing move, combined with creative marketing strategies, propelled the company to success. The rest is history.

Pricing Is Strategic

Recognizing how critical the pricing strategy is to the success of a company, you would be forgiven in thinking that businesses are working hard on the science of pricing to maximize profitability and market share. The data suggests otherwise.

Effective XaaS pricing is not an isolated activity and cannot be designed in a vacuum. Arriving at the right price point is the result of multiple strategic factors including, but not limited to, the target market norms, customer familiarity and acceptability, company strategy, the relative revenue sources of the company (also known as the economic engine or "how a company makes money"), the business' pricing power, the profitability time horizon, and more. In addition to these factors is the leverage derived from the integrated design of the product, offer, and pricing in consumption-based business models. So instead of wading into this complexity, technology providers have taken a simpler route…outcome-aligned pricing.

What is outcome-aligned pricing? *Outcome-aligned pricing is a consumption-based revenue model where a product's pricing is directly linked to the value the customer receives.*

Said another way, the product's value proposition is measurably contributing to the customer's desired business outcome. Outcome-aligned pricing is an under-exploited lever in growing recurring revenue businesses.

In this chapter, we're going to refer to various pricing models and anchors, so it's worth a moment to define them ahead of the discussions.

- **Per-user pricing.** This model is anchored on the number of users with access to the features and functionality of a service for a period of time, typically a subscription.
- **Outcome aligned pricing.** This pricing model is anchored on the number of value units that the customer consumes. Consumption based pricing fits in this category.
- **Outcome-based pricing.** This is pricing that's linked to the customer business outcome that is realized with the use of a provider's technology and services. This can also be thought of as business results risk sharing.

The Directional Trend

As outlined in earlier chapters, the waves of change still unfolding in the tech industry are nothing short of breathtaking. These changes to the digital customer experience are correspondingly playing out in pricing models, as seen in Figure 5.1.

The Risk/Reward of XaaS Pricing Models

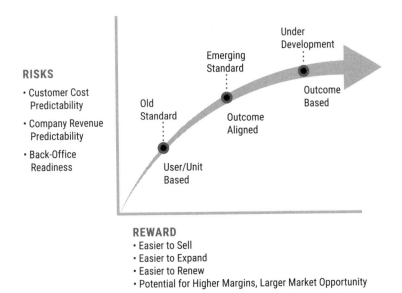

FIGURE 5.1 Trends in Pricing Models

The Past and Present Value Leakage Problem

Given the potential impact of effective pricing to the business, it's truly eye-popping that many companies spend more time selecting their janitorial services than they spend on pricing. This is particularly true for early-stage XaaS businesses. Product teams are very focused on innovating the next shiny object. Historically, that's how tech businesses differentiated and competed on features, functions, feeds, and speeds. Pricing wasn't considered to be such a strategic weapon in a differentiated transactional model.

In fact, pricing was barely on the radar of the product and strategy teams. Marketing and sales took care of it by setting the per-user list price and establishing multiple schedules that typically involved discounts for volume purchases, regional discounts, channel partner discounts, promotional discounts, bundle discounts, and competitive matching. Figure 5.2 documents the dynamic that, over time, there is downward pressure on the list price of a technology as the technology matures. Customers expect to pay less for the same capability.

When new competitors enter the market, there is even more pressure to drop prices. This reality is documented in Figure 5.3.

The combination of commoditization and competition results in a significant reduction in revenue from any given customer over time, as shown in Figure 5.4.

It is interesting that the software technology industry is an industry that, despite creating so much value, has established a

The Problems with Today's per X XaaS Pricing Model

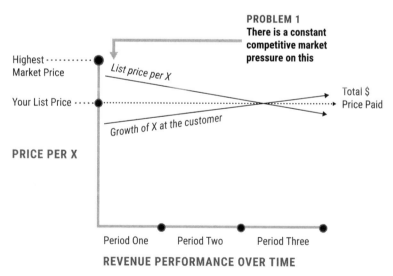

FIGURE 5.2 XaaS Pricing Model – Problem 1

Problems with Today's XaaS Pricing Models - Problem 2

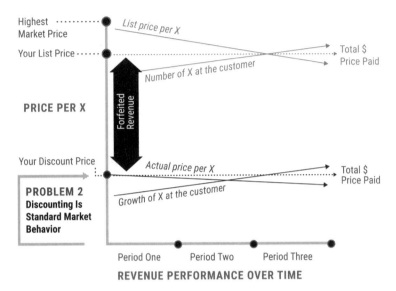

FIGURE 5.3 XaaS Pricing Model – Problem 2

Problems with Today's XaaS Pricing Models - Problem 3

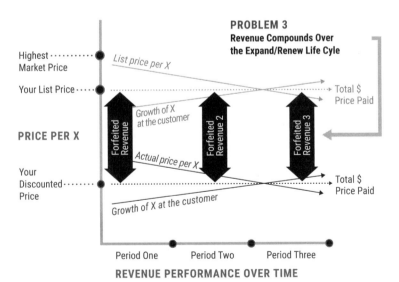

FIGURE 5.4 XaaS Pricing Model – Problem 3

culture of aggressive discounting practices. These practices were established at a time when the incremental cost of delivering an additional unit of software was negligible, and customers knew and leveraged this knowledge in their price negotiations. It is worth pointing out that customers largely have accepted that in the presence of hard-cost goods, like hardware, and human-powered services, their price negotiation power has limits.

It's also no surprise that the supporting life-cycle management process in most B2B companies is called new product introduction. This term has been around in the technology industry for decades, originating with manufacturing companies and with deep roots in engineering, with process phase gates from concept through launch. All this worked reasonably well where compartmentalized and relatively siloed departments worked to develop, launch, and sell new technologies. It was unidirectional—a one-way push of a value proposition.

But this process often creates a big disconnect between the creation of the value, the pricing of the value, and preserving the value at the time of sale. In the end, customers were ultimately responsible for figuring out how to make the most of the vendors' value propositions, which we know most of the time they don't or can't,[3] rendering full customer value realization unfulfilled.

In this traditional model, vendors left money on the table with multiple heavy discounts[4] while they trained customers to demand even more discounts. And customers did demand them because they knew all too well that the vendor's promise of value was only the beginning of the story. The realization of that value would take significantly more in internal IT cost and vendor maintenance and support contracts before the customer realized the full value from their technology purchases, as shown in Figure 5.5.

The Cost of Value Realization

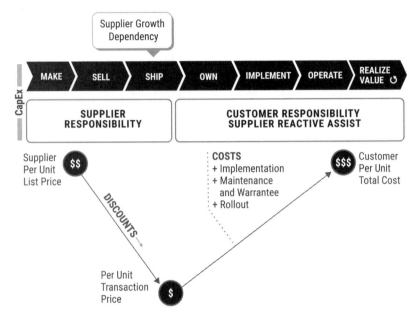

FIGURE 5.5 The Cost of Value Realization

The Customer Burden

At a macro level, technology providers didn't sweat these discounts too much, except for making their quarterly bookings number. Why? Two big reasons. First, with relatively high software gross margins, the discounting practices didn't hurt at all, as the marginal cost of shipping another unit of software was negligible. Second, ultimately, technology providers extracted more money from the customer in the form of highly profitable and mostly reactionary support and warranty contracts. Software companies, in particular, had this exploit down to a T. These contracts were the customer's insurance policy against defects and future software upgrades. These highly profitable support contracts were largely the customer's price to pay for buying a complex technology. Customers expected defects and system failures and paid handsomely to reduce their exposure when these defects and failures inevitably occurred.

Change Happens

Along came connected-cloud solutions that dawned the era of the as-a-service business model simplification for the customer, as technology providers absorbed more complexity. This represented a big value shift in the industry that is still playing out.

With the XaaS model, there's no need for customers to deploy the solution on their premises and a reduced need to engage companies to help them get the basic technology up and running. The suppliers, or their implementation partners, now simply take care of that step, and they incur the related costs. For example, as outlined in the previous chapter, a managed service business may take on the full operation of the solution for the customer, which moves further costs onto the supplier, as seen in Figure 5.6.

In the face of the relationship changes, so too has the complexity and cost shifted from customer to supplier. Correspondingly, the associated risk has also shifted. In absorbing this complexity, suppliers take on significantly more revenue risk, while

Moving the Value Realization Costs to the Supplier

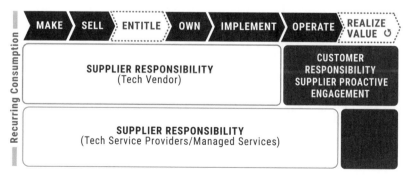

FIGURE 5.6 Moving the Value Realization Costs to the Supplier

seeing their gross margins drop as a result of the increase in COGS with increased hosting and other ongoing service delivery cost obligations.

Further, connected-cloud deployments now provide visibility to the customer consumption patterns and practice behaviors. This gives vendors a unique opportunity to truly understand how the customer is using their solutions. *With this new data, they can see how the customer is using their technology to realize value and no longer have to guess.*

In sum, the changes from the traditional business model to the XaaS business model demand that suppliers reevaluate their pricing models to factor for the changes to:

- Buyer expectations.
- Value propositions.
- Cost structures.
- Customer behavioral insights.

The Impact on Pricing

This was the first time in the industry where there was the opportunity to leverage product consumption visibility to not just talk about value propositions but to align them with what the customer truly values, and ultimately have that reflected in the pricing models.

However, since these early days of cloud deployment, we see that market-following, per-user pricing remains the mainstay of most as-a-service B2B businesses today. Examples abound, such as Salesforce Sales Cloud Suite Editions,[5] VMWare's WorkSpace One (AirWatch),[6] Google Workspace (formerly named G-Suite),[7] and SAP Cloud Analytics.[8] We'll explore some of the reasons for this below.

Ahead of inspecting the practices of the provider-customer value alignment and setting pricing accordingly, let's look at some of the pricing pitfalls that vendors regularly encounter.

We're confident you'll recognize at least a few of these happening in your business.

Pricing Pitfalls in an As-a-Service World

As the hockey puck is moving to consumption models at every level of infrastructure, to platforms, applications, and fully managed services, established businesses are faced with realizing the consequences of the historic practice of paying little attention to pricing. Why does effective pricing matter more now than it ever did with traditional models? Because today's offers are recurring, either consumption or subscriptions attached to either users and/or an outcome.

In these models, it's not one and done, but an ongoing repeated series of transactions over the lifetime of the customer relationship. Pricing done poorly can be the gift that keeps on giving, and not in a good way. Traditional practices are not effective, and many of the conventional approaches can't be relied upon to realize results in the XaaS model. Let's look at just a few common pitfalls that companies regularly experience in XaaS when they apply many of the same old traditional pricing practices while expecting a different outcome.

- Price "SaaS-ification"
- One price fits all
- Pricing complexity
- Following the market exclusively
- Underpricing
- Timing
- Discounting (including applying the same channel discounting model from traditional practices)
- Misaligned values
- Per-user feature buckets

Price "SaaS-ification"

When long-established technology companies decide they must respond to demand for consumption models, they often take the quick step to "SaaS-ify" the pricing of their offers.

What does this mean? Without any changes to their technology offer construct, its deployment posture, or its value proposition, businesses simply allow customers to purchase the same product with their OpEx budget on a subscription basis, instead of, or in addition to, purchasing with CapEx dollars on a perpetual license basis. In this scenario, businesses often define the subscription price using the list price of the perpetual license as their only guide. That is, they take the price of a perpetual license and divide by X, where X is the number of years (usually 3, 4, or 5) over which the perpetual license was typically amortized. An example is illustrated in Figure 5.7.

A "SaaS-ified" Price Example

OFFER LICENSE A A CapEx PURCHASE BY IT BUYER	
Technology Perpetual License Price	$100,000
Attached Support Contract Year 1	$20,000
Revenue Recognized in Year 1	$120,000

OFFER LICENSE B OpEx PURCHASE BY IT OR BUSINESS BUYER	
Technology Subscription Price	$20,000
Support Included	
Revenue Recognized in Year 1	$20,000

FIGURE 5.7 A "SaaS-ified" Price Example

Businesses rationalize taking this approach because:

- It gives investors the appearance of transformation with subscription revenues on the books,
- It is easily explainable to sales, and
- The math is understood by the customer.

The Pitfall

There are many pitfalls here, which all derive from a desire to quickly add or change to a new pricing model with zero consideration for the differences in the underlying business model. In the example above, the supplier has simply applied a random price point to a technology offer with no consideration to the risk shift from the customer to the supplier that's just occurred. Given this risk shift, the supplier must take steps to ensure successful onboarding and adoption. With these costs added to the cost to deliver (at least basic) support, the gross margin takes a hit. Further, if the new offer provides cloud access to the technology, the hosting costs, as shown in Figure 5.8, may impact gross margin even further. All of this occurs even before addressing the competitive posture of the rapid commoditization of the traditional technology value proposition.

One Price Fits All

As noted in Chapter 4, which discussed products that climb the value ladder, a vertical market is a market in which technology providers offer products and services specific to an industry, trade, profession, or other group of customers with specialized needs. Addressing the specialized needs of a vertical market segment with a unique value proposition is a winning play for high offer-market-fit and profitability.[9]

Still, most recurring revenue offers today are not uniquely designed for particular verticals. When they are, however, 68% of those companies with vertically segmented offers also price the

The Business Model Change When Moving
from Product to XaaS

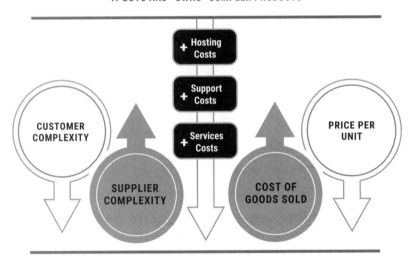

FIGURE 5.8 The Business Model Change When Moving from Product
to XaaS

value delivered in those offers uniquely,[10] as seen in Figure 5.9.
But what about the remaining 32%?

The Pitfall

The pitfall here is applying horizontal pricing methods to dif-
fering value propositions. Assuming suppliers deliver unique
and tailored value to each of their market segments, not pricing for that unique value may leave margin points on the table.
This represents an opportunity for at least a third of the technology providers out there.

Prevalence of Unique Vertical Pricing

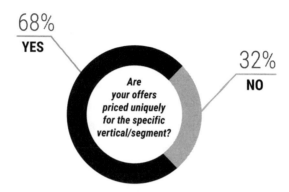

FIGURE 5.9 Prevalence of Unique Vertical Pricing

Pricing Complexity

In Chapter 2: Complexity Kills, the case is clearly made that customers are increasingly expecting simplicity, and the industry is responding. Practices like digital sales and the self-service of configure-price-quote (CPQ) processes are going only in one direction.

Have you ever observed price structures where:

- Sales needs a PowerPoint deck to explain pricing to a customer?
- To quote a price to a B2B customer you need a formula-rich spreadsheet?
- The pricing structure nickel-and-dimes the buyer?
- The prospect has to contact the supplier to clarify the pricing?

Imagine this example: What if, in addition to the term, number of users, and level of feature functionality, Salesforce's price was calculated based on number and type of browser platforms, size of the data stored in the cloud services, number of MS Outlook mailboxes synchronized, and the volume of application program-ming interface (API) calls made?

The Pitfall
There are many pitfalls of a complex pricing model, including delayed or lost sales cycles as a result of customer analysis paralysis while they understand the implications of the model, estimate their ongoing costs of ownership, and translate the cost to the value they expect to realize once deployed.

Following the Market Exclusively
In market-based pricing, suppliers sell at a price point of "what the market will bear." While this works for companies like Apple and other organizations with highly sought-after solutions with market-leading pricing, there is more risk of downward pricing pressure from market followers responding to competitive forces. Reflecting legacy practices, market-based pricing remains highly popular for born-in-the-cloud companies anchored on per-user access to feature functionality by volume.

The Pitfall
While it feels like a winning approach to pay close attention to competitors' pricing, making it a primary focus ejects suppliers out of the control seat and hitches their profitability prospects to their competitors, who may not actually have a well-thought-out approach to pricing. In the face of this race to the bottom, it also signals commoditization of your value proposition.

Underpricing
Often businesses set the price point of their offers well below the customer's willingness to pay for the value and differentia-tion they have worked hard to establish. This can be the result of multiple factors, including the market-based pricing point stated above or intentionally underpricing as a market-share grab strat-egy to get users on board first and figure out how to monetize

later. This is a promoted de facto strategy of venture-backed, born-in-the cloud companies intent on disrupting established markets and businesses.

The Pitfall

When products are priced lower than the customer expects, this can undermine the value of the offer in the eyes of that customer and can bring perceptions of low quality and low value to mind. Business buyers may therefore associate higher risk with the offer, which may or may not reflect the reality. Figure 5.10 Is there a

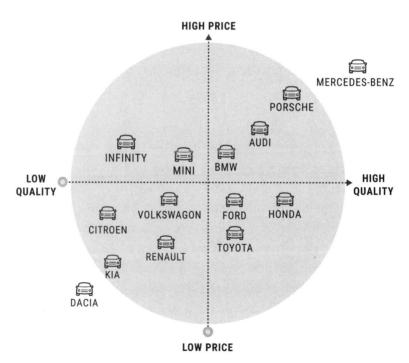

FIGURE 5.10 Example Perception Map of Price versus Quality in the Automotive Industry

source for 5.10? illustrates this point with an automotive example. Further, once the lower price point is established, competitors can have a field day in stoking the flames of these perceptions.

Timing

During the early and high-growth stages of a business or a new offer in the market, where the time horizon to profit may be multiple years away, the effective monetization of related goods and services is often postponed. Startups and XaaS incubators at this stage are often referred to as Future Value Aggregators,[11] where the value accumulated through acquisition of customers is assumed to be monetized at some later date. As the company launches and is focused on high growth, the subscription price often includes support, partially (or non-) monetized implementation services, adoption services, and managed services in support of doing whatever it takes to ensure customer adoption, renewal, and growth. The data validates this. Early-stage SaaS companies often wait until they have over $100 million in revenue beachhead before attempting to monetize the needed services for growth.[12]

The Pitfall

Postponing the assessment of the business' ability to charge for the complete offer may be a big mistake, as the monetization plan will determine if customers are likely to derive enough value from the product to be willing to pay for it. The sooner suppliers can determine the true value of their products to the customer by testing the market and learning the lessons of monetization, the better. Deferring the creation of an effective monetization strategy may also affect customers' perceptions of value, making it more challenging to raise prices when the company's runway to profit shortens. A product or service funded with subsidies (by the company or investors) rather than the revenue captured from value delivered is ultimately not a sustainable long-term strategy, and the piper will be paid eventually.

Discounting

Let's face it, technology sales are addicted to the discounting drug. Why? Because from the time NCR began selling the first cash registers in the late 1880s, sales reps have been offering technology with discounts to entice buyers and create a forcing function to close deals and make their quotas. As outlined earlier in this chapter, enterprises buying technology have learned to expect discounts of all kinds when buying assets with CapEx budgets, most notably, but not exclusively, in software. The channel partners that serve these same buyers want their cut, too.

The technology industry practice of discounting has carried over to the as-a-service business model, where the new business buyer is making a service purchase with its OpEx budget. The vendor's goal is to get the new customer on the platform. It rationalizes that it may lose money on the customer in the first year or two but assumes that eventually the customer will become profitable to the company.

The Pitfall

Suppliers have an ongoing cost obligation to deliver the *service* in anything-as-a-*service*. Discounting gobbles up profit margin, and discounting of services repeatedly gobbles up even more profit margin. And if the customer does not renew in Year Two or Year Three, the company has spent a lot of money servicing an unprofitable customer. Even if the customer stays on the platform, data illustrates that SaaS discounting can lower customer lifetime value (LTV) by over 30%![13] Practiced in the traditional way, discounting in XaaS is detrimental to the viability of any as-a-service business intent on sustainably growing recurring revenue, and for their customers who expect to realize ongoing value from their XaaS contracts. Partners need to be weaned off the old discounting model and be incentivized to compete for delivering value to customers all throughout the life cycle.

Misaligned Values

Alignment of values is when the proposed value proposition is actually realized or has a very high potential to be realized. Offer-market fit is strong, as the value proposition meets the customers' needs. This is one of the most important foundational concepts for effective pricing of recurring revenue contractual offers.

In the traditional model, it wasn't the end of the world if the expectations and values of the customer were different from those of the vendor. In fact, there was no significant motivation for the vendor to expend extensive energy determining if the values were optimally aligned. If the customer was willing to pay the (discounted) price point to acquire the technology, who cared how they used it?

The Pitfall

The pitfall comes when XaaS vendors take that same approach and are not attempting to align their values to that of their customers. Products are hanging out on the lower rungs of the value ladder. Arguably, when vendors focus exclusively on features and function and spend little time trying to truly understand the outcome for which the customer is striving, they miss the mark. Pricing the wrong value proposition misses the mark entirely, as illustrated in Figure 5.11.

In recurring models, there *is* such a thing as a bad customer. It occurs when the motivations of both the customer and the vendor are not aligned. In this case, the customer may or may not effectively adopt the technology and may, ultimately, churn. At best, they will not reach the full potential in lifetime value (LTV) or, worse, they may take the suppliers' product teams

Misaligned Values

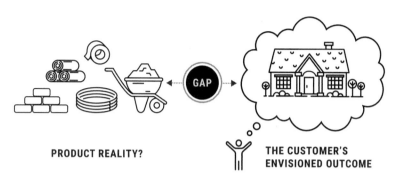

PRODUCT REALITY?   THE CUSTOMER'S
                    ENVISIONED OUTCOME

FIGURE 5.11 Misaligned Values

off course with feature requests that are not aligned with the target markets.

Per-User Feature Buckets

Despite the relationship shift and the related increased revenue risk and increased costs, why do many suppliers continue to price their solutions on a per-user basis for buckets of features?

We see a number of reasons across the industry, which include:

1. Customer model familiarity.
2. Customers believe they can budget easier with per-user models.
3. Supplier failure to recognize the difference in the operating model and related opportunities and cost structures.
4. Fear associated with asking customers for a fair price for the new and/or different value proposition.
5. Inability to tangibly measure the value created and delivered (more on this later in this chapter).
6. Selling feature/function on a per-user basis is what the sales team knows how to do.

7. Customer procurement teams fail to understand or care about "value."

8. The process for value and outcome engineering seems daunting.

9. The internal billing systems don't accommodate new pricing models.

10. There are concerns about revenue recognition changes.

11. There is inertia or the deer-in-the-headlights syndrome.

The Pitfall

Regardless of an individual company's reason for sticking with only per-user pricing methods, it's clearly an unoptimized model when it comes to aligning to customer value. Worse, it can artificially constrain adoption. Examples of companies that have adopted models unconstrained by the per-user paradigm are found later in the chapter.

Let's take a simple example of OpenTable to illustrate the point. OpenTable is a reservation platform whose customers include restaurants, hotels, and casinos. It makes money via monthly subscriptions, bookings, and service fees that reflect the goals and consumption patterns of its customers. What if OpenTable exclusively charged its customers on a per-user basis while providing the features to facilitate taking reservations? The answer: Its revenue growth potential would be significantly capped. More on the OpenTable pricing model later.

Thus far in this chapter we've established the following:

- Pricing is the fair exchange for value delivered.
- Pricing power is a function of your differentiated value proposition.
- Pricing has a huge impact on margins.
- Blindly following competitors' pricing is a failed strategy.
- Discounting has a compounding negative effect in XaaS.

- Pricing complexity kills.
- Data on customer behavioral patterns create new pricing model opportunities.
- Per-user subscription pricing has limitations.

Now that you have drowned in the pitfalls and challenges that must be overcome in pricing in a XaaS world, let's break it down to a set of tactics that suppliers can leverage to tackle an outcome-aligned pricing strategy.

1. Establishing the value metrics
2. Connecting value metrics to business outcomes
3. Setting the outcome-aligned price points

Tackling Outcome-Aligned Pricing

Research shows that the root cause of a subpar pricing strategy is often suppliers simply not putting in the work to determine the most effective economic exchange rate for their value proposition and positioning it appropriately. Once a less-than-optimal price is in the market, suppliers often lack the confidence to change their price point. Part of the new confidence comes from being able to tangibly demonstrate and deliver the value proposition to customers.

When we think about outcome-aligned pricing in the context of the Wave Two digital transformation, as Figure 5.12 references, we can clearly see that it has contextual relevance in the following areas:

- **Users.** Buyers need to budget for planned purchase costs. Partners will build out their solutions to support the supplier's outcome-aligned pricing model.
- **Workflows.** Customer business outcomes and the discover-design-create-launch life cycle: outcome-aligned pricing is the result of *discovering* what the customer values, *designing* the

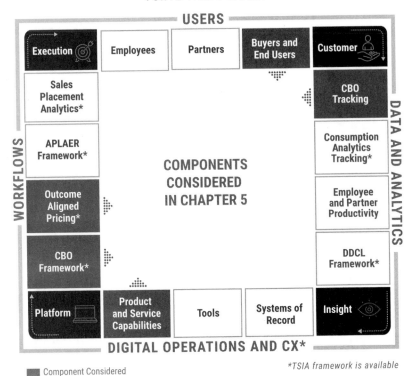

FIGURE 5.12 Outcome-Aligned Pricing in Wave Two Digital Transformation

pricing model of the offers and aligning that to the associated value metrics, *creating* experiences that help continually deliver more value with use, and continually *launching* improvements to those experiences. Outcome-aligned pricing is the fuel for placing, landing, adopting, expanding, and renewing APLAER the solution.

- **Data and analytics.** Consumption analytics are essential to measuring how much value for charge for and to effectively bill for consumed value.

Let's break this down into a few parts.

At the risk of stating the obvious, outcome-aligned pricing is built upon a foundation of tangible outcome contribution. In Chapter 4, we made the strong recommendation that suppliers should identify customers' outcome metrics for every vertical subsegment they are targeting. In the context of understanding what makes the customer tick, this is job number one. Without this understanding, suppliers will be at a disadvantage in the quest to understand their contribution to the outcome that the customer seeks.

What is the difference between value and outcomes? Figure 5.13 defines it for us.

Let's Clarify Our Terminology: Value versus Outcome

"VALUE"
IS THE ELEVATOR PITCH STORY

Value

val·ue / noun / verb (used with object)

1. The regard that something is held to deserve; the importance, worth, or usefulness of something.
"Your support is of great value."

"OUTCOME"
IS THE ACTUAL BUSINESS RESULT

Outcome

out·come / noun

1. The way a thing turns out; a consequence.
"It is the outcome of the vote that counts."

FIGURE 5.13 Value versus Outcome Terminology

Value is somewhat subjective, the price for which is often in the eye of the beholder. More specifically, value and its related pricing is set according to the provider and actualized at the time of sale. As described above in the CapEx model, after all the discounts are shaved, it's pretty clear that buyers are not aligned to the same definition of value as that of suppliers.

It's for this very reason that the focus on measurable outcomes is a more meaningful concept on which to align the customer and the provider. Outcomes and related metrics move from the realm of subjective to objective when it comes to measurements on which pricing can be based.

An outcome metric is the unit of value that can be linked to how much the customer pays for the technology provider's product. Licensing or pricing may be based on the outcome metrics themselves or on related metrics that are an associated proxy for the outcome metrics (let's call these enabling outcome metrics). Defining the outcome metrics is key. If you can't do this, forget about delivering outcome-aligned pricing and find a different chapter to read. Better yet, stop what you are doing now and figure out what your outcome metrics are.

Introducing the TSIA Outcome-Aligned Pricing (OAP) Model

To move beyond per-user pricing to get to the rewards of outcome-aligned pricing, you must first unpack and deal with the risks outlined earlier in the chapter. Figure 5.14 examines the risks associated with outcome-aligned pricing.

In considering the key attributes of good outcome-aligned pricing, you can envision a structure that maps both risk and reward of your pricing, as seen in Figure 5.15 (page 130).

There are six attributes that drive the ability for a technology provider to pursue outcome-aligned pricing.

The Risks of Outcome-Aligned Pricing

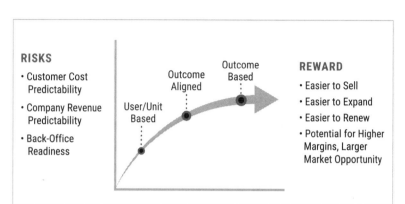

FIGURE 5.14 The Risks of Outcome-Aligned Pricing

1. The outcome is easy for the customer to understand.

When a prospect considers your product, they can immediately understand why the pricing might be designed the way it is. Either they clearly want that metric to grow for their business or they inherently understand that the supplier has costs associated with a resource tied to the outcome metric, or both. For example, the following companies align on these outcome metrics and charge customers based on their growth:

- HubSpot Marketing Hub: Number of marketing emails captured

- Snowflake: Compute resources, data volume

- DropBox: Storage capacity

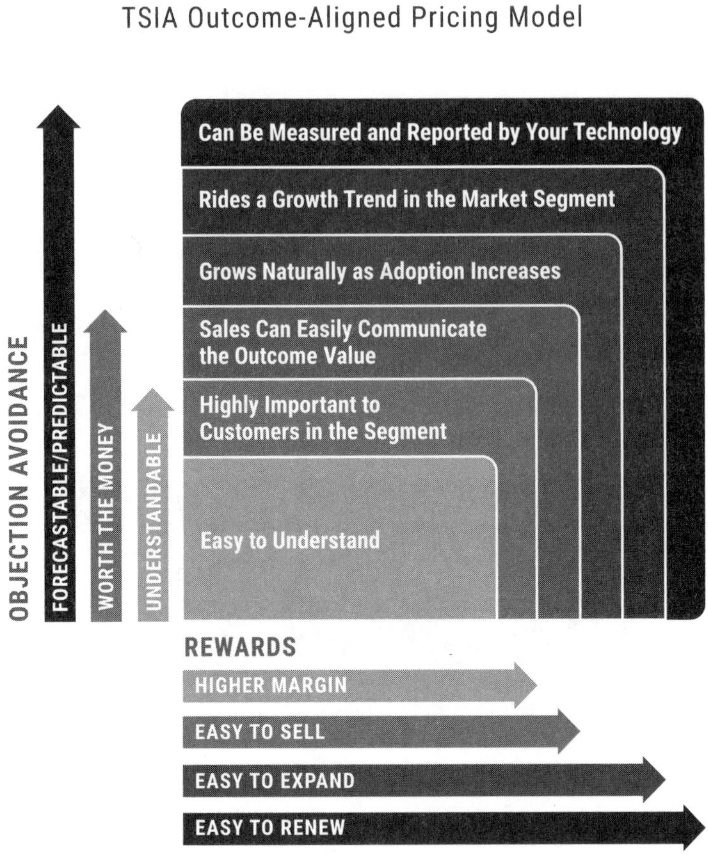

TSIA Outcome-Aligned Pricing Model

FIGURE 5.15 TSIA Outcome-Aligned Pricing Model

- OpenTable: Per-seated diner booked
- Cubic NexBus[14] (transportation): Number of bus riders, bus-on-schedule rate
- A "price optimization application" in specialty retail: Check-out basket size, increased inventory turns/stock-keeping unit (SKU), increased basket size per customer visit

2. The outcome is highly important to the customer.

Let's look at the HubSpot marketing example again. The goal of the demand generation team in the customer marketing department is to generate marketing qualified leads (MQL) for the sales team. As mentioned in the previous chapter, to generate volumes of leads, the contact database must grow multiple times the size of the MQL database. The enabling outcome metric of the number of marketing contacts is perfectly aligned with, and contributes to, the uber outcome that the customer wants to achieve; that is, grow MQLs that result from nurturing the acquired contacts.

In the OpenTable example, the business outcome of the restaurant is to drive up revenue. The OpenTable enabling outcome metric of the number of diners delivered to the restaurant perfectly aligned with that business outcome of revenue growth.

3. Sales can communicate the value of the outcome.

If the customer can easily understand your pricing and its attachment to an outcome they care about, the sales function should have little trouble getting it. Sales does not have to expend energy to map (justify) the value proposition to the intended outcome and, therefore, there is no need for the expense of a value management office (VMO), as discussed in Chapter 4.

4. The outcome grows naturally as the adoption increases.

Let's consider this attribute with a Salesforce automation platform example, such as Salesforce Sales Cloud, NetSuite CRM, Zendesk Sell, HubSpot Sales Hub and others like them. The outcome expected by any customer of such platforms is reliable visibility to the forecasted sales pipeline of the business. Let's imagine that just 50% of a company's salespeople use the designated Salesforce automation tools. In such a scenario, it's not hard to imagine that the company doesn't get the outcome of dependable insight into their total sales forecast. If however, 100% of salespeople use the platform for their sales opportunity management activities, the better visibility the business has to that sales pipeline and are in a significantly better position to realize dependable insight to the sales forecast. This outcome grows naturally with increased adoption by the sales personnel.[15]

5. The outcome rides a growth trend.

Keeping with our mobile use example, the volume of data consumed over the mobile device has been exploding with gaming, content streaming, video calls, e-sports, and health and fitness classes, and is expected to continue,[16] fueled by 3G, 4G, and now 5G, as seen in Figure 5.16.

In our mobile use experience as consumers, today we use voice less and data more, and the younger generation even more

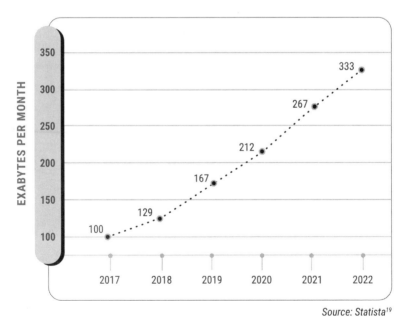

Data Volume of Global Consumer IP Traffic, 2017 to 2022

Source: Statista[19]

FIGURE 5.16 Data Volume of Global Consumer IP Traffic, 2017 to 2022

so, which is another market growth vector. It's no wonder that carrier billing has shifted accordingly. No longer do we consider plans based on voice minutes, but we choose plans based on available data. Carriers have quickly adapted to this market trend growth for their outcome-aligned pricing strategy.

6. The outcome can be measured and reported.

Measurable outcome metrics help providers move from arm waving about value propositions to getting tangible about the value contribution to the customers' desired outcomes. Without measurable data, there's no opportunity to engage in outcome-aligned pricing and no opportunity to inject tangible objectivity into the customer conversation.

The more of these six attributes in play, the more likely a technology provider can achieve the following customer-facing objectives:

- The customer understands the business benefits of the solution.
- The customer believes the solution is worth the investment.
- The customer will be able to forecast the benefits of the solution on their business.

These six attributes also unlock the following benefits for the technology provider:

- High margin on the solution
- Easier to sell
- Easier to expand
- Easier to renew

An additional and critical benefit of outcome-aligned pricing is that it allows your sellers to present your offers as self-funding solutions. A self-funding solution pays for itself right away. If a customer spends X amount of dollars to realize an outcome from your product, be it fully aligned to their uber business outcome or tangibly contributing to that outcome, and then it experiences an acceptable gain from realizing that outcome, continual use is all the more likely.

Lastly, recognizing that predictably forecasting customer cost and vendor revenue can present challenges, vendors with consumption-based and outcome-aligned pricing models are often tackling that challenge by establishing consumption estimates and making an advance commitment for a forward-looking period and drawing down on a pre-paid amount as value is consumed. "Trueing up" at the end of the period and recalibrating for future periods follows. Other methods include blended usage-based subscription tiers, where the baseline may be per user along with outcome-aligned variable tiers. Autodesk, AWS, and Twilio are just a few company examples that offer these flexible billing terms to address enterprise customer budget management cycles and their own deferred revenue schedules (also known as remaining performance obligation).

Aligning Price to Outcome Metrics

With your customer-outcome metrics and your enabling-outcome metrics well defined, this opens a wealth of opportunities for pricing models. There are many good reasons to hitch your pricing to outcome metrics (as opposed to user-based metrics), which include:

- Uncapped growth. Growth is not artificially capped by the number of users (also referred to as seats), where customers may artificially limit use in an attempt to save money.

- Market rewards. In recognition of the uncapped potential, and according to Openview Partner data, public companies with consumption-based offers are trading at a 50% revenue multiple premium over their peers.[17]

- Traditional pricing based on per-user metrics is not aligned with a growth trend:

  o   As digital experiences increasingly automate a variety of human tasks, fewer humans (i.e., users) may be needed to use your technology in the future. As an example, workflow automation vendor Zapier reports that today the majority of knowledge workers rely on automation to get their jobs done.[18]

  o   Artificial intelligence (AI) may further reduce the need for humans to interact with your technology. Hitching your monetization models to the number of users will not futureproof your business. AI company Databricks, for example, recently reported over a million downloads per month of its machine-learning product.[20]

  o   Open platforms deliver value through APIs where no user is needed to realize value. For example, embedded messaging provider Twilio processed 600 billion API-based transactions in 2019.[21]

The transparent sharing of outcome metrics adds a level of objectivity and tangibility to the customer conversation, as it directly connects value delivery to customer outcome. It facilitates the outcome conversation and avoids the big discounting negotiations. In doing so, it preserves more value in the sale and in the subscription renewal process, as seen in Figure 5.17.

Once you've decided to establish outcome-aligned pricing, the actual price point will be a function of many inputs. These will factor in your deep understanding of the complete customer business process and the relative contribution of the outcome metric to the customer's business outcome, i.e., how much is the customer willing to pay for your unit of value when compared with its next-best alternative. That next-best alternative may be a competitive solution, or a "do nothing" decision where the

The Value Proposition

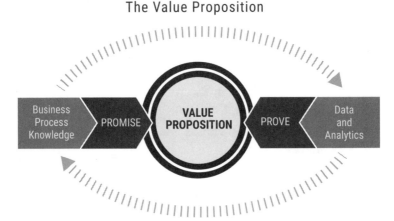

FIGURE 5.17 Outcome Metrics Connect Value Delivery to Customer Outcome

competition is the cost of the customer's current way of doing things. The price point will also factor in your cost to deliver the service—hardware, software, and human resources—and a target profitability profile.

Examples of Outcome-Aligned Pricing

Outcome-aligned pricing is an emerging standard, which we can expect will accelerate rapidly in the coming years. Blended per-user and outcome-aligned usage models are showing up in early-stage businesses and more established enterprise providers like Salesforce, Box, and Zoom. Below are examples of outcome-aligned pricing across a variety of sectors.

OpenTable

OpenTable engages in outcome-aligned pricing in the form of a base platform monthly access fee and a per-diner generated fee (in the industry parlance, that's "per-network cover") when using the digital experience, and the outcome metrics are:

- It is easy for the customer to understand.

- It is aligned with the uber business outcome for which the customer is striving (grow revenue).

- It grows organically with use, as restaurant-goers repeatedly return to the platform because of the ease of making reservations with the digital experience and the accumulation of loyalty points and perks. Restaurants promote it, as they know that users prefer the convenience.

- It rides the market growth trend of increasing expectations of ease and convenience, particularly with younger generations.

In the above example, OpenTable's core principle is to make booking a restaurant reservation super easy. The outcome metric that validates that is the number of reservations made on the platform per restaurant in a given time period. When OpenTable produces the results for its customers, its own revenue grows. As the OpenTable reservation platform becomes even more popular, it can offer competitive insights to restaurant managers, further improving the value of the service to their restaurant customers.

Auth0

Auth0[22] is a middleware provider of digital user authentication and authorization solutions "for everyone but not just anyone." Basically, it makes the customer's login process secure. In addition to the B2E use case, it serves B2C and B2B sectors where customers are growing their business as a function of the number of user accounts on their platforms. The customer outcome metric is the number of accounts—more customer accounts, more user logins to be authorized and authenticated by the Auth0 solution. Auth0 links the pricing of its solution to the number of customer accounts.[23] When the customer grows its volume of accounts, Auth0's revenue grows.

Autodesk

Autodesk, Inc. is a software corporation that makes software application products and services for the architecture, engineering, construction, manufacturing, media, education, and entertainment industries. Autodesk offers a per-user subscription combined with a flexible option to access any part of the Autodesk product portfolio at a flexible daily rate with pre-purchased tokens. Autodesk addresses the need to only pay for what's used and not pay for full user access when customers' projects are time-bound project-based. The customer business outcome metric is minimized spending per project. Surgically addressing the occasional and frequent use cases, Autodesk's Flex program[24] helps customers keep spending to a minimum with pay-as-you-go for occasional product use along with user subscriptions.

Cubic

Cubic is a global provider of mission-critical performance and transportation solutions. Cubic's Nextbus Suite delivers a trio of real-time passenger information, proactive transit operations, and mobile fare payment to municipalities around the globe. Today's public transport passengers expect a full-featured travel experience of real-time, GPS-enhanced schedules, touchless payments, and more. The outcome for the municipalities that Cubic services is to drive up ridership on their bus fleet. The contribution to that outcome is the combination of hardware, software, data, and predictive analytics as a managed service. Pricing is linked to the number of buses on the road (per bus, per month), serving as a proxy metric for the volume of ridership. Cubic Road User Charging Solution[25] is a system where all drivers pay to use the roads. The rate the driver pays is aligned to the distance they travel on the designated roads. Highly congested cities, such as London and San Francisco, are turning to this approach to reduce congestion. Cubic sets up the road tool system, collects the city's tolls (usually electronically), and enjoys a revenue share for providing the service. Designed to minimize up-front costs and risks to municipalities, Cubic's pricing is perfectly aligned with the target outcomes of the customer municipality.

Kaeser

Kaeser is one of the world's leading manufacturers and providers of compressed air products and services. Established in 1919 as a machine workshop in Germany, the company now employs approximately 7,000 people worldwide. Recognizing its customers' need to shift to paying only for how much compressed air they needed, Kaeser Compressed Air as a Service[26] was launched. Instead of a large capital expense, the customer pays a monthly fee to have clean, dry, energy-efficient air at the ready. The customer's business outcome is to lower overall expenses for compressed air and eliminate waste. Kaeser aligned to these outcomes by providing customers the opportunity to purchase with their operating-expense budgets and only pay for the volume of compressed air needed in their business in a given period. This straightforward approach ensures that as Kaeser's customers grow their operations, Kaeser's revenue from the Compressed Air as a Service grows along with them.

Michelin

Founded in 1889 in France, Michelin is the second largest tire manufacturer in the world. In 2016, Harvard Business School published an article about Michelin's journey from selling tires to selling outcomes.[27] Its Tires as a Service enables haulage companies to manage their fleets of semi-trailers as efficiently as possible, reducing the number of tire-related breakdowns and increasing their fuel efficiency. Leveraging the power of Internet of Things (IoT), Michelin has developed several outcome-based managed offers. One of those offers is EFFITRAILER.[28] This offer directly links price to the achievement of their customer's fuel-efficiency goals derived from the use of Michelin's tires and related services. Only when the trucking-fleet customer realizes measurable fuel efficiency gains when using Tires as a Service does Michelin get paid.

There is a lesson in this offer for enterprise hardware and software companies. If a 120-year-old tire manufacturer can successfully build compelling outcome-based offers and outcome-aligned pricing, there is little validity in the assertion that outcome-based offers are simply a bridge too far.

Slack

Slack (acquired by Salesforce in 2021) is an application communication platform that offers teams the ability to collaborate via persistent chat rooms organized by topic, private groups, and direct messaging. Slack's customer-outcome metric includes active collaboration among its customers' teams members. If the number of active collaborators drops, the customer stops paying for the inactive users after just 14 days of inactivity.[29] If a user becomes active after a period of inactivity, the customer only pays from the date of reactivation. With this outcome-aligned pricing model, Slack is very motivated to provide many tools and features to ensure that users stay productive and collaboratively engaged. The Slack team has regular internal objectives and key results (OKR)[30] to focus on driving sticky adoption.

Splunk

Splunk is a provider of software to security, IT, and DevOps teams for searching, monitoring, indexing, and analyzing machine-generated data in a searchable repository. Splunk provides its customers with the necessary tools to generate use-case-specific insights, alerts, dashboards, and visualizations. Splunk offers a "workload pricing" model[31] that aligns to the customer outcome. It is priced based on the compute resources required by the customer workloads that generate insights, alerts, dashboards, and visualizations from their data that has been ingested into the Splunk platform.

It's interesting to note that Splunk's workload pricing has been recently introduced to ensure that value realization occurs ahead of a high paywall. Case in point, a prior value-aligned pricing model, "ingest pricing," is currently not offered to new customers. The ingest model charged for the volume of daily ingested data on the Splunk platform. While aligned with the customer outcome of realizing insights from their own data, data ingestion is an earlier point in the customer journey and a couple steps away from the point of value realization. Further, ingest pricing may have added friction and provide a disincentive for customers to load up the platform with as much data as possible. This Splunk example illustrates that outcome-aligned pricing is a journey.

Twilio

Twilio is a cloud communications middleware platform with over 10 million developers and over 200,000 active enterprise customers. Customers integrate with the Twilio platform to communicate with their customers on the channels (phone, text, email) they prefer. If you have received a text confirmation that a product you purchased online is on its way to you, there's a good chance that notification was delivered through the Twilio platform. Twilio refers to it as "intelligent customer engagement at scale." Twilio's customer-outcome metrics is cost-effective, omni-channel communications. To achieve this, it offers two ways to pay[32] that are easy to initiate and easy to scale: (a) per-active-user-hour pricing that addresses seasonal use, part-time agents, or sporadic business patterns, or (b) named-user-per-month pricing for predictable spend with volume messaging.

Zocdoc

Founded in 2007 and venture-backed, Zocdoc enables individual patients to find and book in-person or telemedicine appointments for medical or dental care. Sometimes referred to as the "Yelp of healthcare," the platform also functions as a physician and dentist rating and comparison database. Its customers are healthcare providers whose desired outcome is growing patient revenue, which is a function of the number of patient appointments. Zocdoc charges based on the number of patient appointments it enables for its healthcare providers. Aligning the pricing with the outcome has paid off handsomely for Zocdoc, making it easier for new providers to get started with the platform, realize value quickly, and align expense with revenue. The outcome-aligned pricing strategy refocused the company toward a sustainable growth path.[33]

Within the cloud-native and early-stage SaaS company category, there are dozens of examples of pure transactional usage-based pricing, usage-based subscription tiers, and even pricing based on pass-through third-party usage. These pricing models are here to stay and may be disrupting your business as you read this.

We Know This Is Hard

Pricing a technology solution based on the actual outcome a customer realizes, or even one aligned to enabling outcome, is scary for most technology providers, because most technology providers have never been forced to price this way. However, this is not an impossible task. Look at the technology providers from all walks of life building this capability! If air and rubber tires can be sold based on the outcome realized by the customer, clearly your sophisticated technology is up to the task. And as is true with many of the assertions in this book, what is the alternative? Discounting your way to success?

The TSIA OAP framework provides scaffolding for product and service teams to start this journey to outcome-aligned pricing. But don't wait too long—both market share and profitability are on the line.

6 | The Data-Driven Sales Force

By Steve Frost and J.B. Wood

The sales organization is under constant pressure to grow revenue and make the numbers. At the same time, it knows that it needs to transform and adapt to the rapidly changing realities of the B2B world. Who is buying is also changing. What they're buying and how they buy it are changing even faster. But how can the sales organization make the changes it needs to make without taking its eyes off the quarterly ball? How can it leverage technology and data to achieve the efficiency breakthroughs that everyone says it should be achieving? And will it be able to manage its own organizational process and skills transformations without additional resources? These are vexing questions facing most every B2B technology company.

In this chapter, we're going to look at these issues in detail. We'll briefly summarize the drivers of change in the market that you probably already have on your radar screen. Then we'll give you some very tangible, new ways you can use to optimize your current go-to-market strategy. Making the changes will require you to focus on new capabilities and use some different tool sets than you use right now. But if you go about it the right way, your sales organization can become a digitally powered growth machine.

Before We Begin

Before we talk about what digital transformation for sales is, let's talk about what it isn't. It is NOT simply slapping a digital veneer on top of a previously analog process. What do we mean by that?

- DT is NOT conducting meetings and sales calls through Zoom. That's just a new way of conducting the same sales meeting you always had, but without getting on an airplane. It's a small improvement to your efficiency and travel costs, but it is not transformative.

- DT is NOT using your customer relationship management system better. Research by Implicit found that the average sales rep already updates 300 CRM records per week. CRM is great, but it was the last transformation in sales, not the next. So, we are taking rigorous CRM use for granted.

In addition, let's also review a constructive, neighboring example of the North Star of Digital Transformation principle that we laid out in Chapter 2 and is shown in Figure 6.1.

TSIA's North Star of Digital Transformation

FIGURE 6.1 TSIA's North Star of Digital Transformation

We are going to start applying this principle to the sales organization in a minute, but first let's consider how DT has impacted sales' longtime "frenemy," marketing.

It wasn't very long ago that the marketing function was often considered the most esoteric, creative, and "fluffy" part of any company. It spent its time working on whiz-bang materials and media campaigns, and its ability to prove the ROI of its effort was questionable. But thanks to digital advertising, marketing automation tools, and all the analytical insight they provide, marketing departments may now be the most data-driven part of their entire company. They know which campaigns turn into conversions, how to optimize them, and can produce reports on all of it within a moment's notice. Their experience with the North Star of Digital Transformation might be explained as:

- *"With this new data, I know how every dollar I spend converts to revenue, and I no longer have to guess where to purchase advertising speculatively based on site demographics or page views."*

  or...

- *"With this new data, I know exactly what keywords I need to purchase for my search advertising campaigns, and I no longer have to overpay for placement on queries that won't turn into conversions."*

A well-run marketing team is already well down the path of digital transformation, and it is far better off for doing so. It has not only changed its processes, but it has also changed its success metrics, and it has raised its internal prestige and importance in the process. In short, *it used analytics to get much smarter about placing its bets.* That is a very important concept. And if it can happen to the marketing organization, it can and will happen to the sales organization. And just like marketing, sales will benefit tremendously from it.

So now that we have boxed in what sales transformation ISN'T, and are armed with a well-known example, we can look at the forces that are pushing the sales function to change its approach.

Drivers of Change in the Sales Landscape

Three big shifts in B2B tech and industrial markets are driving the need for the sales team to further transform:

1. The shift in power from the seller to the buyer.
2. The shift in budget from IT/technical to line-of-business buyers.
3. The shift from transactional revenue to life-cycle revenue.

Let's explore them a bit.

The Shift in Power from the Seller to the Buyer

Buyers are now more empowered than ever. Before the internet (dot-com) era, salespeople controlled the information that a customer needed to make a purchasing decision. This information was wielded as power, and salespeople who cut their teeth during this era were taught to never give out information without getting something in return. In fact, in the late 1990s, it wasn't uncommon to have sales and marketing departments fighting about how much information to put on their websites. After all, if a prospect could find out what they needed to know without talking to a salesperson, how were salespeople supposed to control and guide the sales process? But today there is a plethora of information about your company and your solutions that is available in the public domain. As the dot-com era has progressed into the social media era, customers don't even need to talk to a salesperson for references anymore. They can find them just as easily (and get a more honest story) through their digital network.

So, your customer's buying calculus is experiencing its own version of North Star DT. In their mind: *"With this new data, I can almost make buying decisions for myself, and I no longer have to go through a protracted sales process."*

Customers today like to buy, but they don't like to be sold. It's a fact that the customer no longer needs sales reps who provide basic, early-stage information. What they need and want are specialist expertise and value-added perspective on what's possible. The general seller's influence is rapidly giving way to an ad-hoc team of specialists who come together temporarily based on the unique buyer requirements for a particular deal—people who can actually add value to the process through industry or outcome-based insight.

The Shift in Budget from IT/Technical to Line-of-Business Buyers

Industry consensus is that the purchasing process and budget for new technology is now increasingly controlled by line-of-business buyers, as opposed to being fully controlled by the IT or other technical department. Many TSIA members have confirmed that as much of 80% of the purchasing decisions for their offerings will be made by line-of-business buyers and are often paid for out of their operational budgets rather than a centralized IT/technology budget.

Why is this happening? Like we said in the previous section, buyers are now empowered. As offerings simplify, not only do customers become less reliant on a salesperson to get the information they need, but they also need less help from IT to make it work. The buyer's DT North Star? *"With this new data, I can choose the products that I'm most comfortable using and that meet my specific needs, and I no longer have to rely on IT to complicate my decision or run the software for me."*

Therefore, if your sales process is solely designed to convince IT departments that your technical features are superior, then you probably aren't ready to face this new reality. If your only pre-sales resources are purely technical in nature and can't speak to a customer's actual business problems, then you're going to have resources that don't necessarily match up with the critical interests and priorities of the new customer buying personas. Your whole sales team needs to be able to understand the world of the business buyer. And to do that, you're going to HAVE to show up differently during the sales process.

The Shift from Transactional Revenue to Life-Cycle Revenue

This shift is one that sales leaders recognize but too often try to address with legacy sales processes that don't match up to the new reality. They know that in subscription or consumption pricing models, they no longer get all of the revenue from the customer at the time of purchase. XaaS offers are based on an OpEx framework, where the customer pays for access to the technology over time, but never takes ownership of the asset itself. This is opposed to the traditional CapEx model, where the customer pays the money up front and takes ownership.

Some sales leaders (and the senior executives to whom they report) try to shoehorn the new paradigm into the way they've always done things. They try to get as much money as they possibly can up front, often using large discounts and incentives that compromise the lifetime revenue potential of the customer relationship. They take shortcuts or avoid tough issues that will determine the long-term success of the customer because it slows or complicates the short-term sales cycle. In effect, they are setting deals up for short-term wins in an era of long-term, evergreen revenue models. The initial deal is not nearly as important as what happens during the remainder of the customer journey. What you sell the customer in the first place has to help them solve a tangible problem or reach a well-articulated business outcome. The initial deal must set the conditions for success. That is more important than the size of the commitment. That might be hard to accept, but it's becoming truer and truer every day.

These three shifts mean your sales process, tools, skills, and organization must change. In the past, sales typically responded to changes in the deal landscape by hiring more headcount with the new skills demanded by buyers—more technical specialists, more solutions designers, more value engineers, and, quite often, just more salespeople. And, usually, they never got rid of anyone else when they did this. Sales organizations just got bigger and bigger.

But you can't keep adding and adding forever, especially when there is a digitally powered way out of this cycle.

The Goal of Sales Transformation and the W2DT Model in this Chapter

Every CEO or CFO would agree with the following statement: *I would like to see our sales efforts focused on the important tasks that only salespeople can do.* The sales organization should be working only on high-value, high-complexity activities. That is great in theory, but it rarely happens. It's not because sales leaders don't agree. They, too, want to get their salespeople doing the important things—the things that add big chunks of value for the customer and for their company. But it's a tall order. So, we all need to double down on efforts to make this happen.

We believe three simple concepts should guide your sales transformation:

- Systematically eliminate non-critical uses of sales time.
- Refocus the time savings onto critical sales capabilities.
- Begin your pivot to low-friction land and product-led growth.

Let's begin with the second concept and then circle back to the others. What are the critical things the sales team should focus on? The simple answer is it needs to be spending its time effectively landing net-new customers and doing "major" cross-sells with existing customers. To do this, it needs to focus on a select collection of very high-value activities. These include:

- Industry-specific, business outcome-based discovery.
- Identifying and securing new budgets.
- Gaining the trust and confidence of line-of-business and senior IT executives.
- Aligning multiple internal and external stakeholders.

- Complex price and legal negotiations.
- Managing (only) the large, complex RFPs they are LIKELY to win.

All your digital transformation efforts have to be centered around keeping the sales organization focused and enabled on these activities. Everything else is a productivity crusher. Later in this chapter we are going to examine some of these important tasks in detail. Figure 6.2 highlights the W2DT framework to structure our conversation.

In this chapter we will examine:

TSIA's W2DT Model
Digital Operations Experience Platform

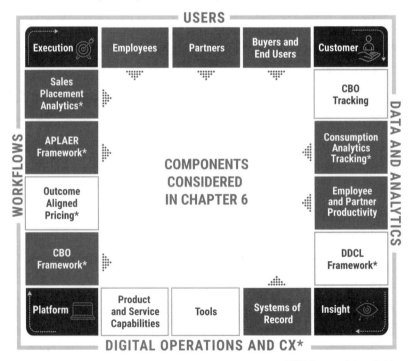

FIGURE 6.2 W2DT Framework - Digital Operations Experience Platform

- Workflows:
  - o APLAER: Place, land, adopt, expand, renew
  - o CBO: Customer business outcomes
- Users:
  - o Employees: Sales, sales management, sales operations, customer success, services
  - o Partners: Sales, sales management, sales operations, customer success, services
- Data and Analytics:
  - o Sales placement analytics

Placement Analytics: The Key to Unlocking Sales (and Service) Productivity

What if you could dramatically reduce non-critical uses of your sales team's time? This one is universally popular. Your sales team would love you for taking some of the tedious work off its plate. You probably already have lots of initiatives underway with this very goal in mind. But we want to explore what it could mean to go ALL THE WAY.

So, let's ask ourselves a question: What if we could eliminate 80% of the inefficient use of the sales team's time? That would be nice, wouldn't it? Well, we first would need to examine what that inefficient time is. We would suggest it falls into two categories:

- Chase time:
  - o Targeting
  - o Prospecting
  - o Qualifying (accounts and buyers)
  - o Finding the right content
  - o Finding the right internal resources
  - o Unnecessary or repetitive presentations

- Wasted time:
  - o   Administrative work
  - o   Unguided prospecting
  - o   Pursuing unqualified leads
  - o   Talking to the wrong buyer
  - o   Chasing losing RFPs
  - o   Using the wrong internal resources

No one would challenge that reducing or even eliminating these time sinks would improve sales force productivity and free up more time for exercising the important sales muscles in the era of XaaS. But how would that work?

A few years back, TSIA proposed a list of goals that would help our members make sure they were doing deals that would be optimized for sales effectiveness and customer success. We called these the "Great 8 Sales Conditions." Now we have evolved our thinking into the notion of "placement analytics" and added a few more conditions for success. Earlier we mentioned that the marketing team uses data and analytics to deploy its resources (marketing dollars) more intelligently and, in effect, place better bets. Well, imagine if the sales team could do exactly the same thing with its resources (sales time). The goal is to put sellers in the right position to win, while putting the right deal in place that will succeed in a perpetual, contractual model. These are the objectives of placement analytics, as described in Figure 6.3.

Imagine the benefits of placement analytics to both your company and your salespeople. You can experience higher win rates, faster sales cycles, more opportunities in the pipeline, less discounting, faster customer adoption, better business outcome success for customers, faster account growth, and greater wallet share.

Then, what if we told you that your company already has all the data you need to execute this model? That's right. You have

The Objectives of Placement Analytics

CONDITION	DESCRIPTION
The right seller	The right skills matched against the profile of the customer (industry/persona)
With the right information	Access to appropriate and relevant material in context of the customer's known issues, requirements, and points of interest
Talking to the right buyer	An individual or team within the target company who is either the decision maker or senior influencer, has authority over the budget required to complete the sale, and is responsible for a defined business outcome
About the right offer	The ability to lead the discussion about the parts of your product and service portfolio that should be the primary, initial focus of the conversation and puts the customer in the best position for immediate success
At a qualified and willing account	The customer is highly likely to be ready and interested and recognizes your company as a valued and quality supplier
On the outcomes that matter to the customer	You can identify and demonstrate that your solution can directly (or indirectly) impact their priority outcomes and deliver financial benefits and track and communicate your success
Ahead of the competition	You have insights that will enable you to proactively pitch your offer ahead of a formal procurement process
With a solution that will reliably be successful	The solution has been reviewed and approved by the people who are responsible for deploying it, ensuring that adoption and consumption are likely
And is the right size for the customer	The solution isn't geared around taking as much money as possible up front, but is based on the technology and services the customer needs to meet the outcome that matters to them
Is motivated and able to set the conditions for life-cycle success	The salesperson has the right comp plan and skill set to guide the customer to a solution that will help them reach their outcome, and is able to be adopted, expanded, and renewed
At the lowest cost of sale	Customer success, channel partners, and e-commerce platforms are all used to keep the cost of sale as efficient as possible
On existing AND new customers	By properly segmenting upsells and cross-sells with customer information, the sales team can be deployed when needed, even with existing customers, only when the deal conditions call for it

FIGURE 6.3 The Objectives of Placement Analytics

the data, or at least you have access to it if you want to make locating and collecting it a priority. You are most likely not leveraging information from your services and customer success teams about what the required conditions for success are in each customer or solution segment. You are not mining your various data sources to find upsell and cross-sell opportunities. You may not even be breaking your offer sales data into customer segments. In addition to the data you do have, there is also information that you have and let evaporate; it never turns into usable data. And, in all likelihood, you don't have an adequate team building your sales data architecture, connecting systems, building analytics, and building a compounding network of inputs and outputs that enable sales placement analytics. OK, you may have a few projects underway. But all taken together, they're not big enough. They are not company-wide enough. There aren't enough resources dedicated to the projects. As a result, you are not truly going ALL THE WAY to take out the myriad inefficiencies of legacy sales processes. Your sales costs are still multiples higher than they need to be. Your new land quotas are still multiples lower than they could be.

Placement Analytics: What Is It and How Could It Work for You?

If you use the tools you have in your kit, you can begin your journey toward leveraging them to place the right resources on the right deals at the right time, with the highest probability of success. The goal of your analytics is to do just that. Figure out where to place your bets that gives you the highest likelihood to win. That's exactly what marketing departments have done with their insight and data. They are buying access to clicks on keywords that give them the highest probability of conversion. They are basing their spends on actual data rather than gut feel or abstract market search. In short, they are placing their resources based on access to people with the highest propensity to take the actions for which they are hoping.

The Oxford English Dictionary defines propensity as: *An inclination or natural tendency to behave in a particular way.* This idea of propensity in the revenue life cycle—that a customer or buyer persona will be inherently likely to have a need that is met by your offering—should be the guiding principle for your sales analytics efforts. The goal is to make your salespeople as smart and informed as they can be before they ever contact the customer, and be as effective and efficient as possible once they do. Based on the behaviors, attributes, and demographics of the customers that have gone before them, they can reasonably use propensity analytics to put the right sales conditions, as outlined above, in place before the sales process even begins.

TSIA sees five major areas where propensity models can help inform not just your salespeople, but your customer success managers, technical account managers, and other customer-facing teams as well. These are:

- Propensity to buy.
- Propensity to consume.
- Propensity to succeed.
- Propensity to grow.
- Propensity to renew.

So, how does this work? Let's look at how we might construct analytics around the first step in the sales process: propensity to buy. We can start by assuming that your current customers are a model of the larger market that they represent. What has happened or is happening to them is also happening to the broader market segment(s) of which they are a part. It's like a drug trial. If you pick your study participants intelligently, you can project their results onto a larger population. That is exactly what we need to be doing. Figure 6.4 shows the life cycle of leveraging sales analytics.

You have probably already done some market segmentation for your business. You may have done it by industry or solution

Sales Analytics Life Cycle

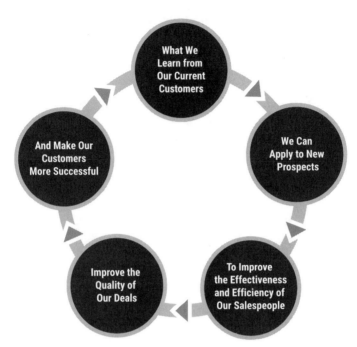

FIGURE 6.4 Sales Analytics Life Cycle

or size. That's a good start. Let's call that macro segmentation. But imagine taking segmentation even further. Imagine doing micro-segmentation inside those macro segments. Sample segmentation criteria may include:

- What was happening at their business (growth rate, new compliance regulations, etc.)?
- What did they buy?
- Was it part of some larger, multivendor solution?
- What partner(s) were involved?
- What persona(s) made the decision?
- What business outcomes were most important to them?

- With whom were you competing?
- How much did they spend?
- What components of the solutions did they implement first, second, and third?
- What training did they buy?
- What services did they buy?
- What role did the partner play in implementation?
- What was their customer health score at three, six, nine, and twelve months?
- What caused their high-severity issues?
- Did they renew or attrit?
- If they did attrit, what were the causes?
- When did we get our first upsell?
- What did they buy in the upsell?
- What was happening at their business (growth rate, etc.) before the upsell?
- What persona(s) made the upsell decision?
- What business outcomes were most important to them in the upsell?

And the list goes on...

If you were collecting this data on every existing customer, you could build a propensity-to-buy model for every company (customers and prospects alike) by industry, size, solution, persona, and growth rate. When it comes to new prospects, you are marrying propensity models with public data about companies and industries. You would know what outcomes to talk to them about and with which solutions to lead (more on that in a bit). You would know what services lead to success. You would know what partners to bring with you and what their role should be. You would know how long to wait and what signals (adoption rate, health score, customer growth) to look for before you dispatch the next salesperson to talk about their upsell.

In short, you would be exercising sales placement modeling with all its HUGE benefits. Not only would you have a much better chance of winning, but your sales cycles will be shorter, and the customer will be happier with their decision. That means they're likely to consume, succeed, grow, and renew. By the way, nothing here is a new motion, at least if you look at the broader picture of the tech industry. Every time you buy something from Amazon, it makes suggestions based on the purchases made by customers who also bought the item you selected. And don't tell us that your business is more complicated than Amazon's. It sells millions of SKUs from thousands of independent vendors. You have more data than you think, and it's more useful than you can imagine.

So why aren't you taking on this project head-on? We would submit that absolutely every piece of information in that list is known somewhere in your company or exists in the public domain. But is it being used to drive sales efficiency at scale? If you are, then you know that:

- *"With this data we can lead sellers to wins and no longer need to waste their time searching for needles in haystacks."*
- *"With this data we can set up the conditions for customer success on every deal and no longer need services and success to pull off customer 'saves.'"*
- *"With this data we can talk to customers about upsells when they are ripe and no longer have to beat the heck out of them."*

The benefits go on and on. And these principles can be applied equally to customer success service resources.

LAER Is Now APLAER

TSIA's LAER customer engagement model has become an industry standard for life-cycle selling. The acronym was first introduced by TSIA in 2014, and the letters stand for land, adopt, expand, and renew. While none of those steps may have been earthshaking in and of themselves, put together they became a road map for how to think of the customer life cycle in a sub-scription, or a recurring revenue, model.

Now, nearly a decade later, TSIA is updating the LAER framework and it all has to do with the power of data and analyt-ics. It's now time to think about digital intelligence with a model that takes better advantage of the wealth of data that is available to your company from your product telemetry, your systems of records, and publicly available data sources. Land, adopt, expand, and renew have never simply been things people do; they are organizational capabilities that companies have to build. They are data-driven workflows. Figure 6.5 offers an illustration of this model.

Every part of the customer life cycle will be enhanced and digitally transformed by data and analytics. So after nearly a de-cade as its foundational framework for customer engagement, TSIA is adding a new layer to LAER. Every motion in the LAER customer journey can be enhanced by data and customer analyt-ics. We are calling this new model APLAER, for analyze, place, land, adopt, expand, and renew. (It's pronounced "A-player," as in, with data and analytics you can turn a B player or a C player into an A player.)

Before any motion in LAER takes place (but especially be-fore the land phase), analytics is doing the prep work and guiding the placement of your resources, giving them the best chance to succeed with the lowest effort and cost. But they're helpful all through the customer life cycle. They're helping you to discover new opportunities with existing customers for cross-sell. They're synchronizing external data and industry data to look for custom-ers who are likely to purchase. They're scouring your marketing databases for patterns and to determine if potential customers are checking you out (and why).

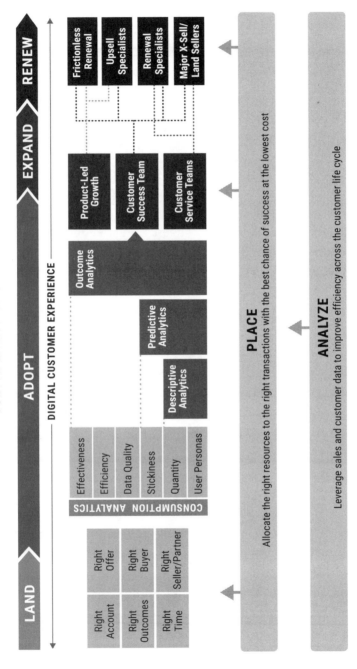

FIGURE 6.5 TSIA APLAER Model

All this analysis is being done so that you can PLACE the correct resource with the right customer at the right time with the right information. It's no longer throwing resources at the wall to see what sticks. Data is guiding your priorities and your actions, just like they've been driving the marketing organization's priorities and actions for more than a decade. It's a new standard for CROs to work toward, but it's critical that they add "analyze" and "place" to their customer life-cycle thinking. Otherwise, it will always just be about people, their skills, and their time. And those are your least scalable assets.

You can read about LAER in more detail in Appendix B, where we have reprised a chapter from our previous book, the *Technology-as-a-Service Playbook.*[1] But you can see how investing in placement analytics will guide and inform every part of the customer life cycle. Once the sales team has sold the right deal to the right customer, the customer success function will understand what motions it needs to take to help the customer succeed. It will know what outcomes to shoot for, how to track its progress toward those outcomes, and how to guide the customer along the way. Given what's happened with previous customers, it will know how likely the customer is to consume what they've bought and adopt it for their real-life needs across the broader organization. Insight into consumption analytics, surfaced in the form of a customer health score (based on a customer success plan), will help you place the right resources needed to help the customer drive adoption and achieve the outcomes for which it bought your technology in the first place. That may be customer success, it may be professional services, it may be support. The point is, adoption requires insight, and you should invest in it. By looking at actual customer behavior, you can see which customers are more likely to grow, and which are in real jeopardy of attrition. When you know if the customer needs a simple increase in capacity or a different feature (an upsell, usually handled by the customer success team) or that the renewal is in jeopardy (too much for a customer success manager to handle), you can proactively place the right resource in the right place at the right time.

Data Creation, Collection, and Analytics-Driven Ontology

"Everything is connected to everything else, and nothing is without consequence."

— David Huddle

So, from where does all of this data come? In many companies, it is all over the organization. Most sales-related data reside in a sales force automation platform or a CRM system. However, much of the data we have been discussing here is not currently collected in CRM systems. Unfortunately, CRM systems typically are used only for data that is measured and used in account and contact management, deal flow, or forecasting. The data mentioned in this chapter are used to perform sales analytics to help more effectively define account strategies, revenue objectives, sales efficiency, and sometimes even sales profitability.

But what if you could collect data streams from across the business and from your partners? What if you could scan the entire customer base, understand exactly what release a customer is on, what features they are using (and not using), if the product is nearing end-of-life or end-of-support, what the customer's credit rating is, how many incidents and outages they've had on every single device and application, how many employees from that company visited your website and what products and services they reviewed, and so on? What if there were relationships among all those disparate data streams from various platforms and systems?

And, yes, there is missing data. It's not because you don't know the information, it's that you let it evaporate. One thing this will force you to do is to capture much more and better data about each won, lost, and stuck deal. We would suggest that every seller be forced to spend up to two hours entering the critical data we mentioned a few pages ago on every opportunity that reaches one of those conclusions. That time investment may sound like a lot, but what if it enabled a propensity model that improved your sales productivity by 25%?

So, the most effective APLAER implementation requires gathering data, structured and unstructured, from as many relevant sources as possible, across all your customer touchpoints. That includes your services and customer success teams, your marketing database, and your electronic touchpoints, such as online performance support and so forth. All that data needs to be managed and governed so the right systems can access the right trustworthy data at the right time. From there, data scientists and artificial intelligence systems can correlate data from these various sources and paint a picture of the relationships among the data streams. This is known as data-driven ontology.[2] These relationships should be tied to very specific, process-driven, actions for the sales team.

We will discuss the technology architecture framework required for APLAER in Appendix A.

Mastering the Critical Sales Capabilities

So now that you are going to start truly reducing both the chase time and wasted time of your sellers and partners by leveraging APLAER, it's time to explore exactly how you are going to reinvest it. Earlier in this chapter, we promised to examine some of these important tasks in detail. The goal is to create a much smarter sales process, optimized for recurring revenue across the customer life cycle.

Focus Salespeople on Land and Big Expand

Focusing salespeople on the land and expand motions of the customer life cycle is a concept with which both CEOs and CFOs would readily agree. There is no doubt that these are the transactions that bring the greatest long-term value to the company. So why isn't the sales team 100% focused on these two activities? In their defense, salespeople were the customer's last resort for shelter from their company's unrelenting complexity. Salespeople, historically, were indoctrinated to the idea that there should be "one throat to choke," usually theirs. To that end (and because they're really worried about outsiders "messing up their deal"), they often worry about giving up a measure of control with their accounts. They have experienced that acting as the customer's champion in difficult times gives them a special relationship status with their buyers.

While that may have been true and valid for decades, things are changing. TSIA research shows clearly that when other groups are involved with driving revenue in the customer life cycle, growth rates skyrocket and overall costs go down. Here are some important statistics you should consider:

- When the customer success organization is primarily responsible for upsells, technology subscription growth rates increase nine percentage points over companies that leave that task to sales executives.

- There is no statistical difference in renewal rate when sales executives are responsible for renewals versus when the customer success team is in charge of renewals.

- However, when sales executives get full quota and compensation credit for renewals, subscription growth rates plummet by more than 10 percentage points.

- Companies that deploy auto-renew terms and capabilities increase their renewal rates by an average of 11.5%, per the TSIA Customer Growth and Renewal Benchmark.

TSIA members have shown that expansions and renewals can be handled by e-commerce renewals specialists and customer success managers and partners, and this ability can be enhanced when they are digitally enabled to do so. We'll go into far more detail on how to go about this in Chapter 7. But the point is this: There will be multiple ongoing touchpoints among various customer contacts and various account-facing roles. These interactions are critical to enabling value realization. Successful sales representatives will embrace these new account relationships and recognize them as a mechanism for account growth. It's important to note that the makeup of this team will look different, based on the segmentation approach that your company adopts. Strategic enterprise accounts will have dedicated resources, and potentially many of them in each of the roles described above. Smaller commercial accounts will probably have shared resources and access to a fully automated experience. The best part? By offloading renewals and upsells to lower-cost and lower-capability resources, the sales team can spend more time on those big, important activities, empowered by data and analytics.

In any case, for customer success managers and renewals specialists to do their jobs, they need to understand why the customer bought from you in the first place. Make sure that you've documented what outcome the customer is trying to achieve before the sale, and definitely before the hand-off. If you can prove that you've met the outcome the customer was trying to achieve when they initially bought your technology, the renewal should be easy. And this brings us to our next critical way to keep sales focused on the most important activities.

Move to Industry-Specific, Outcome Discovery

At the last pre-pandemic, in person, TSIA conference in the fall of 2019, TSIA's CEO asked 2,000-plus technology and industry professionals whether he would find their customers' desired business outcomes captured in the opportunity record in their CRM. Guess how many hands went up? Five. That's just nuts. Why is it so low? Because legacy sales were based on having the best features and promoting them (mostly) horizontally across customer segments to technical buying personas. But increasingly today, it's about selling industry-specific business outcomes to line-of-business buyer personas. And that is a far more complex sales requirement. Why? For two reasons:

- You have to understand the prospect's industry and business model. That allows you to speak in the language of their business. And this infers that salespeople have the knowledge to speak the language of the individual company industry verticals.

- You have to convince prospects, usually executive personas, that there are other companies like them that are getting business benefits from projects that they don't have underway. That is how you create new budget.

Those approaches, outcome selling versus product selling, are two completely different ways of selling and measuring customer success. We probably don't have to convince you that the customer's C-suite couldn't care less about product features. And you might even accept that they don't care about price...as long as the business outcomes are compelling enough.

If you want your salespeople to tap into new budgets or get existing buyers to put more budget on the table, then you had better master outcome discovery. Outcome discovery has three simple objectives:

- Discover and advance the priority business outcomes that your customer wants to achieve.

- Demonstrate how your solution contributes to the achievement of those outcomes.

- Document the customer's desired outcomes so that your success and service teams can actualize them.

As we just said, if you want your salespeople to talk in business language about business outcomes to executive buyers, you had better be speaking the language of the customer's industry. So, industry-specific, outcome discovery is about leading with insights; sharing your knowledge of what other similar companies are doing and adding that to the ideas and priorities the customer already had in mind. Add all that up and you can reach new buyers and new budgets because the addition of your best thinking to their best thinking creates a compelling event for the customer.

In Chapter 4 we asserted that products must climb the value ladder. The sales team also must have the ability to climb the value ladder, and the services team must turn the claim into truth. This framework is seen in Figure 6.6.

TSIA Outcome Discovery Framework

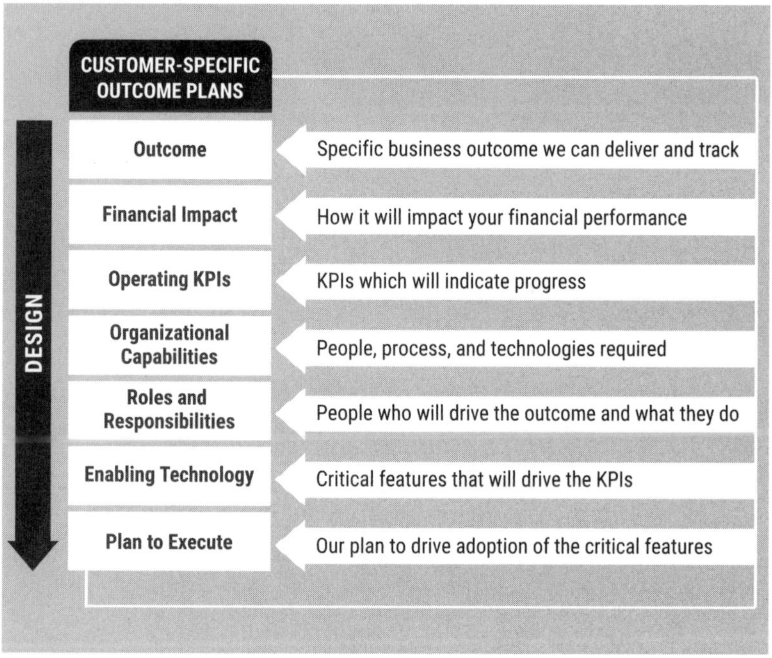

CUSTOMER-SPECIFIC OUTCOME PLANS	
Outcome	Specific business outcome we can deliver and track
Financial Impact	How it will impact your financial performance
Operating KPIs	KPIs which will indicate progress
Organizational Capabilities	People, process, and technologies required
Roles and Responsibilities	People who will drive the outcome and what they do
Enabling Technology	Critical features that will drive the KPIs
Plan to Execute	Our plan to drive adoption of the critical features

FIGURE 6.6 TSIA Outcoming Discovery Framework

And here's the thing: When you are executing on outcome selling, you (the supplier) are providing insight and input as to what those outcomes should be. It's not about saying that you understand their business better than they do; that can come across as arrogant and alienating. However, you're in a position to share your insights and experience based on the fact that your company has worked with dozens, or even hundreds, of similar companies before. It is obvious why this approach would be far more strategic and valuable to the customer, and why it's a great place to focus your digital transformation efforts. As you invest in analytics and tools, you can place the salesperson in the best position to succeed, with your proposal aligning perfectly with the outcome your customer is likely to care about: *"With this new data, I can provide my customers valuable insights on the outcomes that other companies and executives like them care about, and I no longer have to base my sales pitch on competitive features and prices."*

If you've captured the insights you've gathered with other customers in the right way, you probably already know what business outcomes a similar prospect is most likely to care about. You also know which metrics and outcomes are linked to different buyer personas. And you know how your offering can actually help them achieve those outcomes. As you digitally transform your sales process, you need to think about how you document which outcomes and KPIs are most important to which buyers and how you've been successful at driving those outcomes. These outcomes may be financial in nature (lower cost of operation, revenue growth), they may be operational (lack of downtime, enabling key functionality), or even functional (avoiding liability, meeting government regulatory statutes), or even all of the above. Having tools and templates to guide these discovery discussions will be critical to your efforts because you need to be able to present the right outcome to the right buyer at the right time. The DT North Star for this effort would be: *"With this new data, I can show my customers how our technology helped other business buyers improve the KPIs about which they care. Then I can increase their planned investment and sell more of our standard products and services."*

When you sell around outcomes, you're the one leading the dance, so to speak. And for a business buyer, who probably doesn't understand the nuances of technology the way an IT professional does, this is incredibly important. Therefore, as you focus on your digital transformation efforts, a great way to start is to build around outcomes and outcome discovery.

Finally, perhaps the most important thing about leveraging outcome discovery is that it creates a bridge between what happens prior to the sale and what happens afterward to make the sale successful. With the right outcome plan, your professional services team knows what they have to do to make the technology work in the way the customer wants it to work. Your customer success team knows why the customer bought and what they are trying to accomplish. This lets you set the customer journey map for their whole time with you, including when to buy more. It helps your renewal team align what you've actually done to what you said you were going to do in the first place, making the renewal a low-complexity transaction. Outcome discovery, and the digital transformation required to enable it, helps change your mindset from a transactional model to a customer life-cycle model.

In a perfect world, all sellers would be experts in all these things. That should certainly be your continuous goal. But for most companies, those skills are initially added via an overlay rep or a sales specialist. Hopefully over time, the wisdom of the experts is captured and instilled in the general sellers through a combination of tools and training. In fact, that's part of the reason you should be investing so much in analytics. That placement data will really help your generalist salespeople make that transition. Right now, however, we are seeing two new overlays emerge:

- **Industry business outcome experts.** These are experts in the measurable, industry-specific outcomes that your customers are hoping to achieve. They may have deep expertise in a particular vertical or market segment, understand how your customer measures success, and speak their language. They are usually "overlay" reps, meaning they come in to assist account executives with their sale. According to the TSIA Subscription Revenue Effectiveness Benchmark, when companies employ business outcome specialists, their annual subscription growth rate jumps from 16% to 23%, on average. While overlay reps are sometimes thought of as expensive, they're much cheaper than hiring and training a new sale force. And when they're enabled and empowered with technology, they can provide real help at scale. These roles are sometimes housed in a value or customer business outcome management office.

- **Digital advisors.** These are experts in digital transformation. The role is designed to help customers with continuous process improvement. Here is how Microsoft describes this role in a job posting: *Microsoft Digital Advisors bring expertise, commitment, and resources to drive a program of change to build a company's digital business. They guide organizations as they reimagine and transform customer engagements, employee experiences, business models, and operations. Microsoft Digital Advisors work with customer teams to dream and envision their desired future, consider economic value and alternative ideas, and prioritize them.*[3] As the joint team designs, it refines the ideas, identifies dependencies, and eliminates roadblocks. The team continuously delivers innovation as this process, supported by the customer's digital culture and platform, goes from its first success to an embedded, systematic approach that captures the value of the Digital Era.

The Business Dividend of the Data-Driven Sales Force

TSIA speaks to hundreds of sales executives every year and very few of them seem overly concerned about their cost of sales and marketing. They've got numbers to hit, and they worry mostly about hitting them and staying under the budget they've been given. But TSIA is worried about it. Technology unit prices are coming down. Competition is increasing. Companies are adding more and more costly sales overlays. At some point, something has to give. Costs will have to be cut, and the overall percentage of revenue spent on sales and marketing will need to be reduced. Companies will not be judged simply on either growth or profitability, but will be expected to deliver on both.

Companies that are serious about building a data-driven sales force with an outcome sales approach will need to begin with assessing their existing sales force and its skills. Will your current sales team adapt to an outcome sales approach, discussing industry issues and teasing out the critical success metrics of business buyers, or will you need to onboard a new team? Will you invest in training for all or part of your existing sales team to grow its capabilities to have these conversations? Will you give these salespeople the tools they need to discover and document the promises of value that they make in the sales cycle? Will you ensure that your pre-sales technical support teams are retrained into presales solution architects?

The great news is that all the work we have outlined in this chapter is going to give you two amazing options. You will be getting a dividend—maybe a massive one. By leveraging data and analytics, your revenue will go up and your cost of sales will go down. There are two options for reinvesting your dividend in the business, and both stand to reduce your overall sales and marketing (S&M) costs.

You can choose to:

A. Maintain your current level of S&M spending and increase booking quotas (and revenue) from land and big expand sellers. You can choose to grow your way into a lower S&M percentage.

B. Maintain your current level of bookings and revenue but do so with less sales resources. You can choose to cut your way to a lower S&M percentage.

We all prefer option A, but option B has to be considered. The answer is usually some combination of both. But one thing for certain is that if you follow the steps in this chapter, your sales team will have to take on more land quota because it won't be able to make its numbers based on renewals anymore. APLAER will help you to align sales transactions to their most efficient sales channel and to free up your premium sales resources for their highest and best purpose. It's a CRO's dream.

Before we leave this chapter, we want to put one more inconvenient truth on the table. Remember in the first paragraph of this chapter we posed this vexing question: Will the sales organization be able to manage its own organizational and process transformations without additional resources? After all, it has never really been forced to develop a transformation muscle. It's never been outsourced, it's never been offshored, it's never been replaced by bots. So, can it pull this off with current resources?

The answer is, no way. No sales organization has the budget or IT resources or data scientists or project management resources to execute APLAER—or even just to execute sales placement analytics. The data it needs is sitting in systems of record spread throughout every department in the company. These are CEO-commissioned, company-wide projects.

Going ALL THE WAY to a data-driven sales force can only be funded and enabled by the CEO.

7 | Customer Success at Scale

By Stephen Fulkerson, Steve Frost, and Jack Johnson

As we stated in the previous chapter, creating a lean, digital salesforce requires offloading lower-complexity sales motions to automation and lower-cost resources. Guess who those "lower-cost resources" tend to be? That's right, the customer success (CS) organization! But, as many TSIA members have discovered, that's just one of many things that CS is being asked to undertake. If you're not careful, CS can become a "junk drawer" and the dumping ground for every sort of business task. Rather than being a high-efficiency, low-cost, adoption-and-revenue engine, it becomes the place where companies move their mess, without ever cleaning it up.

When customer success is operating maturely at scale, it not only drives low-cost revenue for your company but also helps your customers achieve their desired business outcomes. This, however, can only happen if you set a game plan, and then keep your CS team on offense, not defense. If you're going to scale CS, it has to be something worth scaling. And that starts by having a purpose on which everyone agrees.

In this chapter we will examine:
Workflows:

- APLAER: Place, Land, Adopt, Expand, Renew

Users:

- Employees: Sales, Sales Management, Sales Operations, Customer Success, Renewals Specialist
- Partners: Customer Success, Partner Success Management
- Customers

Data and Analytics:

- Customer Health Scores
- Sales Placement Analytics

Figure 7.1 illustrates these points along the TSIA W2DT Model.

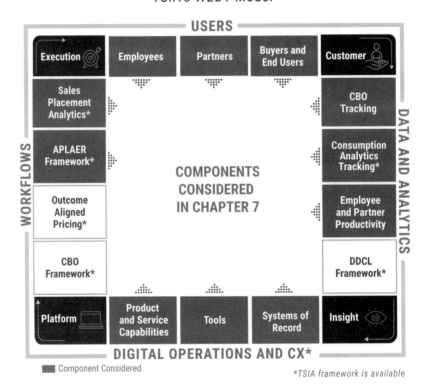

FIGURE 7.1 TSIA's W2DT Model

Customer Success: A Casualty of Digital Hesitation

Too often, the CS function at technology companies is a financial art project. Put simply, it is too small and too underutilized. It either only covers a subset of customers or is chartered to deliver only a subset of its full engagement value.

One major reason for this is that a majority of CS organizations are typically run as cost centers or unprofitable P&Ls, adding downward pressure on the company margins. The second reason is that CS is not being chartered to take on major commercial responsibilities like renewals and upsells. In this chapter, we will take both these sources of hesitation head on, as we are convinced they will ultimately give way to what we call "Big C" customer success.

Every year, TSIA surveys the profitability profile of all the service business lines within tech companies. Figure 7.2 demonstrates the dramatic lag in the financial performance of the CS function. And it begs the question: Why would a company want

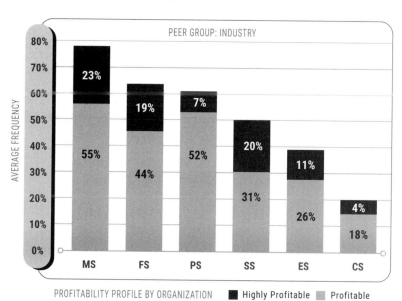

FIGURE 7.2 Customer Success as an Art Project

to scale something that loses money or is highly dilutive to the portfolio? That is not how other service motions, like support or consulting services, have traditionally been run.

To date, the industry has accepted this lack of financial performance under the mantra of "customer health" and "customer adoption." Companies invest in CS to avoid or reduce customer churn by filling the gap between value promised in the Land phase and value realized in the Adoption phase. This approach, however, is stunting the growth and full potential of the CS function within XaaS business models.

The Full Potential of Customer Success

As referenced in the previous chapter, TSIA's LAER customer engagement model has become an industry standard for life-cycle selling. As the handoff from sales to CS becomes more science than art, the product telemetry and systems of records play key roles in helping shape when and how to engage with the customer. The APLAER are data-driven workflows that help with scale and engagement.

We previously discussed that sales should be laser focused on new or big deals, while CS continues to absorb some of the charter of expansion by taking on upsells. Additionally, CS should be taking on renewals as part of its remit, which means that every part of the customer life cycle will be enhanced and digitally transformed by data and analytics, as seen in Figure 7.3.

However, very few CS organizations fulfill this potential. Why? TSIA asserts (and has the data to support the assertion) that if companies hope to cost-effectively scale their CS capabilities, three tactics, seen in Figure 7.4 (page 178) and listed below, must be pursued:

1. Monetize CS offers.
2. Give CS ownership of low-complexity commercial activities (lead generation, upsells, renewals, etc.).
3. Offset the cost of CS by reducing the cost of your sales department.

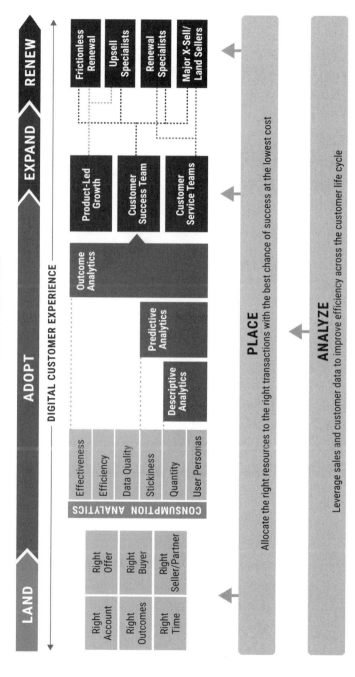

FIGURE 7.3 TSIA APLAER Framework

FIGURE 7.4 Three Pillars of CS at Scale

Monetize Customer Success Offers (Yes, Charge for Success Guidance and Services!)

Yes, you should charge for CS—period! Anything given away is perceived to have little to no value. Some born-in-the-cloud companies choose to give CS away to drive growth, but that is not sustainable, and it usually leads to under-investment in the long term. Monetizing is one of the best options that gives organizations an additional budget to right-size and fund the CS department. Additionally, monetizing supports the ability to deliver value that supports the primary charter of adoption, therefore making your customers successful. CS is the value realization and delivery arm of the organization, and monetization is the easiest and most effective method to fund and scale CS organizations.

Currently, TSIA monetization research reveals that 45% of the industry monetizes CS. TSIA considers anything at 50% or higher as a common practice, so this trend is about to cross the line as a common practice. Why? Because customers are used to having a choice among multitiered offers and paying more for a higher level of engagement, for example, Good, Better, Best, or Silver, Gold, Platinum. Customer organizations that want a higher-level outcome of engagement are generally willing to pay for it. As a result, monetizing your offers into three tiers is a good place for most companies to start, and you may be surprised how often customers are willing to pay for a higher level of engagement when presented effectively. They want this to work, too.

Because of this default service-tier-buying behavior, the naming conventions used often rely on arbitrary categorizations like Standard, Enhanced, Premium, or "precious metal" progressions, failing to intuitively reveal the nature of the incremental value in each service tier. Effectively segmenting the market for service-offer success requires identifying the most common customer business problems in the industry verticals the company serves, across the maturity level of the customers that use the solution. Some suppliers, like PTC, are using more descriptive naming conventions that better illustrate the level of value received and highlighting the core customer business challenge addressed by each offering tier:

- Tier 1: Guided, for customers who want more help using the technology
- Tier 2: Strategic, for customers who have the technology embedded in mission-critical workflows.

Stretching toward more descriptive CS-offer naming opens the door for additional flexibility in the portfolio, potentially adding additional tiers/options for service by identifying new customer workflows where the solution can add value in a simple, standard, and scalable way.

As seen in Figure 7.5, the majority of companies monetizing CS are selling these offers as an annuity that aligns to the technology subscription term. Fixed-fee and time-and-material/SOW models represent a minor but significant portion of the market. For those organizations selling via the annuity model with percentage-based pricing, the median range is 16% for the lowest tier and 20% for the highest. TSIA does see ranges that exceed these,

Monetization Models of Customer Success

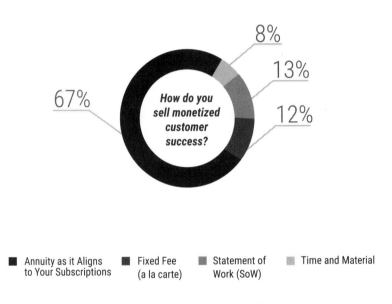

ANNUITY SUBSCRIPTION MODEL TYPICAL
The majority of participants charging for CS sell annuities aligned with subscription terms

8%

13%

67%   *How do you sell monetized customer success?*

12%

■ Annuity as it Aligns   ■ Fixed Fee   ■ Statement of   ▨ Time and Material
  to Your Subscriptions   (a la carte)   Work (SoW)

FIGURE 7.5 Monetization Models of Customer Success

but these are the median ranges to take into consideration for your offerings.

Creating a monetized offering that resonates with your customers demands including the customer in the conversation. It is critical for CS offer leaders to deeply understand their customers' challenges and how the provider solution improves customer KPIs that are relevant to these challenges. Pacesetter organizations develop a CS portfolio that addresses commonly desired outcomes with contributions across the provider organization, including multiple service lines (e.g., education, professional services, support services, and field services) and the core technology itself. Monetizing CS is not charging for the CSM, it's establishing a profitable price point at which the provider can deliver the right combination of technology, services, data, and analytics to support the customer in a well-understood success path. Historically, monetizing specific roles, for example, that of technical account manager, offers value to customers but is rarely scalable. If that scenario sounds like it may be a problem in your organization, consider instead a value-based or role-based offering, as they tend to perform much better with scalability.

TSIA data establishes that service delivery and technology capability are increasingly converging into creatively bundled offers. Often, provider portfolios are exceedingly complex in an attempt to offer broad customer choices and take positions in additional markets. Customers are often challenged to select the right technology from extensive lists of options, and they then face a similar blizzard of choices within each service line. Selecting the right level of support, the right consulting services, and the right training to support their teams can therefore be a challenge.

TSIA data also establishes that service offer managers increasingly have responsibility for more than one service line (service portfolio management), often with CS offers representing the most converged offers in the portfolio. We see a similar trend toward managed services, which also converges multiple service-line capabilities into offers that solve broader and more strategic or critical business problems. While we expect this trend toward convergence to continue, as providers drive complexity out of the portfolio and sharpen their offer-market fit toward better-understood customer problems and workflows, providers continue to require a diverse portfolio as well, especially as customers with traditional buying preferences delay modernization.

The rise of CS offers marks a significant move toward services converging into creative bundles; but single-service offerings like support and maintenance, SOW-based implementation work, or instructor-led training will remain viable offers on most provider portfolios for traditional market segments. Effective market segmentation and the bravery to exit non-strategic or unprofitable markets remains critical. A common misconception from CS executives is that monetizing CS must fund the entire department. That is the wrong way to look at it. A monetized offering does not have to fund the entire CS organization immediately. It probably will take several years to get to that level. However, you must start somewhere, and subsidizing the balance of the CS cost via COS is a common approach during early years. So, if your offering only pays for a portion, then you are in a good place because now you have created a budget to hire for additional staff and/or technology resources to help you scale supporting the customer experience.

Examples of Monetized Customer Success Offerings

One of the more successful organizations in monetizing CS is Salesforce. In 2021, it changed its naming conventions and offerings, but the overall strategy remains the same. Much like the industry standard, Salesforce provides three offerings that encompass "good-better-best." The first tier is a self-serve digital offering, termed Standard, combination offerings include customer support and CS, which Salesforce refers to as Proactive services. Salesforce monetization offerings play a significant role in funding its CS organization. Figure 7.6 outlines their Success Plans pricing.

McAfee is another example of an organization that has three CS offerings that leverage resources from customer support, CS management, education services, consulting services, and senior technical resources. Figure 7.7 (page 184) shares its Customer Success Plans features.

McAfee provides an extensive offering that quickly demonstrates to its customers that they will be guided through their customer journey with a plethora of McAfee resources available to support them. Additionally, McAfee has spread the effort for resource engagement so that it is not a heavy burden to just CS management. Other departments are responsible for delivering

Salesforce Success Plans Pricing

	STANDARD INCLUDED IN ALL LICENSES	PREMIER 30% OF NET	SIGNATURE CONTACT YOUR AE*
TRAILHEAD, HELP PORTAL, TRAILBLAZER COMMUNITY, SUCCESS CENTER	●	●	●
TECHNICAL SUPPORT	●	●	●
24x7 PHONE SUPPORT AND DEVELOPER SUPPORT		●	●
EXPERT COACHING		●	●
TRAILHEAD ACADEMY DISCOUNTS		●	●
PROACTIVE SERVICES			●
ACCOUNT MANAGEMENT			●

Price based on complexity and scale

FIGURE 7.6 Salesforce Monetization Offerings of Customer Success

value to customers. What is important is ensuring that the lanes in the road and the handoffs are well-documented so that customers are not left trying to understand how to navigate the company and the offerings. Note that McAfee also continues to make available traditional support-plus-maintenance offers (purchasing maintenance is, in fact, a prerequisite for all CS offers), project-based consulting services, more extensive training options, and other services independently from the CS bundled offers.

Our final example in looking at information available on the internet is Planview Inc., which provides its customers with two offerings, Standard and Platinum. It does not have a matrix-like visual aid, which makes it more challenging for its customers to see and compare the two plans. However, what makes their Platinum offering interesting is that it has recruited many departments

McAfee Customer Success Plans Features

CUSTOMER SUCCESS PLAN FEATURES	ESSENTIAL	ENHANCED	PREMIERE
ASSIGNED CSM PROVIDES PROACTIVE SUCCESS MANAGEMENT		●	●
ATC PROVIDES ESCALATION MANAGEMENT AND ISSUE MONITORING			●
CLOUD ATC PROVIDES CLOUD MANAGEMENT AND MONITORING	Add-On Option	Add-On Option	●
ASSIGNED REMOTE SAM PROVIDES TECHNICAL ESCALATION MANAGEMENT	●		
DIRECT ACCESS TO TSE EXPERTS	●	●	●
24/7 PHONE SUPPORT	●	●	●
EDUCATION SERVICES	30 Vouchers	30 Vouchers	30 Vouchers
UNLIMITED SITE LICENSE TO ALL E-LEARNING TRAINING			●
ADVANCED SERVICE LEVEL GOALS (SLGs)	●	●	●
DOCUMENTED SUCCESS PLANS		●	●
BUSINESS REVIEWS	Semi-Annual	Quarterly	Quarterly
CONSULTING SERVICES	1 HWS*	40 Hrs 2 HWS*	160 Hrs 4 HWS*
SERVICE REQUEST PRIORITIZATION	●	●	●
PROACTIVE NOTIFICATION SERVICE VIA SUPPORT NOTIFICATION SERVICE (SNS)	●	●	●
DESIGNATED CONTACTS	15 Designated	25 Designated	Unlimited

*REMOTELY DELIVERED HEALTH WATCH SERVICES (HWS)

FIGURE 7.7 McAfee Monetization Offerings of Customer Success

to participate in providing value. Planview leverages senior customer support engineers, CS managers, consulting and training resources, product management inner-circle program access, technical migration services, access to senior executives, and free passes to its annual user conference. Offerings like these, while impressive, need to be measured against the cost of the program to ensure there are no cost overages.

TSIA recommends that organizations have a monetized offering to help fund their CS organization, including resources and technology. In addition to a monetized offering, our research shows that 83% of the industry has multiple tiers, and 57% has three offerings, as seen in Figure 7.8. Previously, we shared examples of monetized offerings and the challenges faced by organizations

Number of Multiple Tier Offerings of Customer Success

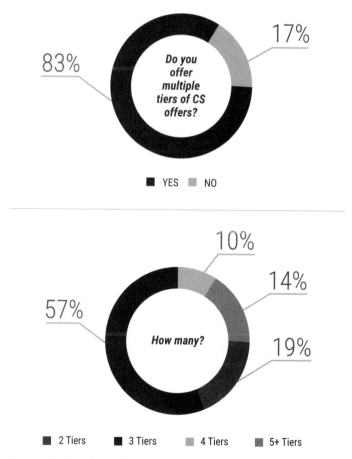

FIGURE 7.8 Number of Multiple Tier Offerings of Customer Success

that have only two offerings, which may not appeal to the needs of their customer base. Only 19% of the industry has just two monetized offerings. This approach limits customers' options and forces them to use only the standard support or single monetized offering, which may or may not meet their needs. TSIA recommends that organizations (at least initially) follow the industry standard of having three offerings, to align with good-better-best, in order to give customers a range of options so they can choose which one aligns with their needs. The best organizations provide three options so their customers can make a better choice as to the level of service and support they need to be happy customers.

Benefits to Companies with Monetized Customer Success Offerings

TSIA Benchmark data shows that organizations that monetize CS have a Net Promoter Score (NPS) that is 17 to 27 points higher than organizations that do not monetize. Second, companies that monetize drive more software subscription revenue. They have customer expansion rates at least 10% higher than those that do not monetize. Last, companies that monetize have an increase in their retention rates of 2% or higher when compared to those companies that do not monetize.

Monetization aligns with the charter of adoption. If your organization has the charter of adoption, then monetization can be a driving force that helps the funding for scale that will help drive greater adoption to ensure the customer experience is successful. With improvements in these three areas, the return on investment is crystal-clear, and it also provides additional revenue to scale CS. Happier customers spend more than those that are not happy. With the increase in fiscal metrics of expansion and retention, the best companies are also using those improvements in fiscal metrics to redirect to funds and scale CS.

TSIA recommends first starting with developing a monetization offering that meets the needs of your customers to help fund motions of adoption. Some 57% of the industry has three tiers, which TSIA considers a common practice. Think of offerings that can be categorized as "good-better-best" and that can help drive a monetized offering to meet the needs of your customers.

Assume Revenue Responsibility

After your CS team has done a great job fulfilling its initial charter of driving adoption (and if you skipped this step, re-read the first part of this chapter and start again), it's almost inevitable that it's going to be asked to take on more commercial responsibilities. About three-quarters of TSIA member companies leverage the CS organization to handle renewals. However, it's now a majority practice for CS to also have expansion responsibility. The question is shifting from "should I have CS take on revenue responsibilities," to "what role should CSMs play in revenue activities." Figure 7.9

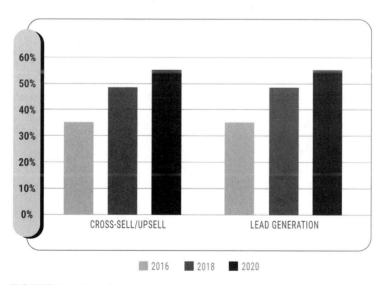

FIGURE 7.9 Time Spent on Expansion Activities by CS Organizations

shows this progression over the last five years. The move to CS taking on more revenue goals is good for your CS team, it's almost always good for your company, and you better believe it's good for your customers.

The First Step: Even Adoption Is a Revenue-Generating Act

OK, so what if you are really uncomfortable with the idea of adding revenue-generating responsibilities to your CS teams? Or maybe you find that your sales team isn't ready or willing to cede any of its commercial responsibility, or it doesn't trust anyone else but its team members. How can you participate in revenue growth if you are not taking an active role? Go back to the basics of the core CS charter adoption. In 2011, TSIA published *Consumption Economics: The New Rules of Tech*,[1] in which the authors discussed emerging factors that may inhibit growth should they go unaddressed. The inability for customers to consume the products sold to them was suggested as a key challenge, and TSIA data today confirms this to be true. Data suggest that a majority of companies believe that between 30% and 50% of their product or product value is not consumed. This is perhaps because those in the sales organization did not scope the deals properly, or they did not understand the customer's ability for consuming the product, or perhaps because the product is too complex to be easily used. If customers cannot consume the value promised in the sales cycle, they are much less likely to buy more of that product, and they are potentially at risk of downsizing at renewal.

A key role of the CS organization, therefore, is to promote revenue growth by unlocking the value of the products sold up front and activating the value that the customers purchased, thereby opening the potential for expansion and renewals. This is a different approach than just simply defending against churn. This is an offensive play to actively promote consumption for the known purpose of unlocking revenue potential. Simply understanding and focusing on driving consumption will undoubtedly result in faster growth at a lower cost. Companies that have built the capability to measure the correlation of consumption to renewal record a double-digit improvement in annual revenue per account growth (ARPA).

Renewals: A Common (and Best) Practice for CS Organizations

Even though renewal is the last letter in TSIA's LAER (land, adopt, expand, renew) customer engagement model, we'll talk about it first because it's a very common practice for CS to be in charge of the renewal. Once the purview of the sales organization or a specialty renewals function, renewals today are moving under CS. More than 76% of CS organizations participate in renewals today,[2] and we see this number rising in the future. Renewals, like expansions, tend to be a factor of product complexity and are balanced by the need for selling skills. Having renewals fully "owned" by CS is a majority practice for XaaS companies today, and the work is placed either in a specialty renewals role or as an additional charter on the CSM generalist.[3]

Renewals have traditionally had a "defend the base" charter. This made sense in the traditional models. Sales sold the product, and the renewals organization renewed the attached support and maintenance. As companies shift to a XaaS model, there is also a significant shift in renewal charter to include expansion responsibilities, and those organizations that own renewals increasingly own an expansion number as well. The traditional gross renewal rate KPI that focuses on retention only is replaced by the net-dollar retention, which includes an upsell or expansion component. This shift affirms the emerging practice of defending and growing at the same time.

And don't forget that in true subscription models, the renewal is an incredibly high-stakes event. In CapEx models, when just the support and maintenance was being renewed, the renewal

was 8% to 28% of total value. In XaaS, nearly the entire contract value is at stake at the time of renewal. CS organizations are
feeling the burden of the revenue goals and stepping up to the
capabilities to effectively forecast, manage, and close the business
at par with traditional sales organizations. But this shouldn't scare
you off. In fact, there is less than 1 percentage point difference in
renewal rate performance between CS ownership of the renewal
and sales ownership.[4]

And while renewal rates are basically the same whether the
CS or sales function handles them, there's a massive impact on
growth rates. Companies that leave their salespeople in charge of
renewals suffer a 14 percentage point reduction in growth rates.
That's because, as we mentioned in the previous chapter, the sales
function is best served when it focuses its efforts on the "hard
stuff." And if you've done your job on adoption, most of the time,
the renewal shouldn't be all that hard.

Helping Will Sell; Selling Won't Help

The main goal of CS is making your customers successful with
your technology, defined as enabling them to achieve the business
outcomes they desired when they bought your product in the
first place. If that requires the customer to buy another module or
add a feature, if it requires additional training or a higher level of
support, or if it includes add-on services or proactive monitoring,
then it's absolutely the right thing for CS to bring this up with
the customer. It's a big reason that TSIA embraces the core mantra
that "helping will sell; selling won't help."

And you're not just helping the customer by tightly integrating your expansion and renewal motions. TSIA research
shows that the number one predictor of success in renewals is
whether or not a company does a good job of expanding the
customers' spend between their initial purchase and the time of
renewal. Expansion and renewal go hand-in-hand. The more
tightly the two motions are intertwined, the better you'll be at

both. The more independently you operate the two, the worse you'll be at both.

In any case, it's almost impossible to embrace the idea of the lean, digital salesforce that we covered in the last chapter without having CS embrace the idea of taking on commercial responsibility. After all, if the sales organization is going to focus on the hard stuff, like aligning multiple stakeholders, justifying new budgets, and driving complex negotiations, someone still has to do the other stuff, like generate leads, handle low-complexity upsells, and drive standard renewals. It all works together to fulfill the promise of the digital customer experience and support CS at scale.

Lead Generation: A Great Way to Get Started

If your CS team is doing its job and lines of communication are good, it will probably come across new sales opportunities with the customer. Most of the time, these leads are discovered within the context of doing its normal duties. But again, in the spirit of "helping will sell," getting the right information over to the sales team for it to act upon benefits all parties, not the least of which is the customer.

Lead generation is one of the key activities that can help justify the funding of CS and cement its value. If CSMs assume this responsibility and do it well, then the budget that the sales and marketing organizations used to fund these motions may be able to be redirected to CS. Sales may likely say, "only if you reduce your quotas," which usually does not happen. The same scenario is true if CSMs can assume the responsibility of upsell or even cross-sell. The budget the sales organization was using for this can be redirected to the CS organization, which has the potential to yield great results, as seen in Figure 7.10. The cost of lead generation by the CSM is a fraction of the cost, at $25 to $50 average, as opposed to sales and outbound marketing, at approximately $200 per lead. Leads generated by CS teams convert to sales 30% of the time, for an average sale of $34,500. There's no way that your

Cost per Services-Generated Lead versus Other Sources

Source: TSIA Lead Generation through Services Survey, 2017 and Hubspot State of Inbound, 2015

FIGURE 7.10 Cost per Services-Generated Lead versus Other Sources

marketing department can come up with any other lead source that can generate new opportunities as efficiently or effectively.

Many CS organizations realize the benefits of generating leads and then make a handful of mistakes in setting up the execution. Primarily, they focus on enabling this motion with training and compensation, rather than focusing on outcomes and processes. TSIA often is asked the question: "How should I incentivize my CSMs for lead generation?" Or, "Do you know a good sales training company to help our CSMs with their sales skills? Well, first, let's talk about compensation. You must be careful about setting hard targets for lead generation with CSMs if you don't want to compromise their status as trusted advisors. Leads are organic and are just one of the activities CSMs can do that will help fuel customer growth.

Adding a cash bonus or SPIF if their leads turn into closed deals can be helpful, but the main motivation needs to be helping the customer and your company hit their goals, not taking leads for the sake of selling more. As far as skills are concerned, don't waste time on standard sales training around prospecting or negotiation. Spend time on soft skills, such as active listening and effective questioning techniques. The last thing you need is a poorly trained, inexperienced CSM trying to do hardcore sales. Remember: Helping will sell; selling won't help. CSMs are just trying to help their customers get to the right offerings to meet their outcomes and solve their problems.

When to Have Customer Success Handle Upsells

Many CS organizations can get comfortable with the idea of lead generation. It is non-threatening, and it's kind of "sales lite" because it doesn't involve closing or negotiating or other activities that could be considered more unsavory. But actually driving deals to closure? Sometimes that's a whole different ball game, and it's harder for CS organizations to make that leap.

Primary concerns from most CS organizations stem from the fear of CSMs losing their status of trusted advisor and being seen as a sales representative. First, let us put your mind at ease with a few things and give you some encouragement. When CSMs have primary responsibility for upsells, defined as selling more of the same SKU, account growth rates improve by double digits. And when CSMs have targets for ARR growth, not only do growth rates improve significantly, but renewal rates improve more than 10% as well. It may not be comfortable, but we encourage you to really think about giving it a try.

So how do you make it work? First, let's consider the difference between a cross-sell and an upsell, as outlined in Figure 7.11.

Think of a cross-sell as a new sale within an existing customer. You're tapping into a new budget, a new department, or a new buyer. For cross-sells, CS should have responsibility for lead generation and can play a supporting role, but it's not on what it should be spending its time. If you find your teams dealing with heavy negotiation or complex and extended sales cycles, they're

Important Sales Definitions

FIGURE 7.11 Sales Definitions that Transcend into Customer Success

probably doing the wrong things, and success will be hard to come by.

Upsells, on the other hand, are prime grounds for CS involvement. In fact, some data suggests that if CS doesn't drive upsells, then no one does. TSIA data and all of our collective years of experience suggest that many enterprise salespeople won't pay attention to a deal that's less than $100,000. Most of the offerings listed in Figure 7.11 under the upsell category are often priced well below that threshold. While that list is incomplete, you'll see that almost all those deal types are additional sales tied to the same buyer and the same budget of the original sale; they don't require much customization, if any; and they are generally executable by the person with whom the CSM is usually dealing in the usual course of business. More importantly, these are offers that help the customer leverage existing technology investments, meet their goals, and reach their desired business outcomes.

In most engagements, we see that complex cross-sell and up-sell opportunities are punted to the sales organizations. And that is the correct process. CSMs do not have the administrative cycles to deal with complex deals. In most interactions, where there are complex deals, they are sent to the sales organization to handle. As we discussed previously, the sales organization takes the hard deals. By doing this, you have removed the concern that CSMs will not be viewed as a trusted advisor. If CSMs are only working on non-complex upsell and cross-sell opportunities from beginning to end, then they will be seen as a resource that can help get work done, much like a trusted advisor.

Be an Expansion "STAR"

So, how do you make it easier for your CSMs to sell without turning them into salespeople? Simply by making the job easier for them. First, limit the offerings they can sell to those that are simple, straightforward, and that don't require customization. Second, don't set them up for failure by asking them to deal with global procurement officers or complex signoff processes. Upsells executed by CS should be transactional in nature. Next, and this is very important, analytics are your friend, and upsells are just another extension of a great digital customer experience. The best upsells are ones that are dictated by the data.

We've all received a call like this from a salesperson: "Hi, this is Bob. I'm just checking in with you." The check-in call only exists so that Bob can legitimately say he doesn't just call when he wants to sell you something. Instead, envision this call: "Hi, this is Bob. I noticed that you've had three different people call us this week with the same problem. We have some ideas on how we can help you." The former call provides no value, whereas the latter one does. But your upsells need to be analytics-driven to pull it off credibly.

Finally, upsells need to be repeatable in nature. Customization is the bitter archenemy of simplicity and frightens inexperienced (at least from a sales standpoint) CSMs from taking on upsells with enthusiasm. Keep it simple and follow the STAR protocol to help you. Figure 7.12 provides a simple reference.

One final point to remember: If it walks like a duck and it quacks like a duck, it's a duck...even if you call it a chicken. And if it has a quota and it has a forecast, it's a salesperson, even if you call it a CSM. Having goals, targets, and MBOs around growth rates for CSMs are in bounds, even helpful. But when you give them hard targets, for which they receive a percentage-based commission and can get fired if they don't hit, then they're in sales, and their primary goal will be selling, even if that charter you've worked so hard on says otherwise.

The STAR Protocol for Effective Upsells

When looking to grow existing customers, what you're selling is just as important as who is selling it or how they sell it. Upsells can be efficient and effective when the STAR Protocol is applied.

FIGURE 7.12 The STAR Protocol for Effective Upsells

Segmentation: Figuring Out Who Does What

One of the real challenges that companies often have when involving CS in the sales process is determining the boundaries between what the sales organization does and what the CS organization does. Companies must make sure goals and roles are clear and well-defined. When looking at what CS teams can do in the sales process, there are two factors that you must consider: the capability of the team and the complexity of the task at hand. We'll talk about both of these in context as we continue this chapter, but you can't think about one of these elements without the other.

Let's start with capability. First, remember that a capability is not an individual competency or skill. Those are part of the equation, but not all of it. A capability is the people, process, and technology that are required to get things done. And when you figure out what role your CS team should play in the revenue process, you need to start by honestly looking at yourself in the mirror. Did my CS team and leadership come from a background of services or support and now they've taken on adoption as part of their remit? If that's the case, then their sales capability is low. They can certainly perform some simple tasks like gathering account intelligence, or relevant data that can be leveraged by sales and your partners for use in the sales process. They can also help with various parts of the process, providing guidance and education. But you may want to stay away from having CS try to close upsells, at least until its capabilities mature.

The other axis on the matrix is complexity. How hard are your expansions and renewals to execute? If you don't have offers designed or optimized for your existing customers, and every expansion is as complicated as a new sale, then the sales team probably has to execute them. Do you provide help to your CS team in the form of analytics and product-led recommendations? If not, and they need to try to do discovery on their own, their chances of success are low. Do you have a CS plan and a defined communication cadence with your customer, including regularly scheduled business reviews? Can you provide insights to your customers on how they can better use your technology to reach their goals? Those are just some of the things you can do to make your expansions and renewals less complex and less difficult to execute, meaning that lower-capability teams can successfully drive them, usually at a much lower cost.

Achieving the Sales Dividend

For most of the history of the technology industry, the sales organization handled all commercial transactions. If there was a commercial transaction to be executed with a customer, a member of the sales team handled it. If transactions were complex and difficult to execute, or at least thought to be so by the sales organization, then only the sales team was qualified to tackle them. No matter the level of complexity, it was on the hook to close the deal. As seen in Figure 7.13, sales sells everything.

When companies begin their journey toward more efficient sales models, they often start with the lowest-complexity transactions they can find. These tend to be renewals and small upsells with their lowest-tier customer segment. In these cases, renewals are driven by either a CSM or are handled via e-commerce transactions, as seen in Figure 7.14 (page 200).

However, as the capabilities of CS e-commerce grow, and companies get better at optimizing their offers and processes around these new motions, more duties can be taken off of the plate of the sales organization and handled by lower-cost, lower-capability resources, allowing the sales team to focus on the "hard stuff" that we discussed previously. Companies may find themselves hiring specialists to help with complex renewals, upsells, or new offerings the sales team may not have the capability to sell. Figure 7.15 (page 201) illustrates this concept.

The end result is a hyper-efficient engagement model, where your highest capability and most expensive resources are focused

Typical Transaction Selling

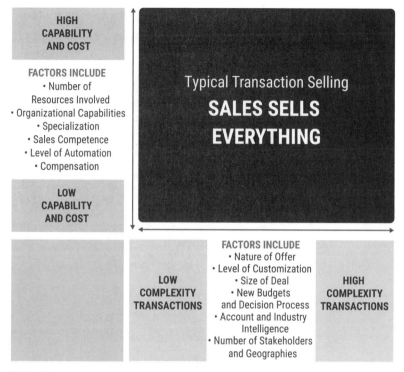

FIGURE 7.13 Typical Transaction Selling

on the tough task of generating new revenue and enterprise deals, and everyone else handles everything else. This means that you hire fewer salespeople and make more money at a lower cost of sale. You're not paying high-cost account executives to handle administrative tasks, close the deals that would already close without them, or work on upsells that are too small to move the needle on their quota but really add up for your company. This "sales dividend" results in either:

- Fewer salespeople covering more accounts, or
- The same number of salespeople carrying higher "land" quotas.

Typical Transaction Selling: Capability and Costs

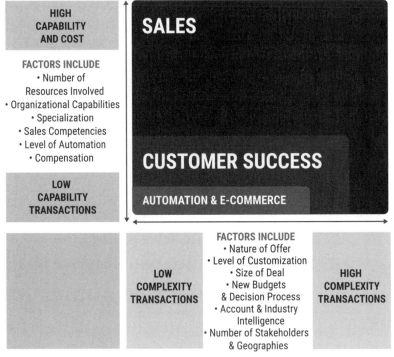

FIGURE 7.14 Typical Transaction Selling: Capability and Costs

This is because the CS organization is handling the other account-related duties at scale. But most importantly, it's the right move for your customers and your company, as the adoption, consumption, and retention of your offerings are paramount in a subscription world. Figure 7.16 (page 202) details the segmentation of CS roles based on complexity and work type.

Leveraging Digital Capabilities to Scale

After hiring CSMs, the next job role to hire in the CS organization must be digital capabilities to help scale your organization's engagement strategy. The exception to this is if your organization already has a plethora of digital solutions that are organic to CS

Typical Transaction Selling: Capability and Complexity

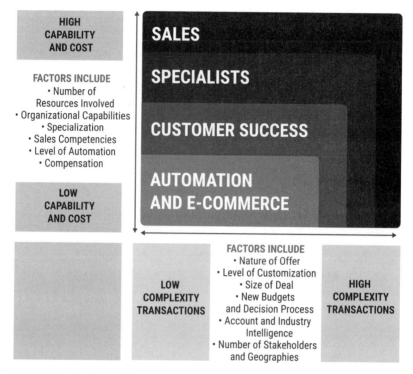

FIGURE 7.15 Typical Transaction Selling: Capability and Complexity

that provides a digital communication strategy or digital touch. What do you already have in hand? The most common organic digital solutions for CS are CRM platforms, CS solutions, and marketing and survey solutions, as shown in Figure 7.17. Historically, CS organizations have leveraged many digital tools available to them from sales and marketing, with the CRM solution (i.e., Salesforce or Microsoft Dynamics CRM) as the major contender at 63%. However, there has been a shift in the industry to the usage of CS solution platforms.

For years, TSIA has been tracking the tools used by CS organizations, and during that time, CS solutions were only leveraged 33% of the time. In 2017, TSIA authored a blog titled "Are 67% of

Segmenting CS Roles Based on Complexity and Work Type

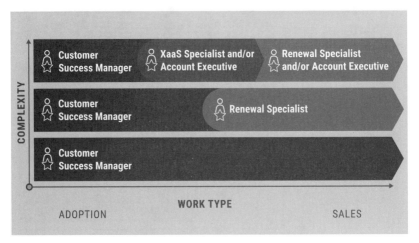

FIGURE 7.16 CS Role Based on Complexity and Work Type

Digital CS Application Growth Used by Customer Success

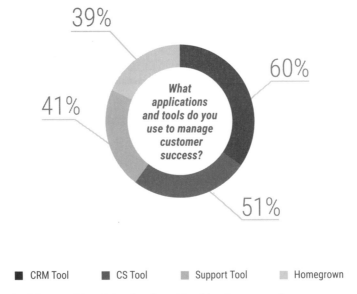

FIGURE 7.17 Digital Applications Used by Customer Success

Customer Success Organizations Wrong?"[5] The data shows that this metric held until the global pandemic of 2020-2021. Since then, we have seen a major change in digital technology usage in CS organizations to the tune of a 15% increase in CS solution purchases. Organizations need help with platforms that help them communicate and reach their customers while also giving them intelligence about the overall health of their customer accounts.

CS software platforms continue to make digital improvements in their capabilities that will propel them over the 50% mark, making their usage a common practice in CS organizations.

Leveraging Partners to Scale

Leveraging partners for customer coverage and engagement is a great strategy for scale that is highly overlooked and underinvested in by most organizations. TSIA research reveals that neither technology providers nor partners are working as a team to share adoption information, as seen in Figure 7.18. Partners supporting customers in order to scale CS is an afterthought for many providers. One of the great challenges in CS and partner relationships is how to enable partners effectively and then monitor partner CS engagement. Without digital engagement, via tools like shared CS solutions, it can be nearly impossible to know how well a partner is taking care of the customer. Those digital capabilities are needed to receive these insights.

There are many decisions, processes, and investments necessary to successfully leverage partners for coverage and engagement in the CS domain. These include:

- Charter definitions.
- Channel conflict.
- Funding CSMs for partners.
- Metrics to be used and tracked by both organizations.
- Partner compensation models.

Sharing Adoption Information with OEMs and Partners

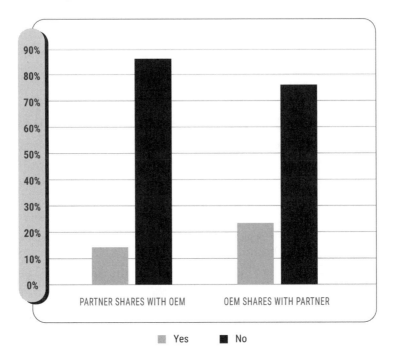

FIGURE 7.18 Sharing Adoption Information with OEMs and Partners

- Responsibility for renewals.
- Sharing adoption systems and data.
- Sharing of journey maps, success plans, and playbooks.
- Training, coaching, and certifications.
- Usage of digital CS solutions.

Yes, there is much to consider when leveraging partners to help make it work, with little to no impact to the customer. But make no mistake about it, leveraging partners is a required scaling technique to extend your coverage model to ensure customers in all markets are receiving value without having to hire additional headcount.

One of the key considerations when leveraging partners to perform the CS function for some or most of your customer base is to help them monetize the CS function, as discussed earlier in this chapter. This is something that technology providers tell their partners to do, but partners do not know where to start on this journey unless they are already doing this for another provider. Partners that have very slim margins to start up new organizations and invest in training and resources are not likely to seriously commit to this new charter unless they can "see the money," and it is up to the provider to work with designated CS partner companies to help them create a path to CS investment payback that aligns with the technology provider's CS compensation model and funding approach.

Without proper investment in the partners' CS capabilities, this will not be a winning play, and the technology provider should not launch plans to extend this capability to partners without sufficient investment and commitment. Whether or not partners are embraced in the CS execution efforts may be a deciding factor for partners to decide "for" or "against" a particular technology provider for any given XaaS market. Keep in mind that partners are often the integrators of multi-provider solutions at the customer site, therefore having them educated and enabled to be your CS extended team is often a winning strategy. Chapter 8 goes into even more detail on how to effectively enable partners.

Leveraging Smarter Account Segmentation to Scale

There will always be more customers than CSMs, and, as a result, it is imperative to develop a segmentation and engagement strategy for scale. Those organizations that do it well have an average retention rate improvement of 9% and an average expansion rate improvement of 7%. It starts by reviewing your customers and understanding the best way to divide them in a way that the CSMs can engage them. Most organizations start with a high-touch model in which TSIA defines a customer-to-CSM ratio of 15:1 or less. Anything above 16:1 is considered a low-touch model.

The most common and immediate way to segment customers is by account size. This is the approach used by 83% of the industry, as seen in Figure 7.19. An additional way to segment is to use categories. Examples include geography, which requires you to look at cultural differences, time zones, and language issues. Growth potential comes in a strong third. This requires your organization to evaluate if the customer has growth potential or if they have spent all that they will with your organization. There are many ways to segment your customer account. You can even segment a segment. We are seeing a shift in the industry from three segments to four segments as most common. It appears that organizations are leveraging digital touch as the lowest level for a self-service option but are leaving the other three segments available for human engagement when and where it is needed.

Segmenting accounts provides a better picture of the resources you have available, which provides insight into how to engage your customers, which defined engagement processes to use, and which available CS resources to employ. Not all customers are equal and not all customers have the same expectations. Do not assume that because a customer is top tier that they want human engagement. We have seen a plethora of situations that would prove this wrong because the customer may have a mature and highly trained team that prefers digital or self-help engagement.

For low-touch engagement, the industry has changed gears from 2018 to 2020 and has made a significant investment in a tech-touch experience, as seen in Figure 7.20. The low-touch coverage model for the customer-to-CSM ratio jumped from 47:1 to 139:1, which shows digital must complement your engagement strategy to give the team a larger coverage model.

Setting customer expectations up front is key, especially if you monetize CS. If the customer wants a high-touch experience with

Segmentation for CSM Coverage

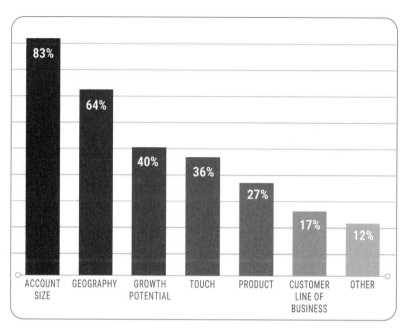

FIGURE 7.19 TSIA Segmentation for CSM Coverage

Comparative CSM Ratios Segmented: 2018 and 2022

CSM SEGMENTATION MODELS	HIGH TOUCH 2018	HIGH TOUCH 2020	HIGH TOUCH 2022	LOW TOUCH 2018	LOW TOUCH 2020	LOW TOUCH 2022
MEDIAN CUSTOMER-TO-CSM RATIO	5:1	7:1	8:1	30:1	50:1	63:1
AVERAGE CUSTOMER-TO-CSM RATIO	7:1	8.2:1	8.5:1	47:1	139:1	124:1
MEDIAN TOTAL REVENUE PER CSM	$5M	$4.3M	$4.0M	$3.5M	$3.6M	$2.5M
AVERAGE TOTAL REVENUE PER CSM	$5.2M	$4.4M	$4.6M	$3.58M	$5.6M	$4.5M

FIGURE 7.20 2018 and 2020 Comparative CSM Ratios Segmented for High and Low Touch

the CSM, then the cost will be more. If they want self-service, then it will cost them less. Customers prefer honesty up front and setting expectations up front. They get frustrated when information is withheld.

There are many ways to segment your customers to provide the greatest coverage model. The key is to start with something. As the expression goes, "perfection is the enemy of good." You may not get it right the first time, but that is OK. At least you learned from the experience. The key is to be in positive communications with your customers to glean feedback and adjust as needed. Then, align the team you have on hand to provide the best possible coverage model protecting the most valued accounts, either based on their account size, total value, logo power, or whatever criterion you decide is most important. When segmentation and engagement are performed well, the outcomes are improved expansion and retention, which are lagging indicators for adoption performed well. Some of the most mature CS organizations, like Salesforce, are even moving toward vertical industry segmentation and specialization of both customers and CSMs.

Outcome Management Is the New Customer Growth Process

What takes place when customers purchase on an "as you go" basis, or, even more pronounced, on a consumption basis, value and outcomes are experienced, or not experienced, daily. The new currency for creating a revenue relationship increasingly lies on the perception of value and outcomes achieved. This requirement places a new responsibility on our CS and renewals organizations. Perhaps you provide reports or dashboards that show consumption or usage. Perhaps you provide case reports to show the status of issue resolution. Maybe automated marketing communications are interwoven with the renewal cadence.

The cost of CS is not effectively assessed per transaction; cost must rather be aligned to the value realized by the customer. To be great under those conditions requires CS organizations to build capabilities to track, measure, analyze, and to nimbly take actions based on the outcomes realized. Revenue growth is as much about helping the customer consume value and achieve outcomes as it is about sales skills. Selling truly is about helping under these conditions, and the overarching charter of the CS organization comes together to connect adoption to expansion to renewal, and effectively, to customer growth.

C-Level Customer Success as the Growth Engine

When CS reports to the CEO, CCO, or C-level executive, great things happen, including revenue growth rate improvements, as seen in Figure 7.21. When a C-level executive has an eye on the customer experience, they are well positioned to promote a positive customer experience, scale teams, and provide the solutions tools and resources necessary to ensure the CSMs are ready for engagement. C-level executives are building organizational teams and alignment to create a customer experience that drives growth, and customer satisfaction is key to driving additional growth from the customer base.

When performed well, C-level CS creates the ethos of the customer experience internally and motivates team members to perform at operational efficiency and excellence. The customer is top of mind, and where there is "old thinking" in the company, it is identified and corrected quickly. *You cannot scale an organization for future profit and growth when employees are stuck in the past.* Organizational structures are designed to create the greatest synergy and growth models. Additionally, frameworks are created and leveraged to build operational efficiencies at scale.

CS management cannot run as a silo. The organizations that surround CS must be aligned to provide balance and to

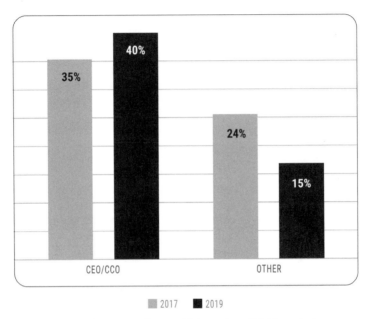

Company Growth Rates When CS Reports
to C-Level Executives

FIGURE 7.21 Company Growth Rates when CS Reports to
C-Level Executives

complement CS efforts so that the customer receives a proactive customer experience. When built out well, CS management becomes the central repository for all customer data, customer intelligences, and customer analytics. That data, which we call The Lean Digital Salesforce in Chapter 5, has the potential to transform sales productivity in a profound way. As a result, the alignment of internal teams working with CS management will need to be constructed to drive greater value through the motions of adoption, expansion, and renewal. When done well, the result is expansion and retention performance improvements.

When C-level CS exists, all the data show increases in financial growth. In some organizations, we have seen yields of 30% to 40% improvement in their growth.

Scaling Customer Success Summary

Scaling CS is foundational and transcends all CS organizations regardless of verticals. Start with the basics by developing the charter. We're not talking about a sentence, ethos statement, or mission statement. We're talking about clearly defining how the CS organization will be constructed, on what it will focus, how that works with all other customer-facing departments, and then align everything else to those charters. Attach the charter to a committed business outcome: Net Promoter Score, expansion, renewal, ARR growth, etc. (You cannot be a financial art project.) From there, funding the CS organization through monetization, fiscal metrics, and efficiencies in sales and marketing determines how many human resources and digital resources you will have to manage the customer experience.

Next, define a segmentation and engagement strategy that allows you to have great coverage of your customers with the limited human resources you have, coupled with the digital capabilities. Incorporate the right digital mix of technology that enables the CS team and touches and informs customers and you're on a much better track for success. Strategically design your partners into your CS strategy and execution plans to ensure you are able to provide CS to all customers with the best, most adept resources possible for their complexity and customer install base needs. When adoption is done well, the result is expansion and retention. When adoption is done poorly, the result is churn. Making the right investments in these areas will help scale your CS organization and create a better customer experience!

CS of the future is an offensive play in which customers not only remain customers through churn mitigation, but they also grow through effective consumption management, expansion efforts, and renewal management. Every opportunity to help a customer is an opportunity to grow a customer. By adopting an active and participating role in the financial health of the company, CS organizations will take some of the load off the traditional sales organizations by generating financial contributions at lower cost.

Digitization of the renewal workflow is a pioneering effort today. Companies are building the workflow using best-of-breed building blocks and connecting them together to form a quote-to-cash process flow. There are very few platform options that manage expansion and renewals end to end, yet those few companies, 33% today, that do automate are experiencing an 11.5-point improvement in renewal rate performance.[6] Digitization of the renewal workflow follows the complexity factor expressed thus far; and, as quotes, products, and offers become less complex, they can be digitized the length of the workflow, thus creating great efficiencies. Customers have been in training for years in how to relate to their suppliers via technology and, in fact, prefer digital communication over a telephone call from a salesperson.[7] Taking the next step is at the tipping point, and the reality is that renewals continue to offer a low-complexity, highly prescriptive work-type option.

The low end of the customer base is a prime target for low-complexity automation and will be the focus for virtually every technology company for the next few years. The real question? What is the ceiling? Can digital strategies that lead the renewal motion in the low end be applied to the high end? It is important to note that a key enabling capability to achieve a sustainable digitization of the renewal workflow is the ability to build simplicity into the product itself, including frictionless paths to purchase alternative adoption and support offerings.

"Big C" Customer Success

As we said in the beginning of this chapter, too often, the CS function at technology companies is a financial art project. Put simply, they are too small and too underutilized. They either only cover a subset of customers or are chartered to deliver only a subset of their full engagement value. With the right financial and executive support, the CS team can have one of the most positive and predictable effects on a company's future prospects when compared to almost any other investment. Companies should resist hesitation and instead be focused on creating a corporate environment that promotes CS at scale so that the end result is profit that matters to the bottom line.

8 | Digitally Enabled Partnering

By Anne McClelland and Thomas Lah

Technology providers that are serious about growing their XaaS business and incrementally accelerating their technology subscription revenue year over year must consider the advantages of leveraging a XaaS partner channel ecosystem as they consider their Wave Two digital transformation strategy. Like the previous chapter on customer success, many technology providers face the daunting challenge of simultaneously scaling and digitally transforming their XaaS channel. But effectively engaging partners around XaaS offers is fundamentally different than engaging partners to sell and service on-premise offers. Here are some of the key differences:

- Partners lose traditional revenue streams from installing and supporting on-premise solutions.
- The skill sets required to sell and service XaaS offers are different.
- The partner enablement playbook for XaaS offers is thicker.
- The technology platform to support XaaS partners is more complex.
- The metrics of success are different for partners selling and servicing XaaS offers.

To navigate these differences, technology providers will need to pursue new tactics to attract, enable, and retain partners that can help drive XaaS revenues. But before partners can be digitally enabled, a technology provider must understand what roles the partner will play related to XaaS offers. This chapter will address the following challenges related to partner management and XaaS offers, which are:

- Defining the role of partners.
- Attracting partners.
- Digitally enabling partners.
- How partners are evolving.

TSIA's Wave Two Digital Transformation Model and Digitally Enabled Partnering (DEP)

DEP requires all the "squares" in the TSIA W2DT model. DEP touches every facet of the company for a *partner-centered technology provider*. Partners can provide so many functions for a technology provider firm. They can participate in land, adopt, expand, and renew motions. They can deliver the planning, implementation, monitoring, and optimization of your offerings for the customers. Partners can also deliver the managed services offerings that contain technology providers' offerings, including providing support services and premium customer account services. Many partners deliver curated solutions expertise via their value-added services and intellectual property integrations that can include optimization of multiple vendors' offerings into the customer's integrated technology solution.

For partner-centered technology providers, every square in the W2DT model lights up for the digitally enabled partnering motion. In a partner-centric technology provider, the partner is functioning as the "hands and feet" of the technology providers that each partner company supports. Success for partners is incumbent upon having seamless access to the provider's data, analytics, support, and services infrastructure as well as a direct line into their requirements processes. Ideally, every partner should have access to the data and analytics they need in order to improve their delivery and service capabilities with customers, such as customer health scores, customer journey analysis, support tickets, and early visibility to updates and changes in product-led growth systems and XaaS offerings releases. Figure 8.1 maps digitally enabled partnering to TSIA's W2DT framework.

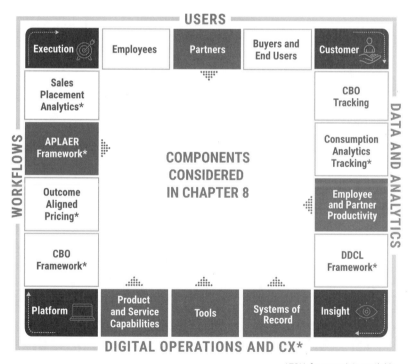

FIGURE 8.1 Digitally Enabled Partnering Mapped to TSIA's W2DT Framework

Defining the Role of Partners
Understanding the Challenges

Most technology providers that have been around for a long time already have an established partner ecosystem that has served them well in the past for their traditional, transactional business. It is a reseller-heavy model, coin-operated, and easy to manage via spreadsheets, a CRM system, and use of targeted incentives to drive behavior.

TSIA has data, taken from our XaaS Partner Ecosystems Trends and Directions Survey, showing that those that create a separate and distinct partner channel strategy to support XaaS are growing their technology subscription revenue at a faster rate than those that do not do this. Creating a kind of "firewall" between the old partner program execution and the new partner program that supports the technology provider's XaaS business is important to ensure success. TSIA's findings include confirmation that many companies will build a focused team of partner business managers, separate direct sellers, separate KPIs, and separate incentive plans for their employees that align with the XaaS business goals. TSIA's correlation data from this survey and others proves this point, as seen in Figure 8.2. This graph shows a strong and positive correlation between having a separate and defined go-to-market strategy for a company's XaaS offer business and the percentage annual growth of XaaS revenue for all direct and indirect channels. Those that have a separate and defined go-to-market strategy will see significantly faster growth in their XaaS revenue over those that do not make these changes to their objectives, KPIs, organizations/roles, and compensation.

Classifying Partners in the XaaS Economy

In Chapters 1 and 2, the examples of Amazon, Amazon Web Services, and Salesforce were described in this march to a digital customer experience. These examples are also very powerful leading indicators of what is to come in the partner channel ecosystem in

Separate GTM Strategy and XaaS Revenue Growth

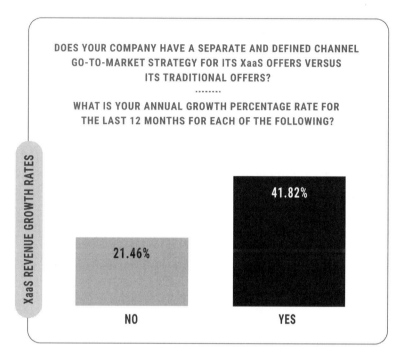

FIGURE 8.2 Separate GTM Strategy and XaaS Revenue Growth

its future state when XaaS is the norm and the traditional, transactional technology acquisition model is a pattern from the past.

Technology providers that are "born in the cloud" have a distinct advantage over companies that have to transform from a heavy, reseller-led partner motion to a XaaS-led partner motion. In XaaS, we see that partnering is less about "sell through" and is more about "sell with" and "sell to." Also in XaaS partner models, we are seeing a significant movement toward giving partners a choice in their options to participate in a technology platform provider's partnering motions, which is preferable to making partners participate in certain ways based on their "partner type." Segmenting by partner type is a thing of the past. Instead, segmenting by "partner motions" or by "partner models" is more appropriate in the age of XaaS. This can be seen in Figure 8.3.

Because traditional partner roles are blurring and technology providers are migrating to delivery of XaaS offers, TSIA asserts that there are really three types of partner technology categories that technology providers need in XaaS. Partners may participate in one or all partnering motions.

- **Sell-through partners.** These partners sell the technology vendor's offerings and own all or part of the sales life cycle. These partners may or may not take physical ownership of the offerings during the sales process.

- **Sell-to partners.** These are partners that buy a technology offer to embed the technology vendor's offer in a solution such as a managed service or an embedded or OEM solution.

- **Sell-with partners.** Partners that are paid a referral fee or marketing fee for providing leads and/or qualified

XaaS Partnering Models

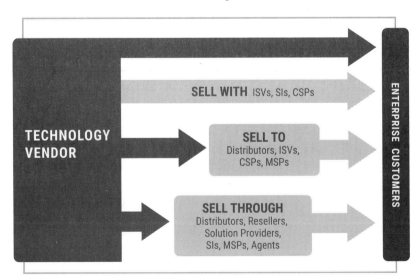

FIGURE 8.3 XaaS Partnering Models

opportunities to the technology vendor. In some cases, sell-with partners do not wish to receive a referral fee, but would prefer non-financial exchanges of value between the parties.

It is important that technology providers revisit their partner segmentation models and their tiering models, and determine how to optimize partner engagement by opening options for their partners to evolve their business models to deliver as much revenue and profit value with and through the technology provider as possible. Gone are the days of dictating how partners must "behave" and therefore how they will make money. Today partners have choices, and your focus should be to ensure that they choose *you* as a technology provider because you have thoughtfully considered how to launch a "partner-first" program that allows them to evolve their business needs to best serve customers in the mode they desire. This is the way of the future.

An interesting example of two companies that have simplified things relative to their partnering motions are Salesforce and ServiceNow.

Salesforce has simplified its program into two categories:[1]

- Consultants
- AppExchange Partners

ServiceNow has designed its partner programs to focus on "what the partners do" versus partner types:[2]

- Sales
- Services
- Technology
- Service Provider
- Public Sector

Other companies are making certain they have a partner program that is extremely simple to enter and engage with and that ensures success. The partner programs of the past that carried complicated hurdles for entry, numerous requirements for moving into higher levels of benefits tiers, and onerous training and certification requirements and partner investments, are no longer relevant. Now, born-in-the-cloud companies are opting for seamless, intuitive partner programs that deliver excellent value to partners in a "just-in-time" fashion, while measuring common-sense XaaS KPIs (such as growing ARR, bringing in new logos and on-time renewals, and influencing customers to invest in the technology provider's platform) to encourage desired behavior and dole out more partner benefits. The most exciting programs publish their "multipliers" to tempt partners to join their ecosystem to get their slice of the opportunity pie.

From a TSIA survey of service provider partners,[3] findings show that their top revenue drivers are managed services; reselling solutions, services, and products; and consulting services. When asked what they see as being the most important growth opportunities in the next two years, they said that helping customers with their cloud migration efforts, helping customers successfully manage their remote workforces, and ensuring a secure work environment are the top initiatives for growth, as seen Figure 8.4. These partners are thinking in terms of providing customers value through technology solutions rather than focusing on the technology itself. This validates that the actual technology inside the solutions is less important than the ability to easily facilitate the provision of value and outcomes with and through that technology.

It is clear from the data that TSIA is collecting that technology providers that are successful in XaaS revenue sales growth are allowing partners to participate in "sell with," "sell to," and "sell through" motions, whichever is most aligned with the partners' business interests and capabilities. Those technology providers that are utilizing "sell with" and "sell to" motions are growing XaaS revenue from partners year over year at rates of 17% and 19%, respectively, greater than those that are not, as seen in Figure 8.5.

Service Provider Reseller Data

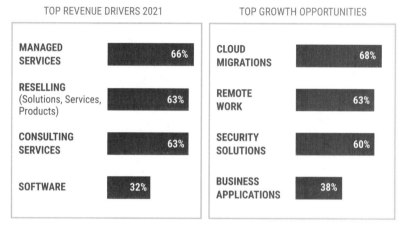

FIGURE 8.4 Service Provider Reseller Data

"Sell With" and "Sell To" Impacts on Subscription Revenue

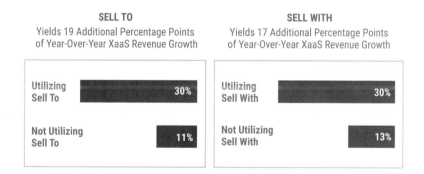

FIGURE 8.5 "Sell With" and "Sell To" Impacts on Subscription Revenue

Some technology providers that are heavily invested in re-seller partners (the "sell through" motion) may find that they are in short supply of the partners they need in this new model. The "sell with" partners that may consist primarily of software companies or systems integrators, or the "sell to" partners that may consist of managed service provider partners, may not be part of the technology provider's ecosystem today. The technology provider needs to create a profile of these partners that are best suited to be successful in their XaaS partner ecosystem and take steps to locate and recruit those partners to join their ecosystem to meet all of the customers' needs and take advantage of all potential revenue streams from having a broad ecosystem.

Attracting Partners
Demonstrating How Partners Can Make Money in the XaaS Model

When making the shift from traditional, transactional business models of the product-centric or perpetual-license-centric selling motions, to the consumption-based pricing models of XaaS, the economics for the partners are different. Therefore, partner companies must make a conscious effort to change their business plans to take advantage of these new models, or they will find themselves disaggregated by other partners that have adapted and morphed to be able to provide the types of life-cycle value-added services that technology subscriptions and consumption models require.

The beauty of the traditional, transactional model is the transactional nature of the model itself. The transaction is central, and making the transaction as large up front as possible from a revenue perspective, is the ultimate goal. This has been beneficial to the technology provider and to the partners. Since the product actually changes hands from the provider to the partner to the customer, the entire bulk of the product revenue can be recognized by both the provider and the partner when the product arrives on the customer premises. Most technology providers and partners leverage their ability to negotiate significant discounts with the customer if a larger delivery of product is agreed to, therefore wooing customers by offering reduced prices to pay more up front than if they pay for the same solution over time. As you can see from Figure 8.6, the heavy nature of reselling

Traditional Channel Economics

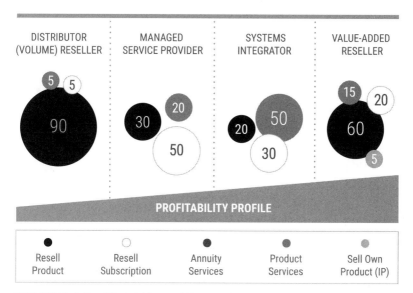

FIGURE 8.6 Traditional Channel Economics

products is predominant in the distributor/reseller value proposition, and there is heavy emphasis on project services for the systems integrator, both of which are indicative of this transactional environment.

In the consumption technology subscription delivery model, revenue recognition is taken when the subscription is (according to its subscription term) consumed, much like professional services. Therefore, when a three-year technology subscription agreement is signed, for, say, a total of $900,000, the commissions paid on revenue at signing is only for the value of the first year of the three, that of $300,000. Potentially complicating matters even more, the finance department likely will "technically" recognize revenue monthly, and new problems arise when a customer cancels their contract during the duration of the contract term. In many companies, the salesperson has to pay back commissions to true up to when the contract ended.

The bottom line here is this means that sales compensation for both the technology provider's sales team and the partner's sales team needs to be reengineered to allow for the payments of the total contract value over the course of the life of the contract. With a true consumption offering, theoretically the customer could cancel and stop paying at any time throughout the three years, therefore revenue (and commissions) is often tied to completing the three-year term and receiving all customer payments in a timely manner across the total life of the contract term.

With this shift in economics, it is critical that partners create other ways to generate revenue and profit that complement the technology subscription offering. These opportunities may come in the form of additional post-sales value-added services, including:

- Monetizing premier account services, such as customer success.
- Partner-sourced intellectual property.
- Complementary technology subscriptions from other technology-provider companies.
- Integration and/or customization services.
- Support services.
- Managed services.

Many partners are still working out how to create more value-added services that will broaden their revenue and profit footprint in this XaaS customer environment.

TSIA talks about the fact that partners, too, need to swallow their fish as referenced in the *Technology-as-a-Service Playbook*,[4] Chapter 10, Changes in the Channel, and in Chapter 8, The Financial Keys of XaaS. Partners' business plans model after the technology provider or OEM company. The partners need to stay afloat while developing their new business by continuing to keep the traditional, asset sale-plus-services business as robust as they can during their transition to a subscription business model to provide them the necessary air cover while they evolve. This requires a committed senior leadership team and investors at the partner company to build, bless, and execute this long-term strategy and get to the other side of the fish model successfully.

Figure 8.7 provides examples of how the economic engines of partners are being shifted by the growth of XaaS offers. It is clear in these models that there is dramatically less transactional revenue from reselling on-premise technology and more revenue sources, including technology subscription sales and annuity value-added services, such as managed services and consulting services.

In a survey of over 800 service-provider reseller partners,[5] TSIA found that the majority of the respondents are providing

Business Model of the XaaS Partner Channel

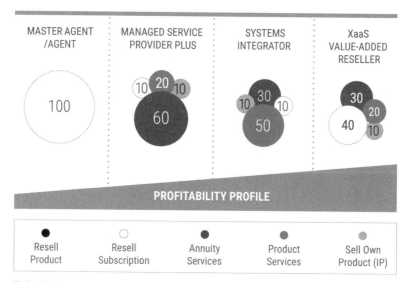

FIGURE 8.7 Business Model of the XaaS Partner Channel

value-added services (94%). Of those partners that provide value-added services, they are growing both cloud-platform revenue and technology provider all-up revenue 15% higher than those who do not provide value-added services. Additionally, they have an 11% higher cloud revenue mix than those that do not.

So, the bottom line is, if partners want to be successful in XaaS, they need to build their value-added services "muscles" to deliver complementary services for their technology providers' cloud platforms and XaaS offerings. This is a fundamental prerequisite to digital transformation for partners. They must first determine how they can add value, then go all in to digitize it.

Helping Traditional Partners Recognize the Need to Transform

Partners are historically excellent at closing sales, and, depending on the scope of their business, they may also be good at traditional project-oriented professional services. What partners coming from the traditional, transactional model are not typically oriented to is post-sale value-added services, such as monetizing the customer success function. Additionally, they may not be adept at delivering vertically oriented services that help customers integrate disparate solutions together from legacy systems with SaaS applications via cohesive user interfaces and experiences to meet line-of-business needs while providing secure, mission-critical-capable solutions across the enterprise.

Technology providers transforming from the traditional, transactional partnering models of the past typically do not have the partners with the necessary skills to be successful in the XaaS construct. A company needs to either enable and assist partners to transform (assuming they wish to transform) or they need to find new partners who are fully capable of delivering against the needed capabilities to be successful in XaaS.

So which partners will swallow their fish and which will not? How do technology providers know where to place their bets? How do providers ensure they are investing in the right partners? And how do the partners themselves, assuming they are committed to migrating their capabilities, swallow their fish from a physical business model migration perspective?

Partners tend to deal in very slim margins; that's why the massive cash flow is so critical (small margins on large sums of money add up), and this gravy train is going to stop, and they know it. Partners themselves have to create a new business plan that, over a period of three to five years, allows them to migrate from their current business that is mostly reliant on sell-through revenue to services-based revenue that complements cloud offerings. In the product-selling model, they take cash in large lump sums (preferably all prepaid up front) through their books to pay commissions and sales and marketing expenses, and they take physical product in (hardware and software), add their "value" to it, and move it through their books to customer buyers at marked-up prices. They need to acquire skills or invest in their current services-delivery employees in order to have the ability to move to a more value-added services-based business model that supports customers' migrations to cloud solutions.

Partners accustomed to delivering as-a-service solutions are not only focused on the initial sale, the land motion, but they are also well versed in driving the adopt, expand, and renew motions of TSIA's LAER model as well.[6] Equally important, these partners are able to translate what happens in the land phase to those resources that will be delivering the adopt, expand, and renew functions, whether they be technology provider resources or partner resources.

This is something that needs to be taught to, and prompted through, the sales/presales team (assuming these are partner sellers) to ensure they are not only remembering to collect this data, but that they do so systematically. Without passing data to the customer success team (whether they are at the technology provider or at the partner), the promise of value made in the presales motion of land will be unfulfilled, because it is sure to be either completely or at least partially forgotten.

In XaaS, partners must be enabled to fulfill a life cycle worth of activities with the customer, and they need to be measured on a new set of KPIs in order to ensure they have focus on this life cycle of activities to pivot from the land motion only to include and embrace adopt, expand, and renew. Partners, in particular those that are delivering project-based services, will also need to be enabled to deliver "PIMO," another TSIA acronym that stands for plan, implement, monitor, and optimize. PIMO is the customer delivery cycle that refers to the focus that customers have on the actuation of business outcomes through the lifecycle approach of taking the technology solution from an initial contract into a living reality of delivery of the results expected to the business due to the installation, adoption, and full usage of the technology throughout the enterprise. Both LAER and PIMO can be seen in Figure 8.8.

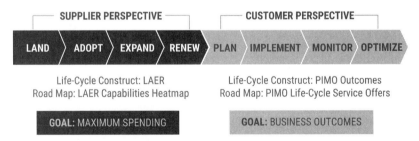

LAER and PIMO: Partners Need to Be Enabled to Cover It All

FIGURE 8.8 LAER and PIMO: Partners Need to Be Enabled to Cover It All

Digitally Enabled Partnering
What Does DEP Look Like?

Recognizing that partnering can occur at any level in a business-to-business context, let's first align on the characteristics of a company that practices DEP.

Attributes of DEP

In Chapter 10 of the *Technology-as-a-Service Playbook*,[7] TSIA made the following assertion.

*The concept here is that customers and partners need a **sophisticated technology platform** that has three main attributes:*

1. *The technology subscription offers attach to the platform. They can be provisioned, used, and managed from it.*

2. *The customers (or downstream partners) interact directly with the platform. They place orders, use products, get marketing and training information, and they can even pay bills. It becomes a significant part of the overall customer experience. Ideally, this platform is multivendor because of the nature of XaaS. Solutions do not consist of one standalone set of offers from one single vendor; they are typically a stack of technology subscription offers from several vendors. However, this XaaS contract, in an ideal world, crosses vendors and aggregates the financial terms and conditions, timing of payments, and, where necessary, smooths cash flow across the multifaceted solution components for the customer (or downstream partners).*

3. *Internal delivery functions such as services success, finance and operations, commissions payments, and co-marketing funding can also leverage the platform. They feed the internal systems with information, events, and data about what to do for a particular customer and when to do it. It is the same for marketing and customer success. Marketing can use the platform to deliver customized messages to buyers and users through the products that are attached to*

it. Customer success can use the platform to validate critical business outcomes and record customer health metrics.

A simplified view of this concept serving the objective of DEP might look like Figure 8.9.

Digitally Enabled Partnering

Digital Prospecting	Digital Sales	Digital Contracts Aggregation	Digital Enablement	Digital Renewals	Digital Services Delivery

TRUE MULTI-TENANT HOSTING PLATFORM (MULTIVENDOR)

CUSTOMER AND PARTNER JOURNEY ANALYTICS

FIGURE 8.9 Digitally Enabled Partnering

This may be a platform hosted by a technology provider with its partner companies integrated into it (such as Microsoft's Azure Marketplace or Salesforce's AppExchange), or it may be hosted by a top-tier distributor that works with multiple providers across many different solution types as part of its differentiated value proposition to its technology providers, downstream partners, and, ultimately, its collective customers. Ideally, this platform is serving up analytics to the technology provider as well as the participating partners about the customer journey through the digital platform, giving insights to a continuous improvement loop to always focus on enhancement of the customer's digital experience.

Building on this vision, let's click into some potential ways that customers and partners engage with this type of digital platform.

Customer View

Below are examples from the customer's perspective when the technology provider offers digitally enabled partnering.

- The technology provider's website is clearly featuring partners as solution providers.

- Partner solutions are aligned to core outcome-based offerings of the technology provider.

- Partner solutions and services are easy to find and connect to via the technology provider's website.

- Partner-provider joint use cases and customer references are featured on the website as well as on other complementary web properties where technology solution line-of-business buyers will frequent.

- Providers engage partners in joint promotions that may include co-branded campaigns and thought leadership.

- Integrated partners' solutions are not only featured, but may be purchased through the technology provider's marketplace on its website.

Partner View

When partners are engaging with a technology provider that is focused on driving an excellent partner experience via digitally enabled partnering, there are several key attributes partners see from their perspective when engaging with the provider.

- Partners have the opportunity to be featured in meaningful ways on the technology provider's website, including through descriptions, joint solutions, and e-commerce capabilities.

- Partners have the ability to manage their presence and their data through their own private portal, therefore having a curated experience with the technology provider's partner relationship management system.

- Partners may manage and earn entitlements, levels, and rewards; download resources; engage in online training; apply for promotional opportunities; manage and send deliverables; and update agreements through the online partner portal.

- Partners may communicate with various technology provider resources online, both from the relationship perspective as well as from the sales and technical support perspective, and they may receive responses, necessary assistance, and have access to data and telemetry to successfully deliver an excellent customer experience through the customer lifetime journey.

- Partners may opt to participate in e-commerce transactions via the technology provider's website of complementary and/ or integrated solutions.

- Partners will have access to applicable customer journey details to improve upon their approach to featuring both their solutions, services, and business-outcome-oriented marketing efforts.

Examples of Digitally Enabled Partnering

Digitally enabled partnering is when the experience for the customer is so seamless that the engagement between the technology provider and its partners feels connected and appears as one synergistic, co-connected ecosystem to its customers. When it is not clear to the customer that there is commission changing hands, or any worries about integration issues, or a visible point where the customer is "handed off" to another entity because the partner and the technology provider's public-facing engagement is so seamless, it is the result of digitally enabled partnering.

A few of the best-known public examples are Amazon and Apple.

Amazon and its partnerships with all of its suppliers, whether they are manufacturers or retail establishments, are so tightly integrated that customers feel like they are buying from Amazon, regardless of whether Amazon is stocking the goods in its distribution center or a third party is sourcing and stocking the goods in its facilities anywhere in the world. It is a synergistic experience, and partners have a seamless digitally enabled partnership with Amazon.

Another excellent public example is the Apple App Store, where the consumer has the seamless experience of dealing with Apple's application providers in such a way that, whether the application was developed in the United States or in China, for example, the look and feel, the method of payment, and the customer experience is identical to the end-user customer.

Let's look at a few examples in the business-to-business technology provider space.

Salesforce

Salesforce was founded in 1999 and now has one of the largest partner ecosystems in the world. One of the most interesting characteristics of the Salesforce partner program and partner ecosystem is how it has evolved the ecosystem to be tier-less and focused on independent software vendors (ISV) and consultants versus being focused on reseller partners. Salesforce continually surveys partners, customers, and other community members about ways it can improve the ecosystem to better serve the 1.8 million-plus Salesforce customers.

According to IDC analysis, Salesforce's ecosystem revenue is somewhere between three to four times that of Salesforce revenue itself. IDC estimated that in 2019, for every $1 Salesforce would make, the ecosystem would make $4.29. By 2024, they predict that figure will be $5.80. In that same report, 64% of the ecosystem value was predicted to come from professional services, and nearly 20% from selling additional cloud subscriptions.[8]

The transaction of the Salesforce software purchase, for the most part, takes place with Salesforce. The partner plays are primarily "sell with" and are complementary software solutions that layer on top of the Salesforce platform. Salesforce launched its

AppExchange in 2006, and there was nothing in the technology industry like it at the time. It offered third-party developers a place to work on their own applications—a place where one could build an app using Salesforce's development resources and find a market for its software. AppExchange disrupted the way customers discovered, developed, and purchased applications.[9] This concept of integrated applications is the glue that makes customers sticky to Salesforce. These ISV applications, once built on the Salesforce platform, cannot be uncoupled from it without a complete re-architecture.

With Salesforce, this DEP effort integrates the applications into the Salesforce platform in a way that is easy to understand and relates to the customer's business outcome needs.[10] Salesforce is thinking in the stream of the vertical and does an excellent job "connecting the dots" between the technology capabilities of its own platform plus its partner offerings to deliver on customer outcome requirements. For example, Salesforce connects technology to business outcomes in the healthcare provider and life sciences domains in this way: a healthcare provider doing research on how to fix the problems it faces with patient communications today will potentially find deliverables from Salesforce that describe the issues and solutions for solving connected patient challenges.[11]

As was mentioned in earlier chapters, a high percentage of the technology buyer journey is happening in a self-directed fashion online. That's why this DCX is so very critical. Salesforce has put itself in the customers' shoes to determine exactly how to engage those customers in their research and provide outcome-based deliverables and customer case studies that answer their questions. Salesforce has gone several giant steps further than most with its integration of partners in this DCX, giving partners the opportunity to actively participate with them in it and sell through it. The "glue" that brings together, in a seamless way, the Salesforce technology stack plus its solution provider partners (via the AppExchange) for healthcare is instantiated in the way it tees up its architectural blueprint for the industry, taking technical concepts and translating them into the "language of the vertical."[12]

The DEP model featured in the Salesforce AppExchange gives partners the ability to control their brand and reach new customers by having their solutions featured, demonstrated, piloted, and sold through the AppExchange.[13] The purchase experience for the Salesforce DEP is connected directly to the AppExchange marketplace. In the analysis of the go-to-market models for the Cloud 40 Index from TSIA, Veeva is listed as one of the high-performing companies, with both healthy NOI and healthy year-over-year revenue growth, and today it is one of the Salesforce ISV partner companies featured on the AppExchange in the pharmaceutical vertical solutions category.[14] One could conclude that being visible on this marketplace likely serves as the "jet fuel" that drives that compelling growth and positive operating income for Veeva.

ServiceNow

ServiceNow is an excellent example when it comes to the seamless way it integrates its partner community into providing customer success services using the tools ServiceNow uses to deliver customer success services. ServiceNow has rich content that is available to customers and partners through its website, within a few clicks. The thoroughness of ServiceNow's Customer Success Center and depth of resources facilitate this DEP experience to seamlessly move from land into adopt, expand, and renew, as it shares openly with partners its breadth of customer success resources. ServiceNow is a believer in facilitating digital workflows, which is the "secret sauce" one needs to successfully engage a partner ecosystem in providing excellence in customer success capabilities. It "eats its own dog food" in leveraging its own tools to facilitate partner engagement. According to the company:

> *"ServiceNow delivers digital workflows that create great experiences and unlock productivity. This is the future of work. Behind every great experience is a great workflow."*[15]

ServiceNow believes, as a part of these core values, that these digital workflows should flow from its company to its partners and back. ServiceNow's aim is to optimize content flow, including processes, guidebooks, deliverables, and data, as evidenced below:

> *"Join and gain access to valuable resources to help you resell ServiceNow Solutions. The ServiceNow Now Learning Platform offers hundreds of on-demand courses to our partner ecosystem, giving users access to our full range of training content, certifications and badges, and hands-on practices. Access useful and relevant sales enablement content in the Partner Success Center, allowing your team to more effectively engage with customers and prospects. Register more opportunities via deal registration, achieve revenue goals, and enjoy the rewards of a successful partnership with ServiceNow."*[16]

The material for its partners and customers to drive the customer success function is available externally to explore through the Customer Success Center on the ServiceNow website.[17] Via this site, one can explore processes, tools, events, webinars, and services, plus receive guided learning paths to be successful in driving full adoption and implementation of a ServiceNow platform installation at the partner's or their customer's enterprise.

It is clear that ServiceNow has tight, collaborative relationships with its partners, such that the partners can represent the ServiceNow brand in everything they do, whether they are selling, servicing, providing a managed service, or providing complementary technology. ServiceNow engages partners intimately and shares the necessary data, deliverables, and tools to ensure success by the entire ecosystem serving their global customer base.

How Partners Are Evolving—With or Without You

Many technology providers ask TSIA questions about how to find these partners that are ready to engage in the XaaS construct of cloud, subscriptions, and consumption. What we see is that the partners are evolving to meet the requirements of the technology providers in XaaS as well as the evolving requirements of customers to identify and articulate specific vertical business outcomes of technology solutions. Depending on which technology providers the partners are working with, and whether or not the partners have vertical expertise, deep solutions, or business process expertise, they are either more advanced or less advanced in their own evolution to meet the growing market needs.

According to a recent TSIA service provider reseller partner survey,[18] those partner companies that are providing value-added services are delivering greater revenue growth for their cloud-platform providers than those that do not provide these services. Those service provider partner companies that stated that between 50% and 75% of their revenue came from value-added services reported marked growth in reseller revenue for their cloud-platform providers, compared to service provider resellers with a lower mix of value-added services.

For a more detailed description of the types of value-added services provided by partners in a XaaS offering construct, read Chapter 10 in the *Technology-as-a-Service Playbook,*[19] specifically the areas on emerging revenue opportunities in optimize services and outcome as a service.

XaaS VAR Solution Provider

TSIA has defined a "XaaS VAR" as distinctive and unique from the value-added reseller (VAR) of the past. Our definition can be seen in Figure 8.10.

XaaS VAR Solution Provider

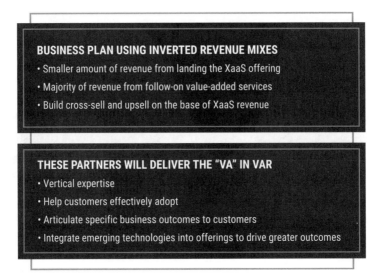

BUSINESS PLAN USING INVERTED REVENUE MIXES
• Smaller amount of revenue from landing the XaaS offering
• Majority of revenue from follow-on value-added services
• Build cross-sell and upsell on the base of XaaS revenue

THESE PARTNERS WILL DELIVER THE "VA" IN VAR
• Vertical expertise
• Help customers effectively adopt
• Articulate specific business outcomes to customers
• Integrate emerging technologies into offerings to drive greater outcomes

FIGURE 8.10 TSIA Definition of a XaaS VAR

This profile looks much like the traditional VAR profile, with some significant differences. Instead of building on-premise solutions, this partner builds value-based technology solutions and delivers services on top of and in concert with the XaaS offering and/or platform of the technology provider that leverage and engage the customer's entire life cycle of a consumption-based technology subscription. These partners will see a decline in project-based services related to implementation, configuration, and customization activities over time, as well as an increase in other life-cycle-related services, such as customer success services and premium account-based services that include identifying and codifying business outcomes and engaging all potential users at the customer to attain maximum customer value.

These partners may behave like what TSIA calls a "managed service provider plus" (MSP+) partner, as they will have an opportunity to grow monetized customer success services and build out consulting capabilities related to helping customers through the digital transformation journey. Additionally, these partners will grow their "vertical muscles" in the verticals that align to their company's competencies and be articulate not only in the business problems faced by the vertical that XaaS solutions can solve, but they are also able to define and calculate business outcomes progress, thus driving customer adoption, health, and satisfaction.

The migration of partner companies is underway. Some companies are more aggressive than others. Some companies are more public about their migration efforts and outcome-focused approach than others. Some are better at acquiring companies and assimilating them into their delivery models than others.

NTT Data has taken a very targeted and agile approach to help customers face the difficult challenges brought on by all of the ramifications of the COVID-19 crisis worldwide. It has made strategic choices in its acquisitions and investments in vertical expertise to be able to articulate these industry challenges in the language of the line-of-business buyer, thus building credibility through thought leadership and its ability to deliver end-to-end solution content and services. A few of NTT Data's recent acquisitions include:

- Nexient, providing application development and modernization.
- Hashmap (a Snowflake premier partner), focused on data-driven and AI solutions.
- Acorio, a pure-play ServiceNow consultancy.
- NETE, a provider of digital design and transformation services for the U.S. Department of Health and Human Services (HHS) agencies.
- Dell Services.
- Carlisle & Gallagher Consulting Group (CG), a business and technology consulting firm that exclusively focuses on the financial services industry.[20]

NTT Data has many impressive examples of meeting customers "where the rubber meets the road" and appears extremely agile in its ability to adjust to the ever-changing cycle of technology requirements due to a myriad of sea changes in recent years.[21] One notable example of how it has adjusted its XaaS VAR Solution Provider offerings is seen in its solutions for the healthcare industry[22] and the education industry,[23] targeting business buyers that have difficult issues to surmount and tackle using technology solutions.[24]

It is clear from this list of acquisitions that NTT Data is honed in on meeting its strategic objectives by acquiring both assets and knowledge workers that will allow it to excel in its key industries and solution areas worldwide. Through this and its annual $3.6 billion R&D investment, NTT Data is clearly delivering on its vision to deliver digital transformations, making the complicated simple and digital transformation drama-free.[25]

Conclusion

Some technology providers believe that the more revenue that comes from as-a-service offers, the less need for a partner ecosystem. TSIA believes that with as-a-service offers, partners still can be the best way to reach customers, large and small, in the most cost-efficient and scalable manner. But, as this chapter covered, the methods to engage partners is evolving with as-a-service solutions. Technology providers that lean into this lever of the digital transformation journey will be better positioned to both capture and protect market share.

9 | Navigating the Transformation to Profitable XaaS

By Thomas Lah, J.B. Wood, and Nathaniel D'Domenicus

This book has outlined critical workflows that we know companies must change in order to realize the full benefits of digital transformation. We know there are tremendous economic benefits to making these changes. We also know so many companies are struggling to even begin this journey. Why? It's partly because of a phenomenon called the Innovator's Dilemma.

The Innovator's Dilemma is a concept that was introduced by Clayton Christensen in 1997.[1] Philippe Silberzahn, an associate professor at Emlyon Business School, provides a succinct summary of the concept:[2]

> *For an incumbent company confronted with a disruption, the innovator's dilemma is the following: either the company embraces the disruption early on and sacrifices its existing activity (which may even represent all of its revenue) to favour an emerging yet uncertain activity; or the company ignores the disruption or embraces it too late, and risks decline or even the company's disappearance.*
>
> *Between the two risks, compromising its present market and compromising its future market, the company adopts the strategy that*

seems the most prudent: protection of its present market. Hence,
choosing to be prudent in order to reduce risks is the cause of its
subsequent failure.

What is especially relevant to the technology providers of today
is that Professor Silberzahn was writing about the Innovator's Dilemma as it related to the demise of Kodak. The Kodak scenario
is instructive because it highlights a second, even more challenging evolution of the Innovatot's Dilemma. This second part is
something TSIA is calling the Innovator's Dilemma Squared (or,
Innovator's Dilemma[2)]. Our definition follows:

> *The Innovator's Dilemma[2] is when an industry is faced with*
> *technology disruption AND the emerging business models appear*
> *less profitable than the legacy business models.*

This is exactly what Kodak faced. Kodak invented the digital
camera back in 1975.[3] The digitization of photography was not
the problem for Kodak. The problem for Kodak was that, in 1976,
it commanded 90% of film sales in the US.[4] And selling film was a
highly profitable endeavor. Selling digital cameras in a potentially
hyper-competitive market was unlikely to be anywhere near as
lucrative. This is the type of challenge that now faces technology providers of all shapes and sizes. More technology markets
are tipping toward as-a-service (XaaS) models, as TSIA has been
documenting for over a decade. However, these new as-a-service
models are typically not generating the same gross margin, operating margin, or free cash flow as the old models.

Mapping the Innovator's Dilemma[2]

The first part of this dilemma is all about technology disruption, as shown in Figure 9.1: Classic Innovator's Dilemma. A new,
superior capability enters the marketplace. Incumbents need to
retool or see their business erode. This reality has been unfolding
for over a decade in the enterprise technology marketplace as
customers shift their buying preferences to as-a-service offers. And

Innovator's Dilemma Applied
To Cloud Products

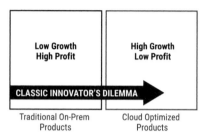

FIGURE 9.1 Classic Innovator's Dilemma

the value proposition of these XaaS offers is not simply financial engineering—migrating from large up-front CapEx spending to pay-as-you-go OpEx spending. As covered in this book, well-designed XaaS offers are leveraging big data, analytics, and AI to unlock new value propositions for customers.

The second part of the dilemma is about business-model disruption as shown in Figure 9.2: Innovator's Dilemma[2]. Technology providers are migrating from business models where they sold products to a customer that owned and operated those products, to business models where the technology provider owns and operates the technology on behalf of the customer.

The brutal reality is that, in the vast majority of the cases, these new as-a-service business models are less appealing to the technology provider on three critical financial dimensions:

- Lower gross margins
- Lower operating profits
- Generate less free cash flow

Let's start with gross margin. If you are a traditional software company migrating from selling software licenses and software

Innovator's Dilemma Squared Applied to
Cloud Products and Business Model Transformation

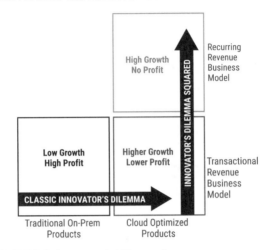

FIGURE 9.2 Innovator's Dilemma[2]

maintenance to selling a SaaS version of your technology, you are taking a significant gross margin haircut, as documented in Figure 9.3.[5]

Shift in Gross Margin:
Software to SaaS

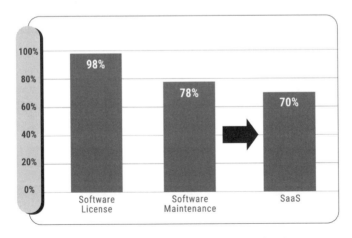

FIGURE 9.3 Shift in Gross Margin: Software to SaaS

Why? Because you now own the infrastructure required to run the software.

If you are a hardware company migrating from selling on-premise hardware and hardware maintenance to offering a managed service where you run the hardware for the customer on-premise or single-tenant off-premise, you are also taking advantage of a significant gross margin haircut, as documented in Figure 9.4.

Why? Again, because you now own and operate the hardware on the customer's behalf.

Moving to operating income, we see in Figure 9.5 that the born-in-the cloud companies tracked in the TSIA Cloud 40 struggle to break even, while traditional on-prem technology companies in the T&S 50 Index comfortably generate double-digit operating incomes.

Shift in Gross Margin: On-Prem Hardware to Managed Services

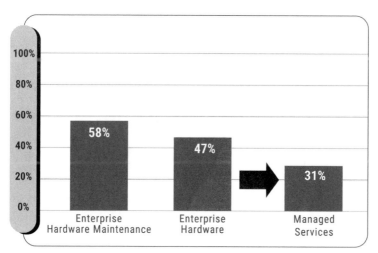

FIGURE 9.4 Shift in Gross Margin: On-Prem Hardware to Managed Services

Q3, 2021

FIGURE 9.5 Operating Income: Cloud versus On-Prem

Why? Born-in-the-cloud companies are spending much more (as a percentage of revenue) on sales, marketing, and general and administrative expenses. These spending rates depress the operating income of these XaaS companies.

Finally, there has always been the argument that as-a-service companies generate fantastic free cash flow. Free cash flow is defined as cash flow from operations, less capital expenditures. In many instances, free cash flow is significantly more than operating profits in an as-a-service business model. However, comparing the T&S 50 to the TSIA Cloud 40, in Figure 9.6, we see yet again that the new business models underperform when compared to the legacy business models.

Now you see the Innovator's Dilemma[2] in all its glory. Technology providers are being asked to not only transform their technology capabilities, they also are being asked to migrate to an operating model that appears to be much less financially appealing.

Free Cash Flow, TSIA Cloud 40 versus T&S 50

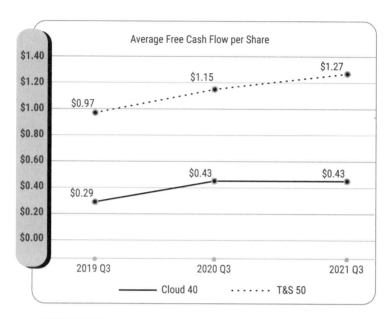

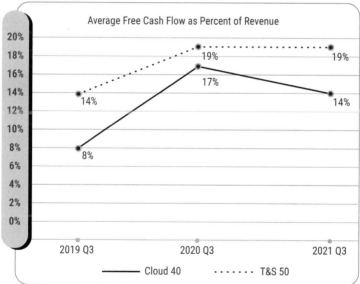

FIGURE 9.6 Free Cash Flow, TSIA Cloud 40 versus T&S 50

Surviving the Innovator's Dilemma[2]

As shown in Figure 9.7, as companies navigate this journey, there are four end states they could experience:

- **Higher Growth, Lower Profit.** The new XaaS revenues are growing (but maybe not fast enough to offset declining product revenues). The investment required to stand up new XaaS offers is depressing profitability.

- **Higher Growth, No Profit.** The new XaaS revenues are driving renewed top-line growth but the lower margin profile of the new XaaS offers, and the investment required to build new XaaS capabilities, impact profitability. This is where TSIA fears a majority of companies will unfortunately end their XaaS transformation journey.

- **Higher Growth, Same Profit.** The company offsets the lower gross margin profile of XaaS revenues by reducing the cost structure of the company.

Navigating the Innovator's Dilemma Squared

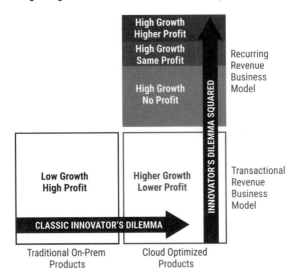

FIGURE 9.7 The Four States of Navigating the Innovator's Dilemma[2]

- **Higher Growth, Higher Profit.** The company actually creates a XaaS business model that is more profitable than its traditional on-premise technology business models. TSIA knows this is possible, but will be a rare scenario because companies will not aggressively pursue the tactics required to achieve this end state.

Let's review real-world examples of companies that have experienced one of these four states.

Teradata: Low to No Growth, Lower Profit

In 2012, Teradata had 49% of its revenue coming from traditional products and the remaining revenue coming from traditional services, such as maintenance and professional services. The company generated an operating income of 21.8%. Today, Teradata products include Vantage, a cloud-based, data-analytics platform. However, analysts have the following observations:

> *According to a Market Research Future report, the global big data analytics market is estimated to grow at 29% CAGR to $132.9 billion by 2026. Teradata (NASDAQ: TDC) is an old player in the market that is trying to reinvent itself on the cloud. The company recently announced its fourth quarter results that shows declining revenues.*[6]

As the company navigates this business model transformation, top-line revenues continue to shrink, and operating profit has declined to 2%.

Palo Alto Networks: Higher Growth, Lower Profit

What about a hardware company that has a business model based on disconnected, on-premise hardware but now wants to migrate to a business model based on connected on-premise offers and cloud offers? In 2012, Palo Alto Networks was a fast-growing company generating 70% of its revenue from selling on-premise

products. The overall gross margin for the business was 72%. Because of high investments in sales and marketing, the operating
income was only 1.5%. In June 2018, the company brought on a
new CEO, who came from Google. He had the charge to transform the company business model. It acquired multiple cloud
startups and aggressively grew its XaaS revenues. By 2021, only
20% of total revenue was coming from traditional products. This
diluted the gross margin downward to 70%—the average gross
margin we see for SaaS companies. This pivot required significant
below-the-line investments that drove the net operating margin to
-7% in 2021. So here is a company migrating to a business model
that is demonstrating lower gross margin and operating margin.
How did investors respond? You can see in Figure 9.8 that investors believe in the potential growth of these new XaaS offers.

Palo Alto Networks Market Summary

FIGURE 9.8 Palo Alto Networks Market Summary

Microsoft: Higher Growth, Same Profit
The task of migrating to a business model that has a lower gross
margin profile without impacting operating income is daunting.

Yet Microsoft has done just that. In 2011, Microsoft had a business model with an overall gross margin of 78% and generated an operating income of 33%. By 2018, the gross margin of the business had declined 16 points, to 62%, as the company began migrating customers to cloud solutions. That is a massive financial hit to a business model! But, in 2021, the company reported a net income of 36%. How did it do it? It was not by making its XaaS offers as profitable as its old on-premise offers. The company squeezed the legacy offers to make them even more profitable, which helped soften the blow of lower gross margin cloud offers. The company then took out 11 points of below-the-line spending by reducing expenses related to G&A and sales and marketing. Figure 9.9 shows the migration of their business model from 2016 to 2019.

Adobe: Higher Growth, Higher Profit

Meet the unicorn of this digital transformation journey: A company that migrates from a traditional software license model to a cloud model and becomes more profitable in the process. In 2010, with a majority of the revenue coming from traditional software, Adobe had a business generating an 89.6% gross margin and a 20% operating profit. Very impressive. But a decade later, with a majority of the revenue coming from cloud offers, the company was generating an operating income of 32%, even though the gross margin of the business had declined by three points to 86.6%. What happened? Like Microsoft, Adobe aggressively reduced below-the-line expenses. as shown in Figure 9.10 (page 255).

Everyone reading this chapter wants to be an Adobe or a Microsoft. Unfortunately, we do not believe a majority of technology providers are going to end up with business models that are as or more profitable than their current model unless they follow the directives outlines in this book. However, *TSIA believes that the technology companies that embark on this transformation and pursue the tactics in this book will be dominant in their target markets.*

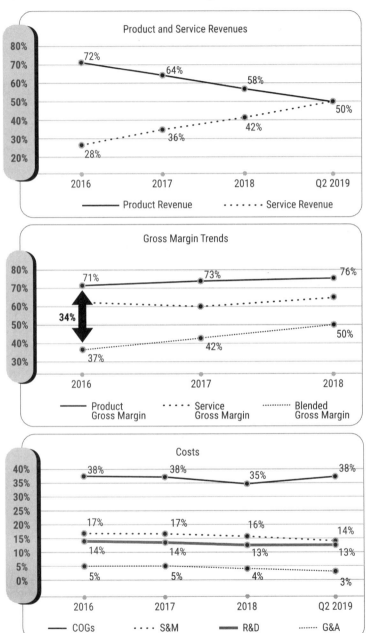

FIGURE 9.9 Microsoft Business Model Migration: 2016 to 2019

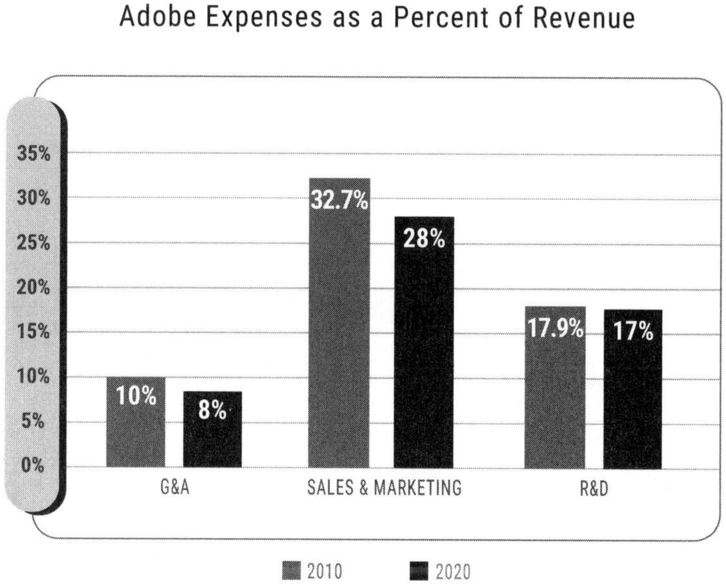

Adobe Expenses as a Percent of Revenue

FIGURE 9.10 Adobe Expenses as a Percent of Revenue

Known Friction Points

Having the unique vantage point of seeing hundreds of companies navigate this specific transformation, we see six common reasons technology companies are failing at digital transformation:

1. **Little "DT" thinking.** Many management teams are fixated on spinning up recurring revenues and migrating technology to the cloud. This is the first wave of this business model transformation. But very few management teams are aggressively pursuing the levers outlined in this book.

2. **Underestimate capability gaps.** TSIA has an inventory of the organizational capabilities required to deliver profitable XaaS offers. When conducting capability assessments for technology companies, it is common for us to identify over a hundred missing organizational capabilities related to developing, selling, and servicing XaaS offers. It takes years

to build out these capabilities. Yet, executive teams falsely believe this journey can be completed in two to maybe three years.

3. **Unwillingness to structure for success.** Most companies cannot flash cut from their old business model to a new business model (e.g., Adobe and Autodesk). They need to support legacy offers while building out new offers. The data is clear that asking existing employees to focus on the old and new simultaneously does not work. The winning strategy is to segment resources and create dedicated teams to develop, sell, and support the new offers. For an excellent framework on how to execute this strategy, read *Zone to Win* by Geoffrey Moore.[7] Despite this reality, management teams are hesitant to break organizational glass.

4. **EBITDA (earnings before interest, taxes, depreciation and amortization) over all else.** Business model transformation and short-term profitability are two mutually exclusive objectives. Business model transformation requires investment. Yet, management teams and boards are focusing on protecting short-term profitability. Then they wonder why the business model is not transforming. Again, we believe the long-term objective is to have a business model that grows and is profitable. However, in the short-term, significant investment is required to build out the missing organizational capabilities. See Appendix A for an overview of the infrastructure required to support a truly digital business model.

5. **Political power of legacy business units.** What played out at Microsoft in a very public way needs to play out in many technology companies. Prior to Satya Nadella's appointment as CEO in 2014, the cash cows at Microsoft were the business units that managed the desktop and server operating systems and the desktop Microsoft Office suite. Cloud computing was an art project. When Satya took the helm, he made it clear

that cloud offers were the future growth engine for Microsoft, and he began migrating resources away from the legacy offers to the new offers. Four years later, on March 29, 2018, the following story was in the press:[8]

> *Microsoft Corp on Thursday, said Terry Myerson, executive vice president of its Windows and devices business, will be leaving the company amid a major management reshuffle that increases the company's focus on its cloud products.*
>
> *The latest transition builds on earlier efforts to unite engineers who work on software with those that oversee hardware. Microsoft is creating two new engineering teams, with one focusing on how consumers use technology and the other on how businesses use cloud computing and artificial intelligence.*

Satya did what many leaders are unwilling to do: break down the legacy power bases of the company to make room for the new growth engines.

6. **Well-intentioned boards that innocently become sea anchors.** Finally, there is a clear pattern that many technology providers are currently being hindered by their boards, not helped. We explore this factor in Chapter 11.

So, these are six common challenges that are preventing companies from transforming their business model. The good news is that there are companies that are successfully navigating these challenges.

Contemporary Exemplars at Digital Transformation

First, there are technology providers that exemplify the type of next-generation technology provider we describe in this book, such as Amazon (AWS). The tactics of these companies should be closely studied by all.

Second, there is a growing list of companies that have demonstrated the ability to transform their business model to leverage the benefits of this digital transformation. To identify these exemplars, we can use criteria that is based on information available in the public domain:

- Percentage of total company revenue coming from recurring revenues (not transactional)
- Annual revenue growth rate (is the company growing top-line revenues?)
- Direction of profitability (is the business model becoming more profitable?)
- Revenue multiplier (the company has a valuation that greatly exceeds the annual revenues of the company)
- Percentage of revenue being spent on sales and marketing (is it extremely high and impacting profitability?)
- Direction of sales and marketing spend (increasing or declining?)
- Aggressively promoting value propositions related to XaaS offers (company is focused on value realization for their customers)

Using these criteria, here are just a few of the companies, with very different pedigrees, that deserve recognition for their progress on pulling the levers of digital transformation:

- Adobe
- Autodesk
- Inuit
- John Deere
- Michelin
- Palo Alto Networks
- Square
- Veeva

Adobe

We have already stated that Adobe is a company that has navigated the transformation and has come out the other side with a business model that is more profitable. That makes Adobe a poster child for migrating from on-premise software to cloud-based software. It navigated the first wave of this journey extremely well. But the data would suggest the company is making real progress on the second wave of the transformation. The company continues to improve profitability while reducing costs related to sales and marketing, as seen in Figure 9.11.

Adobe's Second Wave of Transformation

Company	Annual Report Date	Fiscal Year	Annual Revenue	Market Cap	Revenue Multiplier
Adobe	1/15/21	2020	$12.9B	$289B	22

% Revenue from Recurring	Annual Growth Rate	Net Income Improvement	% of Revenue on Sales & Marketing	Direction of Spending on Sales & Marketing
90%	15%	+25 pts.	28%	-1 pt.

FIGURE 9.11 Adobe's Second Wave of Transformation

The engine for this financial performance is a set of compelling XaaS platforms as itemized in its annual report:

- *Digital Media—Our Digital Media segment provides tools and solutions that enable individuals, teams and enterprises to create, publish, promote and monetize their digital content anywhere. Our customers include content creators, experience designers, app developers, enthusiasts, students, social media users and creative professionals, as well as marketing departments and agencies, companies and publishers. Our customers also include knowledge workers who create, collaborate on and distribute documents and creative content.*

- *Digital Experience—Our Digital Experience segment provides products, services and solutions for creating, managing, executing, measuring, monetizing and optimizing customer experiences from analytics to commerce. Our customers include marketers, advertisers, agencies, publishers, merchandisers, merchants, web analysts, data scientists, developers, marketing executives, information management and technology executives, product development executives, and sales and support executives.*

- *Publishing and Advertising—Our Publishing and Advertising segment addresses market opportunities ranging from the diverse authoring and publishing needs of technical and business publishing to our legacy type and OEM printing businesses. It also includes our platforms for Advertising Cloud, web conferencing, document and forms, and Primetime.*

Of course, the company is being rewarded with an incredible valuation—22 times greater than annual revenues. This company is perhaps the best example of the next-generation business model described in this book. As reported by Macrotrends, and seen in Figure 9.12, Adobe is reducing overall headcount.[9]

As headcount growth slowed from 2017 to 2020, top-line revenues grew from $7 billion to roughly $13 billion! The company is clearly pulling the levers of digital transformation.

Autodesk

Autodesk was the second highly celebrated migration from a traditional on-premise software business model to a cloud-based model. Like Adobe, Autodesk is demonstrating signs of continued progress on the digital transformation journey. Operating income continues to improve while sales and marketing expenses are flattening, as seen in Figure 9.13 (page 262).

The global pandemic accelerated the appetite for cloud-based platforms.[10]

"The outbreak of the pandemic led enterprises to realize the importance of cloud computing in an unprecedented manner. Organizations rapidly transitioned to the cloud to adopt remote work for continual flow in their businesses, which might otherwise have been slowed down by the pandemic-induced restrictions. That led

Adobe Headcount, 2006 through 2020

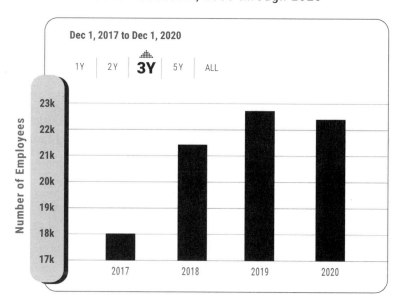

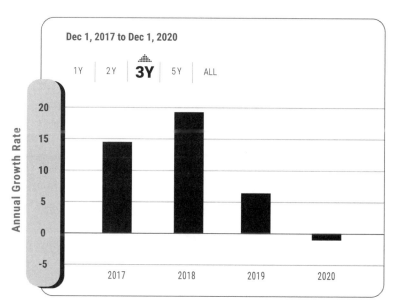

FIGURE 9.12 Adobe Headcount, 2006 through 2020

Autodesk's Second Wave of Transformation

Company	Annual Report Date	Fiscal Year	Annual Revenue	Market Cap	Revenue Multiplier
Autodesk	3/19/21	2021	$3.79B	$65B	17

% Revenue from Recurring	Annual Growth Rate	Net Income	Net Income Improvement	% of Revenue on Sales & Marketing	Direction of Spending on Sales & Mktg.
92%	16%	32%	+26 pts.	38%	-2 pts.

FIGURE 9.13 Autodesk's Second Wave of Transformation

to a spur in demand for several companies that offer cloud-based applications and tools, as enterprises are now more vigilant of the cloud's benefits.

Autodesk (NASDAQ:ADSK) is a global software company that designs software and services used in the architecture, engineering and construction, manufacturing, digital media, and entertainment industries. Amid the increasing adoption of cloud and the company's transition from a traditional license revenue model to a cloud-based subscription model, it has lately emerged as an industry leader."

Being an early mover to the cloud has created significant competitive advantage for the company.[11]

Driving that growth is a surge in deal size. In the past, analysts say they were surprised to see Autodesk make sales that were a few hundreds of thousands of dollars. Now, it has customers spending upwards of $10 million annually.

"It takes a long time to get good at doing the cloud, and we've been doing it a long time," CEO Andrew Anagnost told Protocol. "Our competitors are just waking up to this and are trying to acquire companies to get more cloud-y, but we have a significant head start."

But as Autodesk rides the wave of digital transformation within their industry, the company has been dramatically restructuring the sales and service models to align with the realities of a recurring business model. Callan Carpenter, who was a services executive and then a sales executive at Autodesk during this transformation, delivered an insightful keynote at a TSIA conference on this restructuring, titled "How Autodesk Leverages the TSIA LAER Model."[12]

The transformation for Autodesk has not been frictionless,[13] but it is hard to argue against the success the company has enjoyed by leaning into this business model transformation.

Intuit

Intuit was founded in 1983 at the dawn of the PC revolution. It's initial claim to fame was the ubiquitous Quicken, the highly useful software to manage your home finances.

Thirty years later (30 eons in Silicon Valley time), the company sold the PC-based franchise Quicken to a private equity firm. The 2016 article in *The New York Times* read "Intuit Sheds Its PC Roots and Rises as a Cloud Software Company."[14] In the article, then-CEO Brad D. Smith stated that the company was making a hard pivot to its cloud-based products like Quickbooks online. Why? Because the existence of the company was being threatened by new cloud-based entrants like Xero, a New Zealand company that wooed small businesses and accountants worldwide with a flexible, online accounting system that could be used from a smartphone and would cost as little as $9 a month.

But this transformation to the cloud started at least five years earlier. In a 2011 article,[15] Smith stated:

We are growing Connected Services customers at a rapid pace. Because these customers link into our online solutions, over time we are able to more effectively cross-sell relevant products and services and maximize our revenue per customer.

The same article stated that Intuit gets 60% of its revenue from "connected services"—cloud computing extensions to its core products—and planned to hit the 75% market in 2015.

In a 2021 episode of the podcast "No Turning Back," Smith tells the story of the transformation: "I told my leadership team we have to go mobile, global, and cloud."[16] By aggressively driving a dramatic business model transformation that positioned Intuit to leverage the Wave One and Wave Two benefits of digital transformation described in this book, Smith set the company up to not only survive, but thrive, as demonstrated in Figure 9.14 and Figure 9.15.

Intuit's Second Wave of Transformation

Company	Annual Report Date	Fiscal Year	Annual Revenue	Market Cap	Revenue Multiplier
Intuit	8/31/20	2020	$7.68B	$78B	10

% Revenue from Recurring	Annual Growth Rate	Net Income	Net Income Improvement	% of Revenue on Sales & Marketing	Direction of Spending on Sales & Mktg.
N/A	13%	24%	1 pt.	27%	-1 pt.

FIGURE 9.14 Intuit's Second Wave of Transformation

John Deere

Deere & Company has been around for over 180 years. The financial profile of the company is shown in Figure 9.16.

It is not the first name that comes to mind when thinking of digital transformation. Yet, former CEO Sam Allen was committed to the concept of digital transformation as outlined in the book *The Brains and Brawn Company: How Leading Organizations Blend the Best of Digital and Physical*,[17] by Robert Siegel:

> *Deere is so stable that it's only had 10 chief executives in 183 years. Yet former Chairman and CEO Sam Allen, who led Deere*

Intuit Market Summary

FIGURE 9.15 Intuit Market Summary

Deere & Company's Second Wave of Transformation

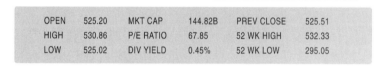

Company	Annual Report Date	Fiscal Year	Annual Revenue	Market Cap	Revenue Multiplier
Deere & Company	**2/17/20**	**2020**	**$35.54B**	**$111B**	**3**

% Revenue from Recurring	Annual Growth Rate	Net Income	Net Income Improvement	% of Revenue on Sales & Marketing	Direction of Spending on Sales & Mktg.
N/A	**-9.5%**	**11%**	**1 pt.**	**10%**	**1 pt.**

FIGURE 9.16 Deere & Company Financial Profile

from 2010 through 2019, was a role model for smart risk-taking and vigilance against inertia and stagnation. He helped this very brawny company and its 75,000 employees simultaneously push the envelope on culture as well as technology.

When Allen spoke to my Stanford class in 2018, I was impressed that despite his decades at Deere, which he joined in 1975, he talked as if he was running a tech company. He believed that advanced hardware and software solutions would drive Deere's future growth by generating more and better data that would help Deere's customers become more successful. He also knew that with trends toward digital agriculture and construction automation accelerating, Deere had to take more risks.

Deere's 2019 annual report breaks out a $1.3 billion revenue stream titled "Other." Here is the description of that revenue:

Other – Includes sales of certain components to other equipment manufacturers, revenue earned over time from precision guidance, telematics, and other information-enabled solutions, revenue from service performed at company owned dealerships and service centers, gains on disposition of property and businesses, trademark licensing revenue, and other miscellaneous revenue items.

These are revenues from new digital services. These services are being enabled by strategic acquisitions. In 2011, Deere acquired Blue River Technology for $305 million. In 2017, it acquired Bear Flag Robotics for $250 million. This push into new digital capabilities is paying off with investors, as shown in Figure 9.17.

Michelin
Michelin was incorporated on May 28, 1889. In 1891, Michelin took out its first patent for a removable pneumatic tire, which was used by Charles Terront to win the world's first long-distance cycle race, the 1891 Paris–Brest–Paris. All these years later, Michelin still sells rubber tires. And its current financials do not look stellar, as seen in Figure 9.18.

So why is it an exemplar for digital transformation? In 2000, Michelin began a business model transformation by expanding its remit from solely being a manufacturer of tires to becoming a service provider through the launch of the Michelin Fleet

Deere & Company Market Summary

FIGURE 9.17 Deere & Company Market Summary

Michelin Tire's Second Wave of Transformation

Company	Annual Report Date	Fiscal Year	Annual Revenue	Market Cap	Revenue Multiplier
Michelin Tires	**2/15/21**	**2020**	**$24.1B**	**$28B**	**1**

% Revenue from Recurring	Annual Growth Rate	Net Income	Net Income Improvement	% of Revenue on Sales & Marketing	Direction of Spending on Sales & Mktg.
N/A	**-15%**	**3%**	**-7 pts.**	**6%**	**0 pts.**

FIGURE 9.18 Michelin Financial Profile

Solutions.[18] This journey has led it to leverage IoT capabilities within its tires to provide compelling outcome-based offers, like Effitrailer.[19] This pivot toward outcome-based offers that reduce complexity for the customer was fueling top-level revenue growth before the pandemic hit, as seen in Figure 9.19.

Michelin: The Journey from Manufacturer to Service Provider

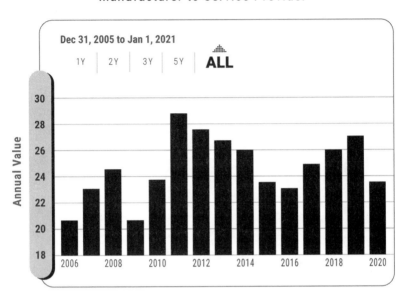

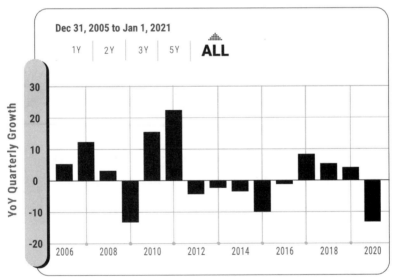

FIGURE 9.19 Michelin: The Journey from Manufacturer to Service Provider

Compare that to the shrinking revenues of competitive tire maker Bridgestone from 2017 - 2019, shown in Figure 9.20.

So, if a company can build compelling XaaS offers around a rubber tire, why, again, is your company not building compelling XaaS offers?

Bridgestone Worldwide Revenue from 2008 to 2020

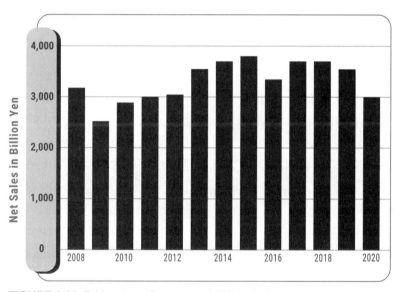

FIGURE 9.20 Bridgestone Revenues, 2008 to 2020

Palo Alto Networks

We have already identified Palo Alto Networks as a company that has invigorated its top-line growth with new cloud-based offers. The company was founded in 2005 and shipped on-premise enterprise firewall solutions. But the company realized that enterprise security technology was moving to the cloud.

In May 2018, the company announced Application Framework, an open cloud-delivered ecosystem where developers can publish security services as SaaS applications that can be instantly delivered to the company's network of customers. Later in 2018, several high-profile tech executives joined Palo Alto Networks:

- Former Google chief business officer and SoftBank president Nikesh Arora joined the company as chairman and CEO.
- Liane Hornsey, formerly chief people officer at Uber, joined Palo Alto Networks in the same role.
- Amit Singh, formerly president of Google Cloud, became president of Palo Alto Networks.

The company then pursued an aggressive strategy to grow recurring revenues through new XaaS offers. By 2020, 69% of total company revenue was from recurring revenue streams, as seen in Figure 9.21.

Palo Alto Network's Second Wave of Transformation

Company	Annual Report Date	Fiscal Year	Annual Revenue	Market Cap	Revenue Multiplier
Palo Alto Networks	9/4/20	2020	$3.41B	$39B	11

% Revenue from Recurring	Annual Growth Rate	Net Income	Net Income Improvement	% of Revenue on Sales & Marketing	Direction of Spending on Sales & Mktg.
69%	18%	-8%	+5 pts.	45%	-2 pts.

FIGURE 9.21 Palo Alto Networks Financial Profile

The company proactively disrupted its legacy hardware offer with a cloud-based software platform. This is a move that many hardware companies struggle to initiate. But cloud-based software continues to eat through on-premise hardware, as emphasized by the comments of this investor analyst who covers Palo Alto Networks:[20]

Meanwhile, the firewall-as-a-platform (FWaaP) market is turning out to be another catalyst for the company. This segment posted 26% year-over-year growth in billings last quarter, driven by a shift toward software-based offerings that accounted for 40% of FWaaP billings. The good news for Palo Alto is that the firewall-as-a-service market is projected to grow at an annual pace of 22% through 2026, according to third-party estimates, indicating that this business can keep getting better.

Now it is clear from the financial data that Palo Alto Networks has work to do regarding its digital transformation. Sales and marketing costs are still increasing as a percentage of revenue, and overall operating income is negative. But the company is pulling the levers of the next wave, including low-friction, free trial offers[21] and the digital customer experience.[22]

Square

Square was founded in 2009 to solve the problem of small merchants not being able to process credit-card payments. The first company product was the little square credit card reader you could attach to a phone to swipe a credit card. Since those humble beginnings, the company has grown into a $16 billion fintech behemoth. Figure 9.22 illustrates this.

Square is different from most technology providers in three ways. First, the company experienced a revenue windfall from fluctuations in bitcoin valuation. Let's put that to the side. Second,

Square's Second Wave of Transformation

Company	Annual Report Date	Fiscal Year	Annual Revenue	Market Cap	Revenue Multiplier
Square	2/23/21	2020	$9.5B	$112.6B	12

% Revenue from Recurring	Annual Growth Rate	Net Income	Net Income Improvement	% of Revenue on Sales & Marketing	Direction of Spending on Sales & Mktg.
16%	101%	2%	-6 pts.	12%	-1 pt.

FIGURE 9.22 Square Financial Profile

the company receives a chunk of its revenue from transaction fees charged when customers use Square to process a credit card. Transaction revenue streams are not common for most B2B technology providers. Figure 9.23 shows Square Revenue for 2020 and 2021.

Square Revenue 2020 and 2021

	Year Ended December 31	
	2020	**2021**
Revenue		
Transaction-Based Revenue	$3,294,978	$3,081,074
Subscription- and Services-Based Revenue	$1,539,403	$1,031,456
Hardware Revenue	$91,654	$84,505
Bitcoin Revenue	$4,571,543	$516,465
Total Net Revenue	$9,497,578	$4,713,500
Cost of Revenue		

FIGURE 9.23 Square Revenue, 2020 and 2021

Finally, Square really has a technology platform business model, which most B2B providers are now just aspiring to create. Per its annual report, its platform business model monetizes in two ways, defined below and seen in Figure 9.24.[23]

Seller Ecosystem: Square offers a cohesive commerce ecosystem that helps our sellers start, run, and grow their businesses. We combine software, hardware, and financial services to create products and services that are cohesive, fast, self-serve, and elegant. These attributes differentiate Square in a fragmented industry that traditionally forces sellers to stitch together products and services from multiple vendors, and more often than not, rely on inefficient non-digital processes and tools. Our ability to add new sellers efficiently, help them grow their business, and cross-sell products and services has historically led to continued and sustained long-term growth. In the year ended December 31, 2020, we processed $103.7 billion of Seller Gross Payment Volume (GPV), which

Square Business Platform Monetization Model

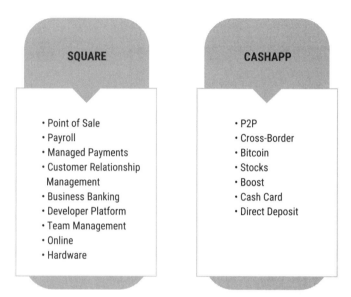

FIGURE 9.24 Square Business Platform Monetization Model

was generated by more than 2 billion card payments from 405 million payment cards. At the end of 2020, our Square point of sale ecosystem had over 210 million buyer profiles and approximately 295 million items were listed on Square by sellers.

Cash App Ecosystem: *Cash App provides an ecosystem of financial products and services to help individuals manage their money. Cash App's goal is to redefine the world's relationship with money by making it more relatable, instantly available, and universally accessible. While Cash App started with the single ability to send and receive money, it now provides an ecosystem of financial services that allows individuals to store, send, receive, spend, and invest their money.*

In many ways, Square does not look like a company B2B technology providers should study. But we disagree. Square is an exemplar in the area of lean digital sales and digital channel enablement.

The company is only spending 12% of total company revenues on sales and marketing as it experiences the incredible top-line revenue growth shown in Figure 9.25.

In reading its annual report, you can see strong reliance on multiple digital levers to grow revenues:

> *We have a strong brand and continue to increase awareness of Square and our ecosystem among sellers by enhancing our services and fostering rapid adoption through brand affinity, direct marketing, public relations, direct sales, and partnerships. Our Net Promoter Score (NPS) has averaged nearly 65 over the past four quarters, which is double the average score for banking providers. Our high NPS means our sellers recommend our services to others, which we believe strengthens our brand and helps drive efficient customer acquisition.*
>
> ***Direct marketing, online and offline, has also been an effective customer acquisition channel.*** *These tactics include online search engine optimization and marketing, online display*

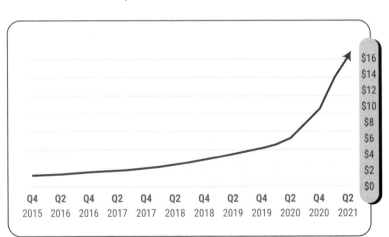

FIGURE 9.25 Square Revenue Growth

advertising, direct mail campaigns, direct response television advertising, mobile advertising, and affiliate and seller referral programs. Our direct sales and account management teams also contribute to the acquisition and support of larger sellers. In addition to direct channels, we work with third-party developers and partners who offer our solutions to their customers.

Partners expand our addressable market to sellers with individualized or industry-specific needs. **Through the Square App Marketplace, our partners are able to expand their own addressable market by reaching the millions of sellers using Square. As of December 31, 2020, Square had more than 700 managed partners connected to its platform.**

Our direct, ongoing interactions with our sellers help us tailor offerings to them, at scale, and in the context of their usage. **We use various scalable communication channels such as email marketing, in-product notifications and messaging, and Square Communities, our online forum for sellers, to increase the awareness and usage of our products and services with little incremental sales and marketing expense.** *Our customer support team also helps increase awareness and usage of our products as part of helping sellers address inquiries and issues.*

Keep in mind, Square is a B2B company—it is selling its products and services to small and increasingly larger retailers, restaurants, and professional service firms. Chief revenue officers, marketing executives, and sales executives should be asking themselves what tactics employed by Square can be replicated in other B2B technology markets.

Veeva Systems

Veeva is a born-in-the cloud SaaS company started in 2007. Its first unique attribute is that it is a PROFITABLE SaaS company, as seen in Figure 9.26.

Veeva Systems' Second Wave of Transformation

Company	Annual Report Date	Fiscal Year	Annual Revenue	Market Cap	Revenue Multiplier
Veeva Systems	3/30/21	2021	$1.47B	$50B	34

% Revenue from Recurring	Annual Growth Rate	Net Income	Net Income Improvement	% of Revenue on Sales & Marketing	Direction of Spending on Sales & Mktg.
81%	33%	26%	-1 pt.	16%	-1 pt.

FIGURE 9.26 Veeva Systems Financial Profile

Its second unique attribute is that it is only spending 16% of total company revenues on sales and marketing. This is less than half the average for companies in the TSIA Cloud 40 Index! One of the factors keeping its demand-generation expenses low is how it goes to market with a digital customer experience that is served up through Salesforce. Combine these two attributes with an annual growth rate of 33% and you get a company valuation that is 34 times annual revenues.

The company characterizes itself as follows:[24]

Our solutions span cloud software, data, and business consulting and are designed to meet the unique needs of our customers and their most strategic business functions—from research and development (R&D) to commercialization. Our solutions help life sciences companies develop and bring products to market faster and more efficiently, market and sell more effectively, and maintain compliance with government regulations.

Customer success is one of our core values, and our focus on it has allowed us to deepen and expand our strategic relationships with customers over time. *Because of our industry focus, we have a unique, in-depth perspective into the needs and best practices of life sciences companies and clinical research sites.*

This allows us to develop targeted solutions, quickly adapt to regulatory changes, and incorporate highly relevant enhancements into our existing solutions at a rapid pace.

Our goal is to become the most strategic technology partner to the life sciences industry and achieve long-term leadership with our solutions that support the R&D and commercial functions of life sciences companies.

We start with a focus on addressing clear and correct target markets. Those are large product markets in which the problem being addressed by our solution is strategic to the businesses of our customers and in which we believe Veeva can become the leader over the long-term if we execute well. **We embrace the concept of running to complexity, an approach in which we strive to solve the most important and challenging information technology problems our customers face.**

The company is pulling several Wave Two levers:

- Customer success at scale
- Lean digital sales force (enabled by a focus on the Life Sciences industry)
- Solutions that climb the value ladder
- Attacking complexity and replacing it with simplicity for their customers[25]

One other unique attribute is that Veeva is a SaaS company that successfully monetizes professional services. This brings in both revenue and margin dollars to fuel this highly profitable business model.

Avoiding Digital Hesitation

We know that the Innovator's Dilemma[2] is making it difficult for companies to transform. We also know that the task is not impossible. How can a management team leverage lessons already learned to increase their probability of success? We have two specific recommendations:

1. Follow TSIA's framework for "swallowing the fish."
2. Study and avoid the top 10 tactical mistakes made by companies during this transformation.

Following the Fish Model

Let's review the recommended four phases of the fish model we outlined in our last book: Technology as a Service Playbook and augment our guidance with four additional phases based on lessons learned since the framework was first published.

Educate

This is a new, pre-fish phase we strongly recommend. In this phase, the management team and board of directors need to educate themselves on the nuances of a XaaS business model. Executives should be reading everything they can about stewarding a business model based on recurring revenues. Exemplars should be studied and discussed. Executive workshops with outside experts should be conducted. We are consistently seeing executive teams underestimate their knowledge gap. Successful, smart leaders are confident they can learn quickly, which is true. It is the volume of new knowledge they underestimate. We have seen this phase last anywhere from months to two years. When management teams skip this phase, they enter the next phase handicapped.

Recruit

This is also a new, pre-fish phase. It is clear that companies that are having success in this transformation are recruiting outside talent that has experience with XaaS business models. This recruitment phase can result in a new CEO, new board members, or simply new leaders responsible for developing XaaS offers.

Align

This is the first operational phase of navigating the fish model. This phase is all about aligning key stakeholders to the journey ahead. There are two lessons to be learned by observing companies that are struggling with this transformation:

1. Don't underestimate the time and effort required to align stakeholders.
2. Get the board on board during this phase (see Chapter 11).

At the end of this phase, all stakeholders should have the same answers to the following questions:

- What is the primary reason we are pursuing new XaaS offers?
- What percentage of total company revenues do we expect to come from XaaS offers three years from now?
- Why will customers buy our new XaaS offers?
- What gross margin do we expect to achieve from our new XaaS offers?

Assess

This is the second phase of the traditional fish model. In this phase, a management team assesses capability gaps. Once gaps are identified, the team determines the order that gaps will be closed. Think in terms of waves: Wave One capabilities and Wave Two capabilities.

Invest

This is a new step in the framework. It is being called out because companies are underestimating the investment required to enable this transformation. In this phase, management teams should be making the following moves:

- Make organizational structure changes required to support the new business model.

- Recast the budget to support the development of the capabilities identified in the previous phase.

- Assess and pursue potential acquisition targets that could accelerate the transformation.

At the end of this phase, the company is well positioned to aggressively execute on the transformation.

Announce
Now, *and only now*, is a company truly prepared to announce its transformation aspirations. From this moment forward, the executive team should relentlessly communicate (internally and externally) the success metrics of the new business model.

Reinforce
This is a new step. In this phase, the leadership team is consistently reminding all key stakeholders of the following:

- The reasons why the company is pursuing the transformation.
- The success metrics of the transformation.
- The status of the transformation.
- To reward good behavior and punish bad behavior.

Declare
Finally, when the new success metrics are being met and real progress can be demonstrated over a sustained number of quarters, the company can declare transformation victory.

The Top 10 Tactical Mistakes
Again, there is a real opportunity for companies just entering this transformation journey to learn from companies that have already embarked on the transformation. TSIA has identified 10 tactical mistakes that companies make as they attempt this transformation.

The good news is that the tactics to navigate these mistakes are well understood so make sure your company steers clear of these ten common pitfalls as it navigates the transformation to profitable XaaS.[26]

1. **Lack of target economic engine.** The company wants to grow XaaS revenues, but the management team does not have a realistic understanding of the profitability profile for the new offers.

2. **Confusing messaging to investors.** The executive team does not clearly define the new success metrics for investors. Quarterly analyst briefings contain a confusing mix of old and new success metrics. Analysts struggle to understand if the company is making any real progress on the transformation.

3. **Me-too XaaS offers.** The company releases new XaaS offers that simply port existing technical features to the cloud. There is no incremental or compelling value proposition for customers to migrate.

4. **Consumption-based pricing models with no idea how to drive consumption.** If the customer is only going to pay for what they use, the technology provider should understand what accelerates customer usage. What services help customers adopt? What product telemetry is required to assess customer adoption? These questions need to be answered before releasing a consumption-based offer into the wild.

5. **Immature compensation models for selling XaaS offers.** The old adage states that sales reps "are coin operated." The old adage is correct. If their compensation is not weighted to sell new XaaS offers, sales reps will default to selling the legacy offers they know well.

6. **No account segmentation for targeting new XaaS offers.** Very few companies are in a position to aggressively migrate all of their customers to new XaaS offers. There are

some existing customers that should not migrate early for various reasons (complexity of their environment, financial buying preferences, immaturity of the new XaaS offer). For this reason, the install base should be strategically segmented into three groups:

- Customers that are perfect to migrate to XaaS.
- Customers that should not be migrated to XaaS at this time.
- Customers that will be evaluated for migration when a new selling cycle presents itself.

The key here is to not let the sales force make these decisions on the fly.

7. **Traditional sales and services approach (no supplier-led, no APLAER).** Selling, expanding, and renewing customers of XaaS offers is different from selling and servicing customers that buy technology and run it themselves. TSIA has written volumes on these differences. Yet, companies continue to build new XaaS offers and stuff them down the existing sales and service channels that were optimized for on-premise transactional offers.

8. **Battle over customer success.** Customer success is a function that gets created to ensure XaaS customers do not churn. After its creation, there is debate over where the customer success team should report. Is it a sales function or a services function? TSIA has definitive data on the answer to this question. If a company wants to effectively scale the customer success function without crippling profitability, it should report into a services executive or a C-level executive (CEO, COO, CRO).

9. **No funding model to scale customer success.** Closely linked to the battle of customer success is the funding strategy over customer success. The answer to this challenge is addressed in Chapter 7.

10. **Forgetting about the partners.** Some technology providers make the mistake of thinking that they must execute the XaaS motion all alone. They believe that partners are either not relevant or they won't understand how to operate in this new construct. However, the most influential and aggressive XaaS companies are leveraging all kinds of partners. The exemplars here include Google, AWS, Microsoft, Salesforce, ServiceNow, Autodesk, and Hubspot. Not only are these leaders leveraging partners, they are making it easier for partners to engage and drive more revenue for all, including initiating partner-to-partner engagement that drives even more excitement in their ecosystems.

Over the decades, technology paradigms shift, from mainframes to client-server to the cloud. There are many longtime technology providers that have successfully navigated several technology paradigms: HP, IBM and Microsoft, to name a few. However, navigating a business model transformation is so much harder than navigating a shift in technology. This is why so many technology providers are struggling right now as highlighted in the opening of this chapter. But there is hope because there are proven tactics to navigate this transformation While they are proven, they require real fortitude and conviction to execute.

10 | The Role of the Board During a Business Model Transformation

By Thomas E. Lah and J.B. Wood

Way back in 2013, in the book *B4B*,[1] we made two assertions:

1. Technology providers will need to transform their business models from being product-centric to being value-centric.
2. This transformation requires companies to swallow a "financial fish."

Now, nine years later, there is no debate whether these two assertions are valid. Technology providers are transforming their business models—and they face a financial fish when doing this. The financial fish involves revenue headwinds as companies migrate from transactional revenue streams to recurring revenue streams. The fish also involves increased investments to stand up new organizational capabilities related to XaaS offers. The result is pressure on overall company profitability. Figure 10.1 tracks the EBIT margin for five companies that have been navigating this business model transformation.

Swallowing the Fish: Impact on EBIT

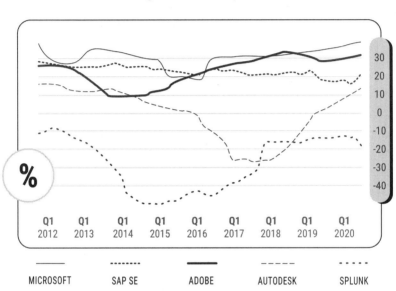

FIGURE 10.1 Swallowing the Fish: Impact on EBIT

When we first started speaking about this financial fish to leadership teams, there was incredible denial.

Executives and their boards were confident this business model transformation could be EBITDA neutral. Today, there is more acceptance of the physics involved in this transformation. Now, everyone is writing about the financial fish TSIA identified:

- "Satya Swallows the Fish"[2]
- "Swallowing the Fish"[3]
- "Choosing the Right Pricing Model for Equipment as a Service"[4]

- "Netflix, Prime, Blue Apron: How Subscription Businesses Are Taking Over"[5]

As more technology companies acknowledge the reality of this turbulent business model transformation, what is the role of the board of directors?

Traditional Role of the Board

If companies are ships sailing in the market sea, historically the board of directors serves as a protective influence similar to a sea anchor. As shown in Figure 10.2, sea anchors keep the ship from drifting too far off its current location.

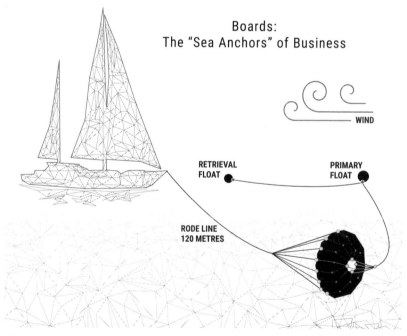

Boards:
The "Sea Anchors" of Business

WIND

RETRIEVAL
FLOAT

PRIMARY
FLOAT

RODE LINE
120 METRES

FIGURE 10.2 Boards: The "Sea Anchors" of Business

But how do boards perform when a company needs to dramatically change course and aggressively increase the rate of change? Typically, not well. In 2012, CBS News published an article highlighting the 10 worst boards of directors in history.

Many of the boards on that list were stewarding technology companies facing business model transformation, which include:[6]

- Kodak, 2003
- Alcatel-Lucent, 2006
- HP, 1999
- RIMM, 2008
- Nokia, 2010

Why do boards struggle when dramatic transformation is required?

The Challenge of Business Model Transformation
Boards help management teams navigate all kinds of challenges. But when it comes to business model transformation, there are two reasons boards can struggle:

1. Lack of vision
2. Lack of relevant expertise

With lack of vision, the board is unclear what the new business model could look like for the company. There is no definition of future success. What is the company running toward? With lack of relevant expertise, the board has experience that is relevant to the old business model but not the new business model.

For example, there is a large and well-known technology company that has been publicly working on a business model transformation for over a decade. And, unfortunately, it continues to be slow going. If you look at the board of this company, you see these two common attributes in every member:

1. They come from a large legacy customer of the company.
2. They are currently retired from the industry.

These board members are wicked-smart professionals. However, their experience is weighted toward the traditional ways of buying and consuming technology. It can be safely assumed they have limited experience with XaaS models. This is a massive problem facing many older technology companies that now face this transformation.

So, is the board a liability or an asset when facing business model transformation? To ensure the board is an asset and not a liability, the CEO and existing board members need to pursue two key tactics:

1. Paint a compelling vision for the new target business model.
2. Recruit board members with relevant experience in that business model.

What Are You Running Toward and Why?

TSIA believes that the first step in making the board an asset and not a liability during business model transformation is to ALIGN the executive team and board of directors on a clear and compelling vision of why the company needs to move to a new business model. Then the board must create a robust strategic plan to chart its course over the next three to five years, plotting out the financial model shift from the current state to the future state over this period of time in order to achieve its end-state goals.

In the case of technology companies, this is tough because the legacy model is so dang profitable! But the old model is dying. Good news, the proof points for migrating to a XaaS business model are growing larger. And there are more companies that are successfully making the transition.

As described in the chapters of this book, TSIA believes there is a clear and compelling vision and strategy for this business model transformation. As a short recap, technology companies need to embrace the XaaS business model transformation for the following compelling reasons:

- Establish recurring revenue streams, not transactional ones:
  o Revenues become more predictable.

o   Recurring revenues are more resilient in economic down-
     turns (we saw this in 2009 and 2020).

o   Valuations for recurring revenue business models are
     higher.

- Create a better customer experience (the digital customer experience or DCX):

o   Reduce complexity for the customer throughout the en-
     tire life cycle.

o   Become better positioned to help the customer adopt the
     technology.

o   Use customer telemetry to unlock new value propositions
     for the customer.

- Generate higher customer retention:

o   Secured through the superior customer experience,
     not the handcuffs of massive investment in technology
     products.

o   Customers will be paying based on consumption or real-
     ized value, not availability.

- Accelerate your ability to capture market share:

o   XaaS companies in the TSIA Cloud 40 are growing 15%
     to 25%.

o   Legacy technology companies are struggling to grow at all.

Ultimately, this transformation is all about winning market share.
Companies that delay this transformation will find themselves on
a path to slow (or fast) liquidation.

Once there is a compelling vision and strategy in place with
the board, executive teams should navigate the four phases of the
fish TSIA has outlined in previous literature, described below and
seen in Figure 10.3.

- **Align Phase.** In this first phase, management teams are still
  discussing how to navigate the financial fish. Executives are
  debating tactics, offers, markets, and priorities.

The Financial Fish of DT and Shift to Subscriptions

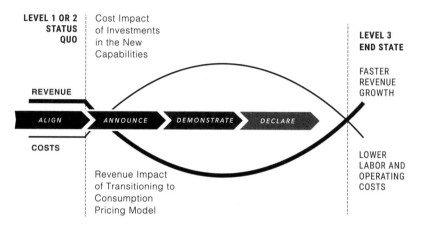

FIGURE 10.3 The Financial Fish of DT and Shift to Subscriptions

- **Announce Phase.** Management team announces both internally and externally how much revenue the company expects to receive from new subscription offers over the next three to five years. The company also identifies the key metrics it will be tracking to assess progress with the new revenue streams.

- **Demonstrate Phase.** The company demonstrates it can successfully grow subscription revenue streams. The company is showing improvement on the new success metrics.

- **Declare Victory Phase.** The company demonstrates it can achieve profitable subscription revenue streams.

These represent our summary view of the best way to navigate through the fish. Conceptually, it's pretty simple: The key is to NOT make public announcements about new XaaS offers or new business models until the board and the executive team have fully completed the alignment phase. Then, you announce what you are going to do, why you are going to do it, how you will measure your progress using new metrics, and what you expect to accomplish by when. If it's a compelling story about future growth and profits in the post-fish era, your stock price will go up a bit. This can be true almost regardless of how ugly the fish is going to be. Then, and this is critical, you must demonstrate that you are achieving your milestones on the metrics that matter. As you do that, each quarter your stock price continues to go up. Investors start to get excited. Growth investors start showing up. If you can do that for a series of straight quarters, then you declare victory. You tell investors that the new metrics are overtaking the old ones. It's a business model reset. Even though you are still in the belly of the fish, your stock price acts like you are in its tail. You have market acceptance and endorsement of your transformation. The more you demonstrate and declare, the more your stock goes up, even if revenues are lagging and expenditures have increased to fund the transformation.

But there is an all-too-common, self-inflicted wound...one you MUST avoid. It goes like this: Executives announce to investors that the company is migrating to a recurring revenue model, is creating new cloud offers, and/or plans to digitally transform its customer experience. Then it does not deliver promised progress on the new metrics. It soon becomes apparent that the entire executive team and the board of directors were not aligned, prepared, and ready to act. Investor confidence is lost in the middle of the fish, the transformation itself is called into question as the financial performance of the company weakens, and the CEO is ultimately replaced.

The fish is just math, plain and simple. Companies can make the decision to make the journey visibly or invisibly. We would highly, strongly, and emphatically recommend being visible. Why? Because, if well executed, being visible to shareholders about your DT and XaaS journey can lead to:

- Greater amounts of money poured into the transformation.
- Faster time through the fish.
- Better, more innovative transformations.

- And, most importantly, higher stock prices during and after the journey.

For more guidance on swallowing this fish and navigating these phases, TSIA members should read these TSIA publications:

- "Swallowing the Fish"[7]
- "Update: Swallowing the Fish"[8]
- "Swallowing Half the Fish"[9]

Making Your Board an Asset

The boards of directors for public companies have traditionally had the following key responsibilities:[10]

1. Recruit, supervise, retain, evaluate, and compensate the CEO.
2. Provide direction for the organization.
3. Establish a policy-based governance system for the business.
4. Govern the organization and the relationship with the CEO.
5. Assume the fiduciary duty to protect the organization's assets and the members' investments.
6. Monitor and control function (hire the auditing firm and review results).

However, during a business model transformation, you need more from your board. You need wind in your sails. Attributes of a board that are an asset during transformation include:

1. It is supportive of migrating to a new target business model.
2. It understands the new metrics of success (renewal rates, expansion rates, adoption rates, etc.).
3. It has expertise related to the new business model.
4. It is not focused on short-term financial performance.
5. It encourages realistic rates of progress based on reality, not a best-case model.

Not every board member may have these attributes, but some board members *must* have these attributes. Historically, board members were recruited nearly exclusively from the ranks of current or retired CEOs or CFOs, or through existing board members.[11] Here is the tough question: Can a CEO or CFO who has limited experience with XaaS business models fulfill all the responsibilities itemized above? Can they help provide experienced direction for the new business model of the organization? Probably not. For that reason, the CEO and existing board members should be aggressively recruiting new board members who have experience with XaaS business models.

Exemplars

There are examples in the wild of legacy technology providers migrating their leadership team and board to support the XaaS business model transformation. The role of Satya Nadella in Microsoft's transformation is well documented. But there are other success stories to consider.

Autodesk

In June 2017, Autodesk appointed Andrew Anagnost as the president and CEO. Before the promotion, he had served in various other roles for the company since joining in 1997. At the time, Autodesk was embarking on an aggressive journey to migrate its customer base to new XaaS offers.

In March of 2018, Karen Blasing was recruited to the board. Blasing was the CFO of Guideware Software. While at Guideware, she led the financial operations of the company and established a technology platform that enhances insurers' ability to engage and empower their customers and employees. Blasing was also instrumental in helping transform the business model from a perpetual license business to a profitable recurring revenue model during her time with the company.

In March of 2019, Blake Irving was recruited to the board. Irving served as chief executive officer of GoDaddy from 2013-2018, where he drove growth and operations. As CEO, he reshaped the domain-name company into a global cloud platform that used predictive analytics and machine learning to power its customer's digital presence. Prior to GoDaddy, Irving served as executive vice president and chief product officer at Yahoo!.

As Autodesk aggressively migrated customers to XaaS models, operating income did suffer, as seen in Figure 10.4.

Autodesk Operating Income, Q4 2005 through Q4 2019

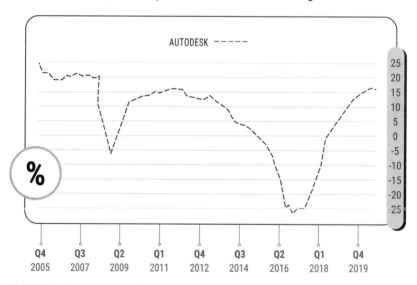

FIGURE 10.4 Autodesk Operating Income, Q4 2005 through Q4 2019

But the board and CEO were clearly aligned on the objectives of the business model transformation. As of 2021, Autodesk has almost 100% of its revenues coming from new subscription-based offers, and its stock price has increased over 400% in the past five years, as seen in Figure 10.5.

Autodesk Revenues, 2017 through Q2 2021

FIGURE 10.5 Autodesk Revenues, 2017 through Q2 2021

Palo Alto Networks

In 2018, hardware provider Palo Alto Networks recruited Nikesh Arora to be the new CEO of the company. Before joining Palo Alto Networks, Nikesh served as president and chief operating officer of SoftBank Group Corp. Prior to that, he held a number of positions at Google, Inc. during a 10-year span, including senior vice president and chief business officer, president of global sales operations and business development, and president of Europe, the Middle East, and Africa.

Arora set a new vision for the business model of the company, one that migrated from selling on-premise, to firewall solutions, to solutions based on AI and that ran in the cloud. To help drive the vision, he recruited Amit Singh to be president. Prior to joining Palo Alto Networks, Singh held several roles at Google, including founding and building Google's Cloud business. In this capacity, he worked to help companies move to cloud-based services, like Gmail, Google Docs, and the entire Cloud platform suite.

In 2019, Lorraine Twohill, the chief marketing officer at Google, joined the board. In 2021, Aparna Bawa, chief operating officer at Zoom, joined the board. Both of these board members clearly have deep experience with XaaS business models.

The company also acquired 10 cloud-based technology providers to help accelerate the transition. Of course, all of this required investment. Figure 10.6 documents the operating margin of the company during this transformation.

Palo Alto Networks Operating Margin, Q3 2012 through Q3 2020

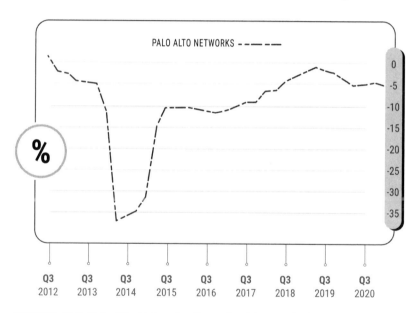

FIGURE 10.6 Palo Alto Networks Operating Margin, Q3 2012 through Q3 2020

Instead of focusing on short-term profitability, the executive team and the board are focusing on the growth of the new XaaS portfolio. And investors have responded favorably.

Since repositioning the business model, subscription revenues have increased from 0% of total company revenue to 43% in May 2021, as shown in Figure 10.7.

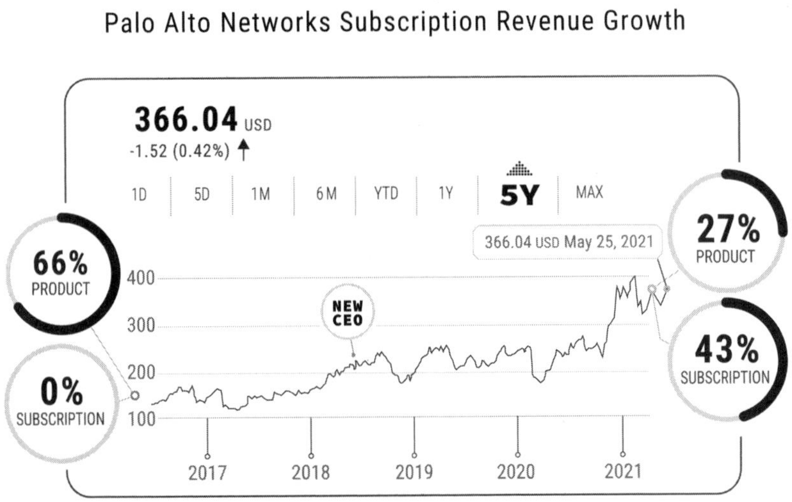

OPEN	368.36	MKT CAP	35.65B	PREV CLOSE	364.52
HIGH	369.68	P/E RATIO	-	52 WK HIGH	403.00
LOW	362.32	DIV YIELD	-	52 WK LOW	217.48

FIGURE 10.7 Palo Alto Networks Subscription Revenue Growth

New Relic

New Relic was already a SaaS company. However, it decided to transform its pricing model from being subscription-based to being consumption-based. This move requires a comprehensive business model transformation.

In August of 2020, New Relic brought new blood onto the board, as stated in a news release:[12]

> *New Relic today announced the appointment of enterprise technology executive Anne DelSanto and Citrix President and CEO David Henshall to its board of directors. In addition,*

current director Hope Cochran was named chair, as Peter Fenton stepped down after over 12 years of service.

"Both Anne and David bring exceptional experience leading cloud companies through transformations, which is invaluable as New Relic continues to drive our long-term growth strategy," said New Relic CEO and founder Lew Cirne. "Hope has been an outstanding member of our board for the past two years, and we're honored to have her serve as our new chair. We are grateful to outgoing chair Peter Fenton for his contributions to New Relic since the company's founding over 12 years ago—an incredible run.

"New Relic has entered a new chapter with its recent set of exciting observability platform announcements," said Hope Cochran. "I welcome Anne and David to our board and look forward to working together and driving the company's growth strategy."

In May of 2021, Lew Cirne, the CEO and founder of New Relic stepped out of the CEO role to become the executive chairman on the board. The press documented this observation:[13]

Lew Cirne, New Relic's founder and CEO, who is stepping into the executive chairman role, spent the last several years rebuilding the company's platform and changing its revenue model, aiming for what he hopes is long-term success.

"All the work we did in re-platforming our data tier and our user interface and the migration to consumption business model, that's not so we can be a $1 billion New Relic—it's so we can be a multibillion-dollar New Relic. And we are willing to forgo some short-term opportunity and take some short-term pain in order to set us up for long-term success,"

Bill Staples became the new CEO. He came from Adobe, where he led the 1,500-plus employee global engineering team behind Adobe's market-leading Experience Cloud. So, now there is a CEO, two new board members, and the board chairman who understand the magnitude of this business model transformation.

By February 2021, New Relic was in the belly of the financial fish, as shown in Figure 10.8.

New Relic Revenue and Operating Income

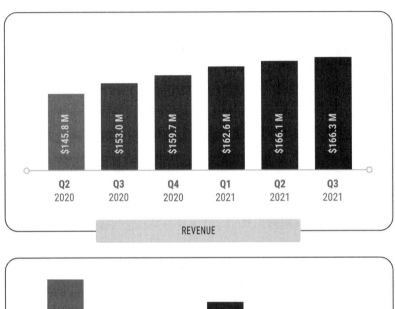

REVENUE

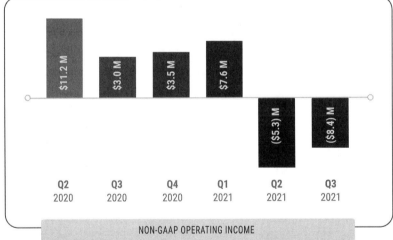

NON-GAAP OPERATING INCOME

FIGURE 10.8 New Relic Revenue and Operating Income

Yet, the chairman of the board was not blinking, as is evident in the below excerpt from the New Relic Investor Letter, from Q3 Fiscal Year 2021:[14]

"The third fiscal quarter marked the first full quarter our reimagined New Relic One platform was in market, and the first full quarter of our transformation from a subscription model to a consumption model. It is critical that investors understand that moving to a consumption model is not just a revenue model transition, it is a commitment from every single function at New Relic to put the customer at the center of everything we do."

At the time this is being written, New Relic investors are yet to reward the move to the new business model—at the same time the stock price did not go down. In fact, the second half of 2021 was a solid period for the company. However, the alignment of the board and CEO should prove a vital asset over the next few bumpy quarters. Figure 10.9 shows New Relics's market summary through Q3 2021.

New Relic Market Summary 2017 through Q3 2021

FIGURE 10.9 New Relic Market Summary 2017 through Q3 2021

Back to Anchors

More than anything, boards need to be forward-thinking. In a *Harvard Business Review* article titled "Where Boards Fall Short," the following observation was made:[15]

> *The majority of 1,500-plus U.S. companies were content to maintain the status quo and dole out roughly the same amount of capital to business units that they did the previous year. These businesses moved forward in low gear as a result. By contrast, the most aggressive reallocators—companies that shifted more than 56% of their capital across business units over that period—delivered 30% higher total returns to shareholders. Boards that combine deep relevant experience and knowledge with independence can help companies break through inertia and create lasting value.*

This article reinforces the main assertion of this appendix: Boards are a critical asset when a company needs to transform its business model. Knowing this, is your board currently an asset or an anchor?

Appendix A

Managed Services: Your Mess for More

By George Humphrey, Vele Galovski, and Bo Di Muccio

·

In this chapter, we will examine the following elements of the W2DT framework seen in Figure A.1:

Workflows:

- PLAER: Place, Land, Adopt, Expand, Renew
- DDCL: Discover, Design, Create, Launch
- CBO: Customer Business Outcome
- PtC: Premise to Cloud Framework

Users:

- Customers
- Employees

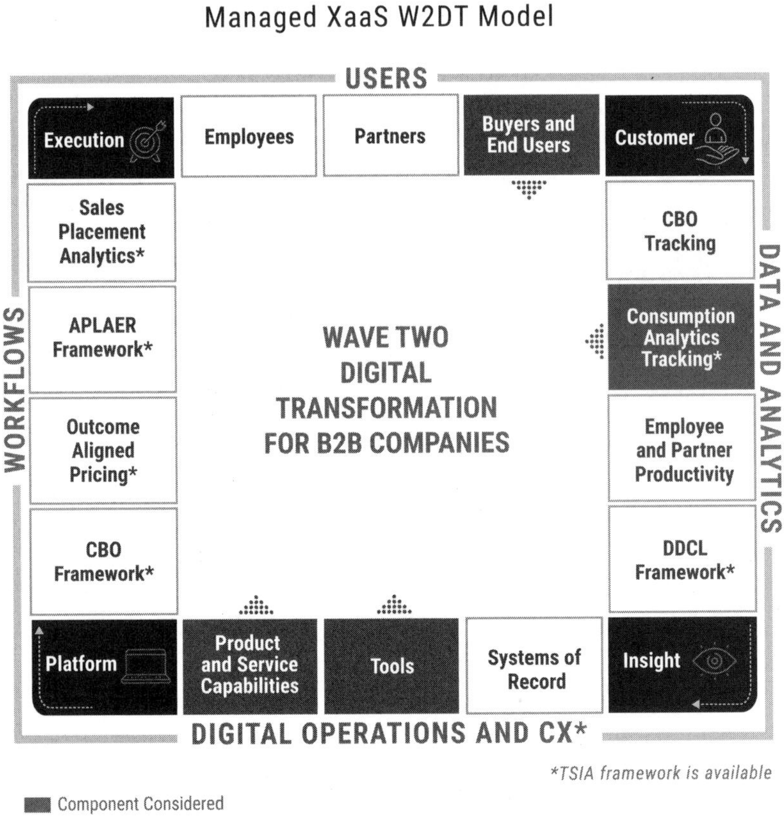

Managed XaaS W2DT Model

FIGURE A.1 Managed XaaS Wave Two DT

Data and Analytics:

- Customer Business Performance
- Consumption Analytics

Digital Operations and CX:

- Operations Systems
- Advanced Analytics
- Structured Data Warehouse

In 2009, TSIA fired a warning shot across the bow of the technology industry when we released the book *Complexity*

Avalanche.[1] The warning was that tech was getting too hot too quickly. Every developer of technology solutions had a single goal in mind: ship as many units or licenses as possible for the sake of the quarter. The fundamental belief was that they could achieve this goal by packing in as many new features and functions as they could with every new release. The challenge was that companies were creating features and functions faster than customers could consume them. This led to the "consumption gap," shown in Figure A.2, that in some ways is responsible for the rise of the current subscription era. Customers want to pay for what they consume. They don't find value in what they don't or can't consume.

Services, on the other hand, should be 100% focused on value. A technology solution is of no value until it is put into production. Professional services are required to design, install, and integrate the solution into a production environment. It is of no value if it stops working; support services are required to keep the solution up and running. Even if the solution has been put into service and keeps working, the customer may not be getting value

The Complexity Avalanche

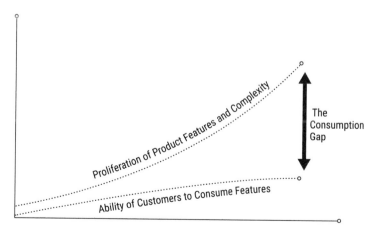

FIGURE A.2 The Consumption Gap

due to the pain of ongoing operational complexity. This is fueling the double-digit growth of managed services. Keeping technology working requires a substantial service-oriented approach. This service-led approach can be incredibly expensive for a company's IT organization or its technology management team. Hence, the value proposition that many providers promoted with their advanced service offerings, such as managed services or outsourcing, has been "your mess for less."

Your Mess for More

"Your mess for less" was a simple phrase used to explain the value of outsourcing the management of a customer's technology environment. Under this banner, there is an expectation that the outsourcing provider will provide the same capabilities an IT organization currently has at a lower price point. Due to the bespoke and labor-intensive model for large outsourcing providers, like Accenture and IBM, that business model ended up being a low-margin endeavor. Thankfully, most hardware and software companies never dipped their toes in those "shallow margin" waters. However, there is an interesting twist of fate now facing some of those same hardware and software companies. They actually need to dive into business models that, on the surface, look and feel like outsourcing. And they are. But they aren't.

This chapter covers topics that are highly relevant to any technology provider that has a majority of its technology still running on-premise within the customer's environment. These include:

- Trends that are eviscerating the traditional on-premise technology business models.
- The promise of "your mess for more."
- The current chasm faced by on-premise technology providers.
- Seven attributes of technology companies that are taking market share (discussed in Chapter 2).

- Three potential paths forward for on-premise technology providers.
- Industry examples of success.
- Crossing the Rubicon: tactics to move forward.

The Current Chasm

There are three factors that are handicapping legacy technology providers:

1. **The technology is on site.** Cloud-based technology providers have incredible customer telemetry because all their customers are on a platform run by the provider. When the customer buys the technology as an asset and operates it on their own, visibility can be challenging.

2. **The technology is not adequately connected.** On-premise technology can be enabled to "phone home." This capability has been leveraged for years by support organizations. However, the most common frustration we hear from service organizations within legacy product companies is that the customer telemetry to which it has access is anemic. It is not rich and robust enough to unlock the attributes described in the previous section.

3. **The technology was sold by the channel.** This last factor is salt in the wound for legacy technology companies. The channel has always been an incredible asset for companies selling on-premise technology. The channel enabled scale. But now that asset is becoming a liability. When a product is sold through the channel, the product provider can lose critical visibility. Who specifically bought the product? Where is it actually installed? Who is using it? Are they still using it? This visibility is required to drive the new value propositions of tech.

This is starting to look very bleak for legacy technology providers.

The Unfair Competitive Advantage of the Cloud

Conversely, there are several factors that enable true SaaS or cloud-based providers to excel at your mess for more:

1. **The technology is in a controlled environment.** The technology is owned and operated by the provider either in a colocation facility or within a purpose-built cloud environment. In this sense, it is much easier to access data, insights, and information from the technology because...

2. **The technology is always connected.** The solution is always on-network, typically serving the customer over the internet. The infrastructure and applications are built upon, or are a part of, a platform that provides real-time, proactive, and predictive analytics.

3. **The service is resold by the channel.** Even if a channel partner sells the solution, the technology/service provider always has complete access to user information and system performance.

So, what is the journey a traditional technology provider can go on to logically move from on-premise, unconnected solutions to the cloud? Figure A.3 is a framework that details the path companies typically follow as they evolve from premises-based technology providers to cloud-based XaaS providers.

On-Prem Not Connected

Although there are exceptions, most technology solutions more than 10 years old were primarily designed to be a single solution deployed for a single customer at the customer's location. The manufacturer made a product, usually a great product. Then it was sold, either directly to the customer or through a channel partner. The product was installed, and someone went through a checklist to make sure the product was ready to be turned over to the customer. The product was simple, and the customer assumed the responsibility to make sure the product kept working. If it didn't, the customer called their supplier to get it fixed, hence the term

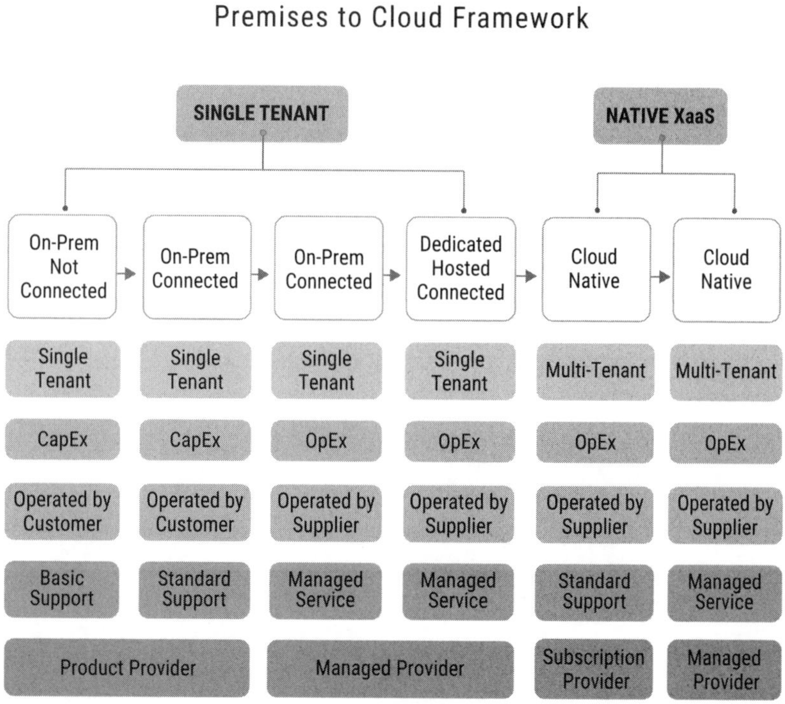

Premises to Cloud Framework

FIGURE A.3 Premises-to-Cloud Framework

"break-fix" maintenance. There was no need for the supplier to connect to the solution.

On-Prem Connected, CapEx

As technology became more complex and the cost to send someone on site to fix issues increased, many vendors started to create "connected" solutions. This would allow manufacturers and technology service providers to remotely connect to the product to diagnose issues, patch software and firmware, and assess overall health. Customers still purchased their technology outright and still operated their own technology environments. Maintenance evolved into "support," where suppliers could provide more help than just break-fix. With the rise in software-centricity and network dependency, complexity continued to increase.

On-Prem Connected, OpEx

Coinciding with the rise of technical complexity, the customer preference started to shift from CapEx to subscriptions. Customers needed more. They wanted to "subscribe" to their technology and have someone else operate it. As of the date of this publication, 96% of the members of TSIA's Managed Services research practice have created subscription (OpEx) versions of their technology offerings that they operate on behalf of their customer. These "operate services" are often commercialized as "managed services." TSIA defines managed services as the practice of outsourcing day-to-day technology management to a third party to improve financial or technical performance. Legacy managed service providers use labor-intensive, on-site operations to operate the technology on behalf of the customer. These models are costly and prone to human error. They depend on the tribal knowledge of the engineer. They are the opposite of scalable solutions. Modern managed service providers are process-oriented, software-driven, and remotely operated.

When technology is located on the customer's premises, there are still many variables outside the control of the supplier. Even though the solution might be sold as a "private cloud" model, the solution is still not cloud-based, and it is still far from the promise of a scalable XaaS solution. The on-prem connected OpEx model is the first step in becoming a your-mess-for-more provider. Insights gathered from connected solutions can be monitored and analyzed to provide business-related insights back to the customer. The more telemetry in the connected technology, the more advanced insights that can be provided.

Dedicated Hosted Connected

As technology and service providers continue their evolution toward cloud nirvana, they still have one major obstacle. The flagship product offering was still designed with a unique instance and individual deployment for a single customer. To eliminate the unpredictable and unknown challenges within the customer's network, the provider often deploys the single instance in a co-location facility or data center. This ensures every deployment happens in a purpose-built environment that has direct access to an "always-on" network connection. The solution provider has the complete ability to access all hardware, software, and the network required to efficiently operate the solution on behalf of the customer. Bandwidth, security, and environment are well understood, consistently employed, and continually optimized. The solution provider has 100% responsibility for all operational performance and can leverage all the data insights, telemetry, and instrumentation of the application and the operating environment. The only barrier to scale is the fact that each and every customer must have their own software instance and, often, their own hardware deployment. The provider has multiple instances to manage, multiple systems to upgrade, and more possible failure points than a true SaaS/cloud-based solution.

Cloud Native

In a cloud-native model, the XaaS solution has been designed from the ground up to run in the cloud, with an inherent multi-itenancy-based model. Basically, that means there is a single software instance that is distributed across all customers. If an upgrade happens to the core software, it happens instantaneously for all customers. Most born-in-the-cloud companies have a technology solution that is multitenancy. Most companies that have been selling hardware and software solutions for more than 20 years do not. Moving to a multitenancy model requires massive reengineering of the product architecture. It is simply not enough to declare you are a cloud provider. Without this shift to a multi-itenancy model, providers will never realize the full potential of scale. Services can only eat so much technical and operational complexity before there is a diminishing return. Products must be re-architected with a "service-oriented" architecture.

Cloud Native, Standard Support

In TSIA's paper, "Emerging Economic Engines of Technology Providers,"[2] we outline the four supplier models of the future: subscription provider, subscription provider plus, managed provider, and managed provider plus. Rather than discuss the entire contents of that paper, let's focus on the two primary models: subscription provider and managed provider. A subscription provider focuses on the platform—the technology. It talks about how wonderful its product is, how it can scale up and scale down, and how it is highly resilient and has lots of amazing features. It's a product play. The provider focuses more on the customer consuming the technology and less on the business value achieved by adopting the service. Most current technology suppliers strive to be subscription providers. Customers previously purchased the technology as an asset, now they subscribe to it. This mentality often perpetuates the reactive "support" model. If a user can't access a feature or is having technical issues, they reach out to their IT team. If the IT team can't reactively resolve it, it reaches out to the subscription provider. If the issue is not directly related to the core technology, the issue is handed back to the IT organization to troubleshoot, perform root-cause analysis, and resolve.

In a standard support, cloud-native model, the customer is still responsible for ensuring the technology helps them achieve their business goals. Nonetheless, the cloud-native provider technology is always connected. The provider has direct-, developer-, and administrator-level access to the technology. It can more easily and effectively analyze performance, consumption, and adoption data. It can provide utilization insights to the customer and even create analytics-driven offers to provide value to the customer that a not-connected or premises-based provider could ever hope to create. This is a critical step in mastering the your-mess-for-more provider model.

Cloud Native, Managed

The second major economic engine model described in "The Emerging Economic Engines of Technology Providers" is called the managed provider. A managed provider focuses on removing all technical and financial challenges to consuming technology. It focuses specifically on business objectives and the desired outcomes of the customer. It leverages the connected nature and scalability of cloud-native solutions. The cloud-native provider leverages data and insights from every available source and adopts the "Four Ps" of a next-generation service model: Proactive, Predictive, Prescriptive, and Preventive. TSIA's Four Ps framework is illustrated in Figure A.4. Not only does the cloud-native provider strive to prevent bad things from happening operationally, but it also understands that there

The Four Ps of a Next-Generation Service Model

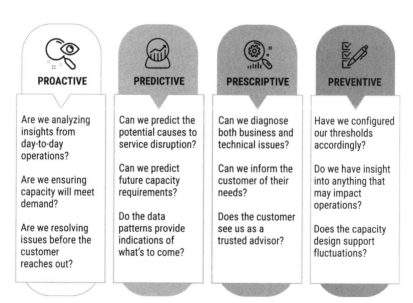

PROACTIVE	PREDICTIVE	PRESCRIPTIVE	PREVENTIVE
Are we analyzing insights from day-to-day operations?	Can we predict the potential causes to service disruption?	Can we diagnose both business and technical issues?	Have we configured our thresholds accordingly?
Are we ensuring capacity will meet demand?	Can we predict future capacity requirements?	Can we inform the customer of their needs?	Do we have insight into anything that may impact operations?
Are we resolving issues before the customer reaches out?	Do the data patterns provide indications of what's to come?	Does the customer see us as a trusted advisor?	Does the capacity design support fluctuations?

FIGURE A.4 The Four Ps of a Next-Generation Service Model

are significant, quantifiable business impacts from a service not performing as intended. It understands that technology solutions are put into place to help achieve specific business results. In a managed cloud model, the technology and the service must work in orchestration. In fact, many managed providers directly drive the functional requirements of the technology and the underlying platform.

Three Potential Paths Forward

TSIA asserts that there are three paths forward for companies that have a majority of their revenue coming from on-premise technology solutions.

1. Transform to a XaaS provider.

On this path, the company migrates a majority of its offers to the cloud. This is exactly what legacy software companies like Autodesk, Microsoft, PTC, and SAP are doing. TSIA has a robust library of research on tactics to "swallow this fish" and navigate this specific business model transformation.

It must be noted that not many traditional hardware companies have leaned into this option. Why? One reason is that this path requires the most investment and structural change. A second reason is that some technology simply cannot be migrated to the cloud. Another major challenge with a shift from premises-based, product-centric organizations to as-a-service models is the risk in accelerated margin erosion in an already commoditizing business. The average margin for managed services is currently well below the average margin for on-premise enterprise hardware and hardware maintenance contracts.

2. Transform to a your-mess-for-more managed provider.

On this path, the company keeps a majority of its offers running on-premise. There are lots of reasons this may be a requirement of its marketplace. However, the technology provider makes two key investments on this path: (1) invest in connectivity and robust customer telemetry, and (2) invest in new managed service offerings. On this path, the technology provider is willing to operate on-premise equipment for the customer. However, this is *not* the traditional your-mess-for-less outsourcing business model. These managed offers are designed around unlocking business value for the customer that includes:

- More utilization of capabilities.
- More value realization.
- More employee productivity.
- More security.
- More system uptime.

These next-generation managed providers are creating offers that have some or all of TSIA's "great eight" attributes of compelling XaaS offers. These are essential to arrive at the top rungs of the value ladder discussed in Chapter 5.

1. **Operational simplicity.** The XaaS offer is not hard to technically implement or run. Any operational complexity is assumed by the vendor.

2. **Pay as you need.** The customer does not pay for capacity or features that are not being utilized.

3. **Enhanced insights.** Leveraging new telemetry generated by a XaaS platform, the technology provider can apply analytics and AI to provide new valuable insights to the customer.

4. **Accelerated adoption.** The vendor is adept at helping key roles within the customer's organization effectively utilize the capabilities of the technology.

5. **Process optimization.** The technology helps optimize and digitize key employee or customer-facing processes.

6. **Specific KPI improvements.** The adoption of the technology can be linked to the improvement of KPIs within the customer's environment.

7. **Quantified financial gains.** The adoption of the technology can be linked to specific financial improvements that are tracked and quantified.

8. **Accelerated business outcomes.** The adoption of the technology can be directly linked to helping the customer achieve strategic business objectives.

The section on Industry Examples, which follows, will overview some of these new your-mess-for-more offers.

3. Maintain the current business model.

Finally, technology companies selling on-site technology offers, mostly through the channel, can decide to retain their current business model. Clearly, many of these companies are in this posture today. If this is the chosen path, management teams must be prepared for the following realities:

- Declining margins as offers become more commoditized.

- Significant cost reductions (as margins decline).

- Industry consolidation (high volume will be a requirement for survival).

Option 1 and Option 2 are hard. Very hard. They require substantial and deliberate investment, along with rigorous realization and life-cycle operation capabilities. Option 1 and Option 2 fundamentally begin to change the DNA and identity of the company. They cause companies to become service-led providers rather than product-led providers. The product is developed specifically to optimize the service, as opposed to services being optimized for the company's product portfolio.

For these reasons, some companies opt for Option 3.

One of the reasons we see companies fail to complete these transformations is that they are missing one of three critical levers of transformation:

1. Top-down direction-setting from the executive team. We call this "setting the economic engine" target for the company.
2. Bottoms-up tactical plan by all workstreams required for the transformation. (See TSIA's report, "Update: The XaaS Transformation,"[3] for more on this.)
3. Complete alignment on the timing and execution of all workstreams.

Without all three of these levers activated at the same time, there is a slim-to-no chance of a successful transformation.

The bottom line is that the entire business must align around the objectives before they attempt to execute the vision of the strategy. Companies would be wise to heed Jack Welsh's warning: "If the rate of change on the outside is greater than the rate of change on the inside, the end is near."

Industry Examples: Your Mess for More

There are numerous examples of companies that have built your-mess-for-more offers around their on-premise technology. To make the point that even the simplest of product offers can be converted into a your-mess-for-more model, we will start with two examples that are not enterprise hardware or software related.

Kaeser's Compressed Air as a Service

Kaeser's Compressed Air as a Service provides a reliable supply of compressed air tailored to customers' needs. Instead of a large capital expense, the customer pays a monthly fee to have clean, dry, energy-efficient air at the ready.

The benefit of this service includes:

- Custom analysis of the specific air requirements of the customer.
- Fixed pricing based on the estimated quantity of air the customer requires.
- Fixed contractual price for additional quantities when larger amounts of air are needed.
- Installation and operation of the compressed air system.
- Availability of compressed air at all times.
- Savings by moving from a CapEx to an OpEx purchasing model.

In this offer, the customer is only paying for what they need. This offer is promoting the following compelling attributes:

- Operational simplicity.
- Pay as you need.
- Enhanced insights.
- Quantified financial gains.

Michelin's Transportation Solutions

In 2016, Harvard Business School (HBS) published an article about Michelin's journey from selling tires to selling outcomes. Leveraging the power of the internet of things (IOT), Michelin has developed several new outcome-based managed offers. One of those offers is EFFITRAILER. This offer generates a Type 2 outcome and directly links price to the achievement of fuel efficiency.

This is a telematics solution dedicated to semitrailer fleets that has many real-time functionalities, including:

- Geolocation.
- Data transmission.

- Measurement of the pressure and temperature of the trailer tires.
- Collection of usage data (braking, mileage, load, etc.).
- Door-opening detector.

The solution enables haulage companies to manage their fleets of semitrailers as efficiently as possible, reducing the number of tire-related breakdowns and increasing their utilization rates, regardless of the brand of trailers and tires. The solution also enhances the safety of loads and increases the reliability of deliveries, while benefiting from the personalized support of a dedicated logistics analyst. The implementation of the solution is simple: The assembly of embedded telematics and sensors are fitted within the customer company by specialists from Michelin solutions.

This offer promotes the following compelling attributes:

- Operational simplicity.
- Enhanced insights.
- Accelerated adoption.
- Specific KPI improvements.
- Quantified financial gains.
- Accelerated business outcomes.

There is a lesson in this offer for enterprise hardware and software companies: If a 120-year-old tire manufacturer can successfully build compelling outcome-based offers, there is little validity in the assertion that outcome-based offers are simply a bridge too far.

Philips Healthcare: Enterprise Monitoring as a Service

Philips Healthcare produces sophisticated patient monitoring devices that, obviously, need to be deployed on site. Philips has engineered a new your-mess-for-more managed offer called Enterprise Monitoring as a Service, seen in Figure A.5.

Philips' Enterprise Monitoring as a Service

A CATEGORY-REDEFINING WAY OF DOING BUSINESS

FROM A TRADITIONAL CapEx APPROACH
We recognize that to have a fully functional patient-monitoring system and effectively manage patient care, you need a strategic partner equally invested in your successful standardization, adoption, and continuous improvement of system use.

TO A FLEXIBLE, ACUITY- AND USE-DRIVEN MODEL
That's why we created a shared-risk, pay-for-use service model that enables access to the capabilities that are aligned to your performance goals—without the burden of equipment ownership and continual reinvestment. In EMaaS, Philips industry experts help you reach these goals by experiencing our challenges right alongside you to identify opportunities and to problem-solve as a team. As an agile partner, we enable you to flex your monitoring and care capabilities to meet your changing needs every single day, while forging paths to realize your long-term operational and clinical ambitions.

Source: Philips Healthcare

FIGURE A.5 TSIA's North Start of Digital Transformation

With this service, Philips manages all its monitoring devices for the healthcare provider. More importantly, Philips leverages product telemetry to drive optimal adoption of its technology within the healthcare provider's environment. In the world of healthcare, optimal adoption results in saving lives.

This offer promotes the following compelling attributes:

- Operational simplicity.
- Pay as you need.

- Enhanced insights.
- Accelerated adoption.
- Quantified financial gains.

HPE GreenLake Cloud Services

HPE argues that there are many enterprise applications that cannot migrate to the public cloud:

> *The vast majority of apps and data—70%—are "systems of record" that run the enterprise—ERP, CRM, and more. They must live in data centers and colocations for data gravity, latency, application dependency, and regulatory compliance reasons, and lack the agility of the modern cloud experience.*[4]

For this reason, HPE has created a new offer that blends on-premise and cloud-based infrastructure into one pay-as-you-go service. HPE itemizes the benefits of this approach as follows:

- *Pay per use. HPE GreenLake speeds insights to unlock data's value, with pay-per-use and financial flexibility for new ventures and business operations, so you can free up capital and boost operational and financial flexibility.*

- *Scale up and down. HPE GreenLake helps you create essential data and analytics core to digital transformation, as a service in your locations. HPE speeds insights for data science teams to unlock data's value with pay-per-use, scale-up-and-down freedom.*

- *Simplified IT. Centralize operations and insights across your hybrid estate from a single intuitive self-service platform, HPE GreenLake Central. Get a unified view, monitor usage, cost performance, compliance, and more.*

- *Managed for you. Offload monitoring and management of your on-premises cloud and public clouds, securely managed from our world-class IT Operations Centers, helping you free up your resources to be more productive.*

In the tough year of 2020, GreenLake was the fastest growing offer in HPE's portfolio. According to the company:

> *HPE grew its annualized revenue run-rate (ARR) to $528 million, up 11 percent from the prior-year period. GreenLake services orders finished the quarter with a record 80 percent year-over-year growth.*

This offer promotes the following compelling attributes:

- Operational simplicity.
- Pay as you need.
- Enhanced insights.
- Quantified financial gains.

Diebold ATM as a Service

Obviously, ATM devices cannot be moved to the cloud. They are, by their very nature, hardware devices that must be deployed at the local level in cities and towns around the globe. Through their DN AllConnect Services, Diebold Nixdorf offers completely managed ATM technologies while allowing financial institutions to redirect their CapEx expenses to OpEx models.

Diebold's service-led approach focuses on holistic management of cash-based systems as the physical and digital world of financial systems continues to blur.

Not only does the service include a subscription model for the ATM devices, but it also includes complete fleet management, field resources, payment processing hardware and software, and secure network connectivity solutions.

The service is also supported by DN's Branch Lifecycle Management services, which provide complete branch life-cycle solutions to transform legacy hardware solutions into next-generation, network-connected, data-ready, and analytics-driven solutions.[5]

Diebold Nixdorf has already employed the solution with international financial institutions such as Bank99, JoFiCo, and others.

Dell Technologies Data Center as a Service

Dell Technologies' Data Center as a Service is a fully managed, premises-based solution that combines VMware Cloud software along with Dell EMC VxRail hardware. This enables companies to take an OpEx approach to deploying next-generation hyper-converged technologies. The value proposition includes some of the classic-managed services' value propositions, such as:

- Controlled costs.
- Simplified operations.
- Risk mitigation.

It also includes the value propositions of next-generation cloud services, such as:

- Rapid deployment with next-generation innovation to drive business growth.
- Flexible movement of workloads to any available host.
- Deployment of cloud-native applications on premises-based infrastructure.

Another key, and very timely, value proposition, is the enablement of a remote workforce through rapid deployments of virtual desktop infrastructure (VDI).[6]

Tactics to Cross the Rubicon

Julius Caesar's crossing of the Rubicon River on January 10, 49 BC, precipitated the Roman Civil War. Today, the phrase "crossing the Rubicon" is a metaphor that means to pass a point of no return.

Companies that continue to sell on-premise technology are at the edge of their own Rubicon River. They must decide if they want to cross over to a new XaaS-oriented business model. Like Caesar's crossing, there is no going back. Once this decision is made, a company must aggressively forge ahead.

But there is a difference from Caesar's experience. The real Rubicon River is a relatively small tributary. Caesar's physical crossing was trivial. The symbolic Rubicon that is facing on-premise technology companies is deep and wide, with deadly currents. Only the strongest and most committed companies will successfully make this crossing.

TSIA has a wealth of resources to help management teams navigate the XaaS transformation. On that journey, companies ultimately need to perform three transformations:

- **Offer transformation.** Define new, compelling XaaS offers.

- **Go-to-market transformation.** Modify direct and channel sales models to sell XaaS offers.

- **Customer engagement transformation.** Modify customer engagement models to ensure adoption, expansion, and renewal of XaaS offers.

For companies with on-premise technology, there are five specific tactics that should be pursued to start this business model transformation:

1. **Segment the product portfolio.** The company should review all on-premise offers and segment them into one of three categories:

   - Commoditizing: These are products that will remain on premise and will never be connected to provide meaningful telemetry.

   - Migrate to Managed: These are products that will remain on premise but can be connected. These are prime candidates for compelling your-mess-for-more offers.

   - Migrate to XaaS: These are products that can be migrated to the cloud.

2. **Embrace owning the assets.** The company should establish the financial infrastructure to own assets that are deployed

on the customer site. No funny financial engineering here. Companies should not be selling their products to themselves by establishing a separate entity that buys the products used in managed service contracts. This is an act of denial! You are no longer a product company. Cross the gosh–darn Rubicon and do not look back.

3. **Prioritize product telemetry.** Resources must be prioritized to start enabling on-premise products with the telemetry required to support new XaaS offers.

4. **Identify compelling XaaS offers.** Product and service offer teams should collaborate to identify new compelling XaaS offers. The "great eight" attributes should be one of the tools the teams leverage during that collaboration.

5. **Accelerate equipment migration.** This is similar to the concept of giving away the razor to sell the blades. Hardware companies should consider absorbing the cost of replacing non-connected legacy infrastructure with next-generation, connected solutions when the customer signs up for the new XaaS offer. The customer benefits from the new capabilities of these solutions while the provider benefits from software-driven, connected solutions in a recurring revenue model. The technology becomes a "cost of service" element.

6. **Don't forget about professional services (PS).** One of the worst mistakes a transforming technology provider can make is to allow critical capabilities that they already possess to atrophy. Professional services (advisory, consulting) is one of those capabilities. The fact is, you need a highly mature PS capability to enable XaaS transformation in just about any context. In most cases, PS is required for solid platform implementation and successful initial adoption. When done right, PS also provides an additional revenue stream that helps drive account expansion. Every data point we have suggests that professional services in the deal increases renewal rates. Yes, there are tough

questions to address regarding how to organize for PS, including what's the best financial concept for PS, given the proper, overriding focus on the total offer and a seamless customer experience. But if there's more than very little complexity in your product, professional services aren't a "nice to have," they are a "need to have." So don't forget about them.

The main TSIA assertion in this chapter is simple: There are three main paths on-premise technology providers will follow over the next five years. Which path will your company traverse?

Appendix B

The Digital Operations and Customer Experience Platform

By George Humphrey

Contributions by Jeremy DalleTezze and Laura Fay

Throughout the chapters of *Digital Hesitation*, we have continually focused on the need to completely rethink the company's end-to-end digital approach. We've touched on the importance of leveraging data-driven insights from all aspects of the business to drive informed decisions, reduce operational complexity and latency, and accelerate the customer's business outcomes for the sake of value realization. The TSIA research team also documented the need to shift to a "digital operations and customer experience." As ServiceNow CEO Bill McDermott said during a TSIA conference fireside chat, "We must eliminate the soul-sucking work for our employees and customers." We must eliminate the friction in the sales, adoption, expansion, and renewal processes. We must give sales the ability to leverage data to *prescribe* the right solution.

So how does the entire business do that? What are the steps the company has to take to fully realize the benefits of a true digital transformation? The days of managing a business from Microsoft Excel must come to an end. Whoever owns the data, owns the customer. Whoever masters data, increases growth, productivity, profitability, and retention.

> *"The core advantage of data is that it tells you something about the world that you didn't know before."*
>
> *– Hilary Mason,*
> *Data Scientist and Founder of Fast Forward Labs*

This appendix is intended to be a general overview of the technology required to enable a digital transformation.

What Is the Business Challenge?

The fundamental challenge for companies on the digital transformation journey is the fact that it's hard. Very hard. It requires investments that the company has historically not had to make. It requires skills that most companies still do not possess. It requires a cultural shift for the leaders of every line of business (LoB) and every supporting business function to align on a common set of goals and objectives. It requires a fundamental understanding that, even though not apparent, every aspect of a business has the potential to impact all other aspects of the business.

Today's business systems, operations systems, products, and services are all built completely separately from one another. In many cases, data from one system sits in complete isolation from others. Worse yet, many systems being used by organizations are based on legacy technologies that don't easily allow for data exchange and integration. Unless you started with a blank sheet of paper and were born in the cloud, there is no single, unified philosophy for what data should be captured, how it should be captured, and what should be done with it once it is captured. Some companies, such as AWS and Salesforce, are starting to come much closer to this, but the bottom line is that there is substantial underinvestment in data science, data technology, and data ontology.

What Is the Solution?

The solution is a platform that leverages data and analytics to create business-oriented relationships, known as ontology, and uses those relationships to accelerate efficiency in all aspects of business, partner, and customer operations. The platform enables all applications to communicate with each other, to share data, interface with external systems, and presents relevant information to the end user in a way that is most useful to the activities they are attempting to conduct. Simply put, it is an enterprise-wide operating system or a digital operations and customer experience platform (DOCX).

The DOCX is composed of four major modules, as illustrated in Figure B.1. Each of these modules typically contains standalone

Digital Operations and Customer Experience Platform

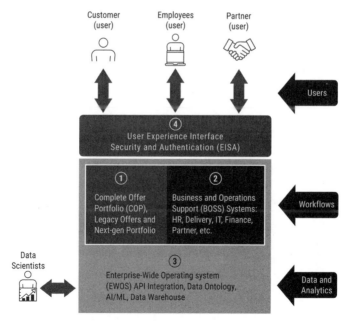

FIGURE B.1 Digital Operations and Customer Experience Platform

systems that often work in isolation from each other. This appendix will identify each major module.

The Complete Offer Portfolio (COP) Module

The COP module seen in Figure B.2 contains all systems and applications used to bring new products and services to market as well as those products themselves. Today's technology companies often have both legacy technology solutions deployed with their customers as well as next-generation technology-as-a-service (XaaS) solutions. As described in Chapter 9, legacy technologies residing in a customer's location may still be unconnected. XaaS

Example of Components in the Complete Offer Portfolio

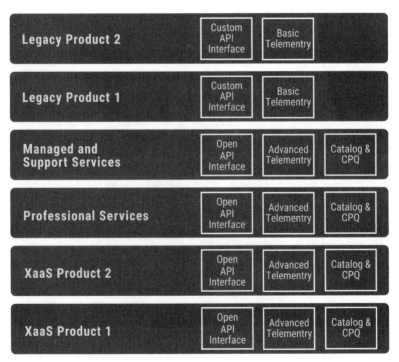

FIGURE B.2 Example of Components in the Complete Offer Portfolio

solutions, in most scenarios, are connected back to the provider's operations center. These organizations also have product and service applications that are required to bring these solutions to market, such as product life-cycle management (PLM); product and service catalog; configure, price, quote (CPQ); project management; and research and development (R&D). Technically these are considered business support systems and will be captured in the next section.

Many companies that are growing their presence in XaaS solutions are doing so through acquisitions. Each of these companies typically has its own product and service offer management toolset, its own UI applications, and more.

Rationalization of these applications and toolsets is crucial in order to drive consistent customer experiences and scale of operations. The good news is that these already exist. The bad news is that they often don't integrate with each other or to the other existing business and operations support systems.

The elements within Figure B.2 are only a small portion of the tools, applications, products, and services that exist within technology companies.

The Business Operations and Support Systems (BOSS) Module

Business support systems and operations support systems are typically used to support specific functions within the business. It is not uncommon for every organization within a business to have its own set of applications and tools used to support the business. These include systems such as enterprise resource planning (ERP); finance, billing, and collections; delivery operations; human resources (HR); information technology (IT); sales; and customer success, as seen in Figure B.3. It is also uncommon for these systems to seamlessly integrate with one another, even though what happens in one system or operation will likely

Business Operations and Support Systems

Product Lifestyle Management	API Interface	R&D Tools	Offer Database
Salesforce Automation Platform	API Interface	Customer Database	CRM Software
Partner Management Platform	API Interface	CRM	CPQ
Delivery Operations Platform	API Interface	ITSM	Discovery & Monitoring
Customer Success Platform	API Interface	CS Management	
Revenue and Financial Management Platform	API Interface	Billing	
Supplier Management and Procurement Platform	API Interface	P&L	
HR and Resource Management Platform	API Interface	HR Management	
Corporate IT Systems	API Interface	Service Integration	System Integration

FIGURE B.3 Business Operations and Support Systems

impact other organizations, operations, customers, and partners. Once again, if a company has grown through acquisition, it is not uncommon for there to be multiple iterations of business and operations support systems adding to the layers of complexity.

The elements within Figure B.3 are only a small portion of the systems, tools, and applications that exist within technology companies.

The Enterprise-Wide Operating System (EWOS) Module

This is where it gets tricky. The systems, tools, and applications in the Product Module and the Business and Operations Systems Module, for the most part, already exist. As discussed, these systems don't typically play well together. They lack an "orchestration" model. This is where the EWOS comes into play. There are two major components of the EWOS: the foundational layer providing API-based integration, data repository, data ontology, and algorithmic-oriented analytics, as seen in Figure B.4, and the

Enterprise-Wide Operating System Foundational Layer

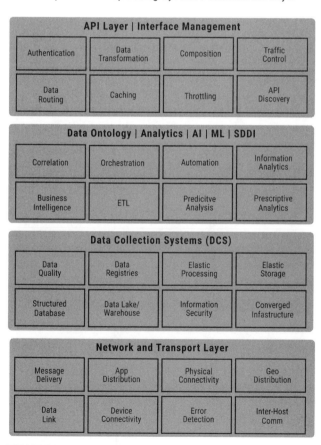

FIGURE B.4 Enterprise-Wide Operating System Foundational Layer

presentation layer providing the digital experience all customers, employees, and partners use to interact with all products, services, and systems, shown in Figure B.5. Each of these layers will be explained in more detail.

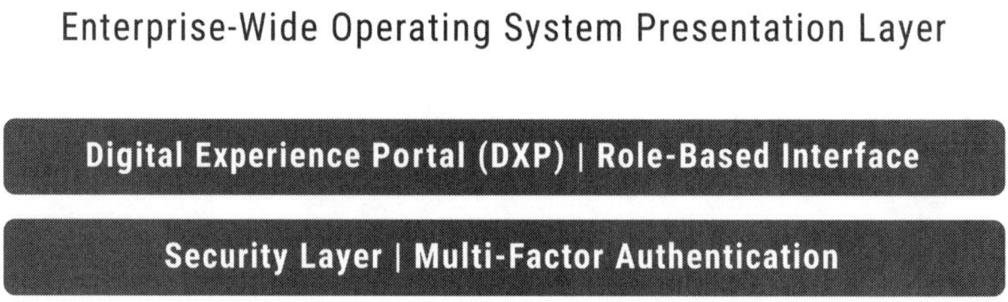

Enterprise-Wide Operating System Presentation Layer

Digital Experience Portal (DXP) | Role-Based Interface

Security Layer | Multi-Factor Authentication

FIGURE B.5 Enterprise-Wide Operating System Presentation Layer

The Application Programming Interface (API) and Integration Layer

The days of developing closed, proprietary systems have become a practice of the past. In order to get value out of data from systems and applications, they must be able to talk to each other. In fact, data is the language of digital communication. However, many systems have their own languages, known as closed APIs, and many legacy systems lack the ability to speak any of these languages. These API-less systems will require the development of custom APIs through software-defined data integration (SDDI). The need for data from systems has driven the requirement for open APIs[1] that most software developers code to today.[2]

Think of it this way: a traveler going from Italy to Australia for the first time will need the ability to communicate with local residents and merchants. Without the ability to translate from Italian to English, the traveler would have a difficult time navigating the country and getting the most out of their experience.

The API and integration layer does more than just translate machine language. Due to the sheer number of data streams (signal liquidity), API layers must provide additional functions, such as authentication (from what system or application am I getting this data?), basic transformation (stripping out unnecessary data), routing and control (efficiency of information flow), and API discovery that provides important metadata (what else is out there that I may want to talk to?). Without the API layer, there is no way for crucial data to be communicated from one system to another. And just because technical people will be the primary "customers" of the API, do not skimp on investment in thorough documentation, as there are good APIs, and really, really bad APIs. Figure B.6 represents the API layer.

Application Programming Interface and Integration Layer

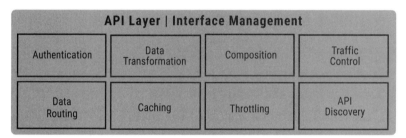

FIGURE B.6 Application Programming Interface and Integration Layer

Data Warehouse and Hyper-Converged Infrastructure

If volumes of data are generated, where do the volumes of data go? For most companies, the answer is either (a) into a closed or self-contained system's database, such as the configuration management database of a delivery operations platform, the database of a sales force automation system, or some other operational database store (ODS), or (b) it evaporates into the ether. Effective cross-functional data ontology and analytics is critically dependent on the collection, storage, retrieval, and hygiene of data. This is the primary purpose of the data warehouse. Sources of key information are identified along with the interfaces to access the data through the API layer. Data then flows through the ontology and analytics layer and into the data warehouse through a process known as extract, transform, and load (ETL). Data is organized according to such logical groupings as finance, marketing, sales, and production, as well as such columnar relationships as start of service data, entitlements, product license, service function, and so on.

Historically speaking, these data warehouses were built using storage-specific appliances and infrastructure. Today's technologies have paved the way for converged infrastructure that combines the functions of storage, compute, virtualization, and software-defined networking. Many companies have even opted for cloud-based data warehousing solutions to avoid expensive capital investments and the cost of operations labor to support the storage solutions.

Data warehouses can be a large investment, particularly when it comes to time, as the organization and IT figure out how to optimize and stitch together connections. Because of this potential bottleneck, companies also leverage data lakes via ETL. These lakes allow data to live in their natural form and are much quicker to build than warehouses. So long as the API layer is able to provide the data and metadata, data lakes can enable key stakeholders across the company to access any data immediately with context, and then over time learn how to optimize the data insights accordingly. To be clear, you still need business-driven engineers and analysts to transform the data in the lakes, but this can be done over time and it will not overburden your applications.

Figure B.7 illustrates the data collection system (DCS). The DCS includes the infrastructure where the data resides as well as

Data Collection System

Data Collection Systems (DCS)			
Data Quality	Data Registries	Elastic Processing	Elastic Storage
Structured Database	Data Lake/ Warehouse	Information Security	Converged Infastructure

FIGURE B.7 Data Collection System

data-centric applications ensuring proper structure of data, quality of data, and security of data.

Data Ontology | Analytics Application Layer

The data analytics application layer is one of the most exciting opportunities for organizations to master. Information technology, business support systems, operations support systems, and cloud services all generate massive volumes of data. The data generated is rarely translated into interrelated business intelligence. Most organizations generate data in silos, and that data is often not collected and analyzed for patterns. When companies have a hyper-converged infrastructure, though, they are ready for digital transformation, as the right data *can* be available for the right person at the right time. The data ontology layer is all about making the right data available for the right person (employee, customer, partner) at the right time. Technology companies should think of these data insights as force multipliers.[3]

It may help to visualize a real-world example of leveraging the data ontology and analytics layer as follows:

In order for a product team to develop and launch a new offer, it must build a business case in order to receive approval to proceed. That business case includes critical assumptions that include product development, services development, financial assumptions for the business (revenue and profit), sales readiness and forecast planning, delivery resource planning, and customer success staffing plans. Once the offer launches, each of these areas typically has its own systems in place to govern post-launch, day-to-day activities. Rarely are these systems seamlessly connected with free-flowing data among them. If one of the organizations misses a key deadline, such as staffing the delivery team with the proper, accredited technical experts, there are ripple effects across all the other organizational units. Often those impacts occur in real time, causing a reactive series of events to mitigate impacts, adjust business plans, miss revenue targets, and more.

Now imagine all those systems are connected with free-flowing, real-time information exchanged across them due to a hyperconverged infrastructure. As schedules are built in product development, the sales forecasts are updated automatically and reviewed and approved by the sales team in their system of records. The HR platform automatically receives feeds of the business plan along with units shipped (or licenses activated), allowing the HR team to understand exactly what skills are required to deliver the offer and how many resources are available (or need to be hired) to meet the delivery demand. If the sales organization increases its forecast, data is automatically synchronized with the product management systems and financial systems to increase the revenue targets for the business. Additionally, the HR system is notified that there is an increase in delivery demand with specific training and certification requirements for individuals. The entire organization begins to work in complete orchestration. Music to our ears!

Another potential scenario is that the microchip components required for circuit boards that are used to service existing infrastructure may have moved into a supply-chain delay. The hardware inventory system would immediately feed those insights into the revenue planning system for support services, and the sourcing department would be notified and could take action to find alternative suppliers. The customer success team would be notified that there may be a customer impact (resulting in an unhappy customer), and it could take proactive steps to inform the customer of a potential delay in servicing a system.

Both scenarios require data insights across multiple systems. They require an understanding of how a single scenario may impact operations across multiple organizations. Those scenarios not only require software defined data integrations (SDDI), they also require mapping of the relationships of the data (ontology) among those systems. Figure B.8 is an illustration of the data ontology layer.

This layer is responsible for the correlation of data streams and events across the business. Computer intelligence identifies which

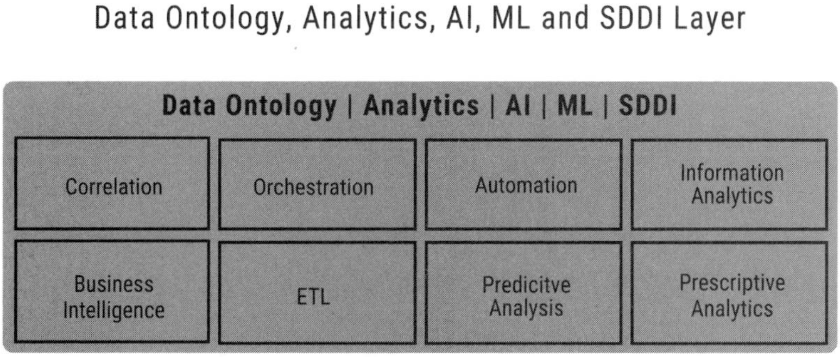

Data Ontology, Analytics, AI, ML and SDDI Layer

Data Ontology | Analytics | AI | ML | SDDI			
Correlation	Orchestration	Automation	Information Analytics
Business Intelligence	ETL	Predicitve Analysis	Prescriptive Analytics

FIGURE B.8 Data Ontology, Analytics, AI, ML, and SDDI Layer

events happened at the same time, from which systems they came, and what the triggers were. This requires orchestration across the various business systems, product systems, and operations systems. Analytics are then applied and mapped to business and operations intelligence to identify if there is already a known resolution to the correlated events. If there is an automation capability to rectify the situation, it is invoked, and the issue is resolved. If there is not a known solution, the intelligence gathered is then directed to an operations employee to resolve the issue manually. The steps taken by the engineer are documented and fed back into the knowledge management system. High-frequency occurrences are automatically identified and prioritized for further automation. Every manual fault results in an opportunity to drive more automated efficiency, and insights are fed back into the product management system to engineer improvements directly into the next release of the product.

The Experience Interface Secure Authentication Module

So far in this appendix we've made the assertion that companies going through a true digital transformation need to have an enterprise-wide operating system that enables all product, services, and business and operations support systems to connect to each other. We've also discussed there needs to be a data collection system that captures all relevant data streams from these systems.

Lastly, we've discussed the need for a data-science approach to correlate, orchestrate, and analyze the data collected. No operating system is complete without a graphical user interface that allows a user to easily interpret the data, interact with a myriad of complex technologies, and guide individuals through their activities.

This is the purpose of the experience interface secure authentication (EISA) module. Many companies obsess over the customer experience, spending millions of dollars on graphical user interfaces. Few, if any, think about a holistic experience for all users leveraging all applications, systems, and data. Think about it. The list of individuals who interact with your company's systems and applications is quite long: customers, partners, delivery engineers, product developers, finance, procurement, IT, executive management, sales, customer success, and more. Every individual on this list has a different experience, and that experience varies by every product, system, and application they're using at that time. Companies need to define user experiences by their roles, accessing data in a consistent manner that is presented to them based on their business objectives. Simply put, it's presenting the right data to the right user at the right time, as shown in Figure B.9.

Enterprise-Wide Operating System Presentation Layer

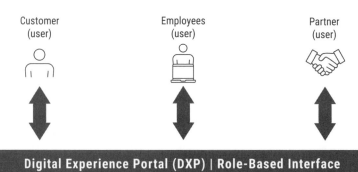

FIGURE B.9 Experience Interface Secure Authentication Module

There have never been more technology options to accomplish this for businesses than there are today. A simple example is the Liferay Digital Experience Platform.[4] Liferay's platform aggregates multiple application interfaces into a purpose-built "single pane of glass." This single pane of glass is simply a roles-based user interface accessed through a web browser.

The EISA interface allows users to log in to the company's website using standards-based authentication and identity management. Based on the identity of the individual accessing their site, the user is presented with guided insights relevant to their specific tasks. The more integrated the backend systems are, and the more data gathered and analyzed by the ontology module, the more guided the user experience will be.

For example, the CFO can access critical financial information through their portal that flows from the supply chain system, the procurement platform, the sales forecast, and the product P&L. More advanced intelligence within the analytics module would allow the CFO to run multiple, "what if" scenarios to model potential impacts of a product manufacturing issue.

Another example is that the services operations leader could view the backlog of implementations based on the sales team's over-performance. From there they could activate incremental job postings for more installation engineers or identify any capacity availability from partners that are also integrated within the system.

Buyers logging in to their portal could see the current capacity of their existing systems and identify which products they've purchased are nearing end-of-support status. The portal would direct them to the offer portfolio with new options and allow them to subscribe to new solutions. They could also augment their technology solution with recommended training from the on-demand training catalog and request a consulting expert contact them for more strategic future planning. All from the same interface!

Further, as elaborated in Chapter 3, the end-user omnichannel experience is similarly integrated and frictionless, with relevant purchase and micro-learning opportunities being presented to users at the appropriate time.

Once a company taps into the potential of the digital user experience for *all users*, through the blending of intellectual property and information technology, the possibilities are endless. It is only limited to the imagination of data scientists and software engineers and the processes that support them.

Where to Start

Here are the following steps you can take to begin the journey of creating a more integrated DOCX that can deliver on the vision of a true digital transformation.

Build the Blueprint

The first step in building a DOCX platform is to invest in a dedicated team that defines the corporate experience model, frames the technical architecture, and documents all existing products, services, and systems. From there, this team will build the blueprint leveraging the high-level model in the opening image of this appendix.

Document the Current Systems

This is a major inventory exercise. All products, services, and systems should be grouped into major categories, such as HR systems, IT systems, delivery operations systems, and so forth. The graphical blueprint should be supported by a detailed document-based inventory with the following details: category, business purpose, and whether or not the system or application supports standards-based APIs (Y/N).

Platforms supporting standards-based APIs are "data exchange ready." These APIs will forward structured information to the data-collection system. The data will then be ready to be accessed by the data ontology layer where meaningful connections and business-related data maps can be generated.

Platforms that are not ready for data integration through standards-based, open API interfaces will need to go through a scoping process to document requirements for private (non-public/non-open) code development. Establishing an API-first strategy is foundational. The private APIs developed will enable legacy systems to gather and relay basic telemetry insights to the data collection system and be leveraged by the analytics engine.

Define Data Integrations Based on Business Objectives

To realize the full benefits of systems integration, digital transformation leaders must define business objectives and requirements *with* the data science and engineering teams. This is a meeting of the minds. The business owners need to discuss the top business challenges. The primary focus should be on areas that require cross-functional support and that are causing substantial pain in the business today. The objective is to drive as much efficiency as possible. In the EISA section of this appendix, several scenarios were provided showing data relationships among multiple systems that today don't naturally exist. The data science and engineering teams, after hearing the pain and challenges of the business owners, must then prescribe the data relationships among the disparate systems. This creates business-challenge-oriented maps that have software-defined data relationships. The result is highly automated process digitization that alleviates business pain and accelerates business results.

Once software-defined data relationships and integrations are established for the top business challenges, organizations can begin to document additional systems integrations that will improve performance, reduce cost and latency, eliminate friction, and accelerate growth for the business.

With the investment in an artificial intelligence and machine learning function, eventually software agents can be leveraged to identify patterns and create software-defined data relationships that are not obvious to humans. While still in its infancy, this is an exciting and blooming development opportunity for suppliers.

The Roles-Based Digital Experience Portal

We've referred to the foundation of the DOCX as the EWOS. Using both Microsoft and Apple as examples, one can understand how critical the end-user experience interface is to the success of an operating system. Most companies today are obsessed with the "customer experience," spending substantial amounts of dollars on how customers interact with their solutions. While this is critically important, it is also equally important to design the user experience for employees and partners. After all, are they not also users of the company's systems and solutions? We would assert that software engineers and user-experience designers should spend as much time, energy, and investment on leveraging both the IP and IT investments for a superior, blended employee and partner experience as they do on the customer experience.

The user experience should be context- and roles-based to ensure the right data from the right system is presented to the right user at the right time. The user interface should be containerized and presented through all relevant omnichannel interfaces aligned with the brand experience of the company.

In Closing

Digital transformations are hard, hence the reason most fail. Digitization can't happen in silos as art projects that are buried within each organization. The true power of a successful digital transformation is a more scalable, informed business that delivers a unified experience to all users. This requires a unified approach driven by the highest levels of the company, up to and including the CEO. The company must be committed to hunting down and destroying complexity in every area of the business, wielding data, analytics, and automation as their weapons of choice. To emphasize an earlier sentiment, it's all about getting the right data to the right user at the right time in a consumable, easy-to-digest format. Companies that have succeeded in the digital transformation emerge stronger, faster, and smarter than their peers and their competitors and are prepared for a sustainable future.

Appendix C
LAER
By Thomas Lah

This appendix provides an overview of the TSIA LAER framework.

LAER

TSIA's LAER model was first introduced to the industry in 2016 and quickly became the de facto standard model for customer engagement for recurring revenue businesses of all kinds.

TSIA's LAER model is the supplier's internal perspective of the customer journey and consists of four distinct customer life-cycle objectives. The model consists of four separate engagement phases:

- **Land** includes all the sales and marketing activities required to land the first sale of a solution for a new customer as well as the initial implementation of that solution. When you land the customer, you've successfully convinced the prospect to become a new customer of yours.

- **Adopt** includes all the activities involved in making sure the customer is successfully adopting and expanding their use of the solution. This is the step where you help the customer who just bought your technology successfully use it to achieve their business outcomes.

- **Expand** includes all the activities required to cost-effectively help current customers expand their spending as usage increases, including both cross-selling and upselling. As you become more invested in the customer's outcomes, it becomes easier to tie your technology to other projects and initiatives, thereby encouraging your customers to buy more products and services from you, the supplier.

- **Renew** includes all the activities required to ensure the customer renews their contract(s). It involves convincing your customer to renew their relationship with you when it comes time to repurchase the technology.

Who Is Responsible for the Different Activities Across LAER?

While the LAER model will continue to evolve as more businesses begin to embrace it as part of their day-to-day operations, following is an example of an established LAER-based customer coverage model that breaks down the traditional roles and responsibilities between sales and services. Please note that we've reversed the expand and renew phases in the following examples to make it easier to map roles to them.

Land

Landing the customer has historically been handled by your sales team (Figure C.1). Its sole responsibility is to engage prospects and

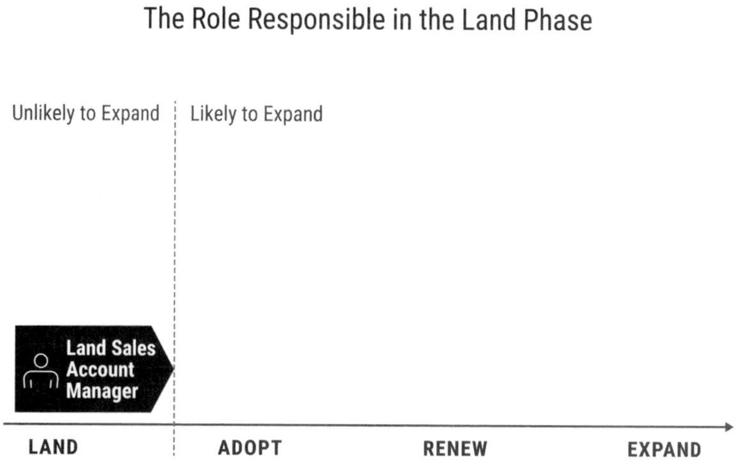

The Role Responsible in the Land Phase

FIGURE C.1 The Role Responsible in the Land Phase

turn them into customers, but it doesn't tend to focus on expand selling activities.

Adopt

Once a customer is using your offer, there should be a role focused on helping that customer successfully adopt the technology, such as a customer success manager (Figure C.2). Your customer success, education services, and support services teams are all able to help ensure your customers successfully adopt the technology. They are also well-positioned to aid in the renewal process, because highly adopted customers that are happy with their purchase are more likely to renew their contract. However, it's important to keep in mind that not all levels of adoption are created equal, and the key here is to make sure individuals in these roles are promoting "effective" adoption of the technology.

Renew

One of the great debates in the industry is centered on the role of a customer success manager in the renewal process. Can this role own the renewal commercials? TSIA data is showing that not only

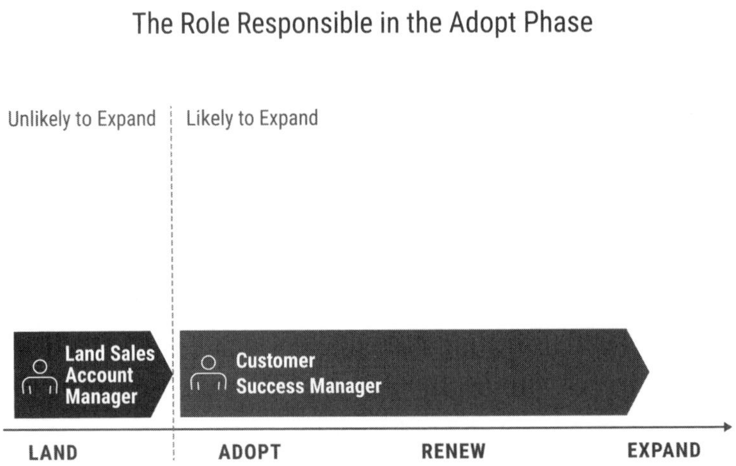

The Role Responsible in the Adopt Phase

FIGURE C.2 The Role Responsible in the Adopt Phase

can the customer success manager own renewal commercials, they also are proving to be the most cost-effective mechanism for collecting renewal dollars. However, if the customer success manager responsible for renewal runs into challenges, they may need assistance in communicating the value proposition of your technology to the customer. In this case, a renewal specialist may need to be engaged. These individuals specialize in addressing the challenges of existing customers, finding solutions, and ensuring they continue to find value in your offers and keep coming back.

Expand

If you have highly adopted customers successfully using your technology, there is clearly an opportunity to sell more to your existing customer base. Customer success managers should always be looking for these opportunities, but other parts of your services delivery teams may also identify ways that other offers within your portfolio can help your customers achieve their goals. The sales, customer success, and marketing teams can work together to drive customer growth.

The roles responsible in the renew and expand phases of LAER are seen in Figure C.3.

The Role Responsible in the Renew and Expand Phases

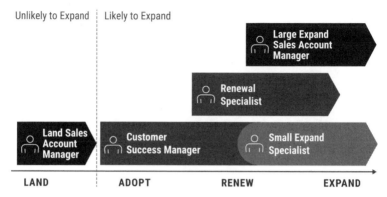

FIGURE C.3 The Roles Responsible in the Renew and Expand Phases

Endnotes

Chapter 1

1 Wood, J.B., Todd Hewlin, and Thomas Lah. 2013. *B4B: How Technology and Big Data Are Reinventing the Customer-Supplier Relationship.* San Diego, CA: Point B, Inc.

2 LAER stands for land, adopt, expand, renew, as defined in the *Technology-as-a-Service Playbook*, by Thomas Lah and J.B. Wood. 2016.

3 For a list of the companies in the T&S 50 Index, visit https://www.tsia.com/members/tools/financial-sets/financial-sets/summary

Chapter 2

1 Chen, James (Reviewed By Michael J. Boyle). December 23, 2020. "Neural Network." Investopedia. https://www.investopedia.com/terms/n/neuralnetwork.asp Accessed January 19, 2022.

2 Coined by Amazon CEO, Jeff Bezos, "two-pizza teams" are so named because they're small: 6 to 10 people; you can feed them with two pizzas.

Chapter 4

1 TSIA 2019 Sales Model Transformation Survey.

2 TSIA Sales Poll, April 2021.

3 TSIA 2020 Monetizing Customer Success Study.

4 The Innovator's Dilemma is a term coined by Clayton Christensen in 1997. It describes the decision that businesses must make between catering to their customers' current needs or adopting new innovations and technologies that will answer their future needs.

5 TSIA Value and Outcomes Poll, May 2021.

6 Levitt, Theodore. 1983. *Marketing Imagination*. The Free Press.

7 TSIA Annual Organization Survey.

8 Non-Functional requirements define system attributes such as security, reliability, performance, maintainability, scalability, and usability. NFRs ensure the effectiveness and viability of the entire cloud-hosted system.

9 TSIA XaaS Product Practices Poll, May 2021. Respondents include PM communities from large established tech firms and cloud native companies.

10 Wood, J.B., Todd Hewlin, and Thomas Lah. 2013. *B4B: How Technology and Big Data Are Reinventing the Customer-Supplier Relationship*. San Diego, CA: Point B, Inc.

11 Next Bus website. https://www.cubic.com/solutions/transportation/nextbus

12 The term product-led growth was originally coined in 2016 by Blake Bartlett of Openview Venture Partners, an expansion-stage venture capital firm.

13 Autodesk, Inc. website. https://www.autodesk.com/products

Chapter 5

1 Harvard Business Review website. https://hbr.org/1992/09/managing-price-gaining-profit

2 Marn, Micihael V., Eric V. Roegner, and Craig C. Zawada. February 1, 2003. "The Power of Pricing." *McKinsey Quarterly.* https://www.mckinsey.com/business-functions/marketing-and-sales/our-insights/the-power-of-pricing

3 According to the (2021 H2) TSIA Support Services Gold Standard Benchmark, 76% of vendors sell applications that require a high degree of technical and business expertise to operate.

4 According to the 2020 TSIA XaaS Product Management Benchmark, 97% of vendors offer discounts.

5 Sales Cloud Pricing, Salesforce, Inc. website, 2021. https://www.salesforce.com/editions-pricing/sales-cloud/

6 VMware, Inc. Workspace ONE. 2021. VMware website. https://www.vmware.com/products/workspace-one.html

7 Google Workspace Pricing. Google website. 2021. https://workspace.google.com/pricing.html

8 SAP Cloud Analytics Pricing. SAP website. 2021. https://www.sap.com/products/cloud-analytics/pricing.html

9 Lah, Thomas, Steve Frost, and Martin Dove. 2018. "Why Improve Your Vertical Leap." TSIA.

10 TSIA 2020 Offers and Pricing Survey.

11 The term "future value aggregator" is derived from the *Technology-as-a-Service Playbook: How to Grow a Profitable Subscription Business*, by Thomas Lah and J.B. Wood. 2016. San Diego, CA: Point B, Inc.

12 TSIA Organization Survey, 2020.

13 ProfitWell website. https://www.priceintelligently.com/blog/saas-discounting-strategy-lowers-ltv-by-over-30-percent

14 NextBus Real-Time Passenger Information, Cubic website. 2021, https://www.cubic.com/solutions/transportation/nextbus

15 "How to Control How Much Data Netflix Uses." 2021. Netflix, Inc. Help Center. https://help.netflix.com/en/node/87

16 Clark, Stephen, November 23, 2020. "How Much Data Does Spotify Use?" WhistleOut. https://www.whistleout.ca/CellPhones/Guides/How-Much-Data-Does-Spotify-Use-Canada

17 Mendoza. N.F. March 23, 2020. "Data and Voice Usage Spike as More People Work from Home During the Coronavirus Pandemic." TechRepublic. https://www.techrepublic.com/article/data-and-voice-usage-spike-as-more-people-work-from-home-during-the-coronavirus-pandemic/

18 Global Internet Traffic Forecast Highlights. Cisco Systems website. https://www.cisco.com/c/dam/m/en_us/solutions/service-provider/vni-forecast-highlights/pdf/Global_2021_Forecast_Highlights.pdf

19 Statista website. https://www.statista.com/statistics/267202/global-data-volume-of-consumer-ip-traffic/

20 Poyar, Kyle. November 5, 2021. "Playbook: Scale to $100M+ ARR with a Usage-Based Pricing Model." OV Blog. https://openviewpartners.com/blog/usage-based-pricing-playbook/

21 Zapier website, 20201. https://zapier.com/

22 Databricks website, 2021. https://databricks.com

23 Twilio website, 2021. https://twilio.com

24 Auth0 website, 2021. https://auth0.com/

25 Ibid.

26 Autodesk Flex Program. Autodesk website, 2021. https:// www.autodesk.com/benefits/flex

27 Cubic website, 2021. https://www.cubic.com/solutions/ transportation/road-user-charging

28 Kaeser Compressors website, 2021. https://us.kaeser.com/ services/compressed-air-as-utility-service/

29 Nadim, Emad. November 17, 2016. "Michelin: Tires-as-a-Service." HBS. https://digital.hbs.edu/platform-rctom/ submission/michelin-tires-as-a-service/

30 "MICHELIN–Effitrailer–Semi-Trailer Management Solution–EN." September 7, 2018. YouTube. https://www. youtube.com/watch?v=cXtym0KmTTg

31 Slack Flex Pricing website, 2021. https://slack.com/help/ articles/218915077-Slacks-Fair-Billing-Policy

32 OKRs stand for objectives and key results, a goal-setting methodology that can help your team set and track measurable goals.

33 Splunk, Inc. Workload and Ingest Pricing https://www.splunk. com/en_us/software/pricing/faqs.html#workload-pricing

34 Twilio Pricing https://www.twilio.com/flex#pricing

35 https://medium.com/zocdoc-corp/zocdocs-turnaround-from-an-unsustainable-path-to-profitable-growth-c3fc7ce2314d

Chapter 6

1 Lah, Thomas, and J.B. Wood. 2016. *Technology-as-a-Service Playbook: How to Grow a Profitable Subscription Business*. San Diego, CA: Point B, Inc.

2 In computer science and information science, an ontology encompasses a representation, formal naming, and definition of the categories, properties, and relations between the concepts,

data, and entities that substantiate one, many, or all domains of discourse. More simply, an ontology is a way of showing the properties of a subject area and how they are related, by defining a set of concepts and categories that represent the subject. Wikipedia. https://en.wikipedia.org/wiki/Ontology_ (information_science) Accessed January 21, 2022.

3 Microsoft website. https://careers.microsoft.com/us/en/ job/1219297/Director-Digital-Advisor-Healthcare-Life-Sciences Accessed January 21, 2022.

Chapter 7

1 Wood, J.B., Todd Hewlin, and Thomas Lah. 2011. *Consumption Economics: The New Rules of Tech*. San Diego, CA: Point B, Inc.

2 TSIA Customer Success Benchmark Data. 2021.

3 TSIA Rapid Response Research Poll: Who Owns Renewals. July 2020.

4 TSIA Subscription Revenue Effectiveness Benchmark Data. 2020.

5 Phil Nanus and John Ragsdale. August 24, 2017. "Are 67% of Customer Success Organizations Wrong?" TSIA Blog.

6 TSIA Renewal Workflow Automation Survey Data. February 2021.

7 TSIA Rapid Response Research Poll: Customer Experience Preferences in the Renewal Cycle. May 2021.

Chapter 8

1 Salesforce, Inc. website. 2021. https://partners.salesforce. com/s/education/general/Partner_Program

2 ServiceNow website. 2021. https://www.servicenow.com/ partners.html

3 Anne McClelland. October 2011. Service Provider Resellers Insights. TSIA. https://www.tsia.com/resources/service-provider-resellers-insights

4 Lah, Thomas, and J.B. Wood. 2016. *Technology-as-a-Service Playbook: How to Grow a Profitable Subscription Business*. San Diego, CA: Point B, Inc.

5 Anne McClelland. October 2011. Service Provider Resellers Insights. TSIA. https://www.tsia.com/resources/service-provider-resellers-insights

6 Land, adopt, expand, and renew describe the motions in TSIA's well-known LEAR Model, a framework for technology business growth, as defined in the *Technology-as-a-Service Playbook: How to Grow a Profitable Subscription Business* by Thomas Lah and J.B. Wood.

7 Thomas Lah and J.B. Wood. 2016. *Technology-as-a-Service Playbook: How to Grow a Profitable Subscription Business*. San Diego, CA: Point B, Inc.

8 John F. Gantz. October 2019. "The Salesforce Economic Impact: 4.2 Million New Jobs, $1.2 Trillion of New Business Revenues from 2019 to 2024." IDC. https://www.salesforce.com/content/dam/web/en_us/www/documents/reports/idc-salesforce-economy-report.pdf

9 "The Ultimate Guide to Salesforce AppExchange." April 13, 2020. Inspire Planner. https://inspireplanner.com/blog/salesforce-appexchange-ultimate-guide/

10 Salesforce website. 2021. https://appexchange.salesforce.com/

11 "Connected Patient Report: The Trail Map for Understanding Today's Digital Patient." 2017. Salesforce Research. https://a.sfdcstatic.com/content/dam/www/ocms-backup/assets/pdf/industries/2017-connected-patient-report.pdf

12 Scale Care Management. 2021. Salesforce website. https://www.salesforce.com/solutions/industries/healthcare/providers/scale-member-management/

13 Salesforce AppExchange website. 2021. Healthcare & Life Sciences. https://appexchange.salesforce.com/mktcollections/industry-collections/healthcare

14 Salesforce AppExchange website. 2021. Veeva CRM. https://appexchange.salesforce.com/appxListingDetail?listingId=a0N300000016ZRTEA2

15 ServiceNow website. 2021. https://www.servicenow.com/company.html

16 Sales Partner Program Data Sheet. 2020. ServiceNow. https://www.servicenow.com/content/dam/servicenow-assets/public/en-us/doc-type/resource-center/data-sheet/ds-sales-partner-program-info-sheet.pdf

17 ServiceNow website. 2021. https://www.servicenow.com/success.html

18 McClelland, Anne. October 2011. Service Provider Resellers Insights. TSIA. https://www.tsia.com/resources/service-provider-resellers-insights

19 Lah, Thomas, and J.B. Wood. 2016. *Technology-as-a-Service Playbook: How to Grow a Profitable Subscription Business*. San Diego, CA: Point B, Inc.

20 NTT Data website. 2021. https://www.nttdata.com/global/en/about-us/ntt-data-history

21 NTT Data website. 2021. https://us.nttdata.com/en/

22 NTT Data website. 2021. https://us.nttdata.com/en/industries/healthcare-and-life-sciences

23 NTT Data website. 2021. https://us.nttdata.com/en/industries/education

24 "Getting Students Back to Campus: Enabled by the Accelerate Smart Platform." 2021. NTT Data. https://us.nttdata.com/en/-/media/assets/infographics/ntt_covid-acceleratesmart_student.pdf

25 NTT Data website. 2021. https://us.nttdata.com/en/digital/digital-with-no-drama

Chapter 9

1 Christensen, Clayton M. 2017 (Reprint). "The Innovator's Dilemma: The Revolutionary Book That Will Change the Way You Do Business." Harper Business.

2 Silberzahn, Philippe. September 16, 2018. "Do You Really Know Why Kodak Failed?" Diateino.https://www.diateino.com/blog/2018/09/16/do-you-really-know-why-kodak-failed/ Accessed February 20, 2022.

3 Trenholm, Richard. May 31, 2021. "History of Digital Cameras: From '70s Prototypes to iPhone and Galaxy's Everyday Wonders: The Digital Camera Has Come a Long Way. CNet." https://www.cnet.com/tech/computing/history-of-digital-cameras-from-70s-prototypes-to-iphone-and-galaxys-everyday-wonders/#:~:text=The%20first%20actual%20digital%20still,invented%20Fairchild%20CCD%20electronic%20sensors Accessed February 20, 2022.

4 Hudson, Andrew. August 29, 2012. "The Rise & Fall of Kodak: A Brief History of The Eastman Kodak Company, 1880 to 2012. PhotoSecrets." https://www.photosecrets.com/the-rise-and-fall-of-kodak Accessed February 20, 2022.

5 These gross margins are industry averages based on TSIA benchmark data.

6 March 15, 2021. "Cloud Stocks: Teradata Trying to Reinvent Itself on the Cloud." One Million by One Million Blog.

https://www.sramanamitra.com/2021/03/15/cloud-stocks-teradata-trying-to-reinvent-itself-on-the-cloud/ Accessed February 20, 2022.

7 Moore, Geoffery. 2015. *Zone to Win: Organizing to Compete in an Age of Disruption*. Brilliance Audio.

8 Paresh, Dave. March 29, 2018. "Microsoft's Windows Head to Leave Company Amid Reorganization." Reuters. https://www.reuters.com/article/us-microsoft-moves/microsofts-windows-head-to-leave-company-amid-reorganization-idUSKBN1H52C1 Accessed February 20, 2022.

9 Adobe: Number of Employees 2006-2021 | ADBE. Macrotrends. https://www.macrotrends.net/stocks/charts/ADBE/adobe/number-of-employees Accessed February 20, 2022.

10 July 13, 2021. "Investors Doubling Down on Autodesk's Digital Twin Platform." TipRanks. https://finance.yahoo.com/news/investors-doubling-down-autodesk-digital-131800067.html Accessed February 20, 2022.

11 Williams, Joe. July 9, 2021. "Autodesk Is Dragging the Industrial World Into the Cloud — and Showing It the Future." Protocol. https://www.protocol.com/enterprise/autodesk-cloud-cad-profile Accessed February 20, 2022.

12 "How Autodesk Leverages the TSIA LAER Model." August 17, 2016. https://www.youtube.com/watch?v=hswP56VnvcM Accessed February 20, 2022.

13 Pacheco, Antonio. July 30, 2020. "Autodesk Responds to Revit Criticism." Archinect. https://archinect.com/news/article/150209385/autodesk-responds-to-revit-criticism Accessed February 20, 2022.

14 "Intuit, Inc. Sheds Its PC Roots and Rises as a Cloud Software Company." April 11, 2016. *The New York Times*. https://www.nytimes.com/2016/04/11/technology/intuit-sheds-its-pc-roots-and-rises-as-a-cloud-software-company.html

15 Dignan. Larry. May 22, 2011. "Intuit Well Along on Transition to Cloud, On-Demand Software." ZDNet.https://www.zdnet.com/article/intuit-well-along-on-transition-to-cloud-on-demand-software/ Accessed February 20, 2022.

16 Brad Smith on Intuit and Giving Back to the Community. "No Turning Back." Apple Podcasts.https://podcasts.apple.com/us/podcast/brad-smith-on-intuit-and-giving-back-to-the-community/id1527309309?i=1000530142111 Accessed February 20, 2022.

17 Siegel, Robert. 2017. *The Brains and Brawn Company: How Leading Organizations Blend the Best of Digital and Physical.* McGraw-Hill Education.

18 Nadim, Emad. November 17, 2016. "Michelin: Tires-as-a-Service." HBS. https://digital.hbs.edu/platform-rctom/submission/michelin-tires-as-a-service/ Accessed February 20, 2022.

19 September 7, 2018. "MICHELIN - Effitrailer - Semi-trailer management solution – EN." YouTube. https://www.youtube.com/watch?v=cXtym0KmTTg Accessed February 20, 2022.

20 Chauhan, Harsh. July 14, 2021. "Buy Palo Alto Networks Stock Before It Lifts Off." The Motley Fool. https://www.fool.com/investing/2021/07/14/buy-palo-alto-networks-stock-before-it-lifts-off/ Accessed February 20, 2022.

21 Palo Alto Networks website. https://www.paloaltonetworks.com/prisma/request-a-prisma-cloud-trial Accessed February 20, 2022.

22 Palo Alto Networks website. https://www.paloaltonetworks.com/cyberpedia/what-is-digital-experience-monitoring Accessed February 20, 2022.

23 Square, Inc. 10-K. December 31, 2020. UNITED STATES SECURITIES AND EXCHANGE COMMISSION.

https://www.sec.gov/ix?doc=/Archives/edgar/data/
1512673/000151267321000008/sq-20201231.htm Accessed
February 20, 2022.

24 Veena Systems website. https://ir.veeva.com/investors/finan-
cials/annual-and-proxy/default.aspx Accessed February 20,
2022.

25 Veeva   website.   https://www.veeva.com/resources/urogen-
streamlines-clinical-and-regulatory-operations/   Accessed
February 20, 2022.

26 For every one of these challenges, TSIA has published research
papers with recommended tactics to address the challenge.

Chapter 10

1 Wood, J.B., Todd Hewlin, and Thomas Lah. 2013. *B4B: How
Technology and Big Data Are Reinventing the Customer-Supplier
Relationship*. San Diego, CA: Point B, Inc.

2 Tzuo, Tien. December 2, 2019. "Satya Swallows the Fish."
https://tientzuo.medium.com/satya-swallows-the-fish-
7aaa5bb31b0a

3 October 23, 2019. "Swallowing the Fish." ESG Customer
Success   website.   https://esgsuccess.com/pillar/swallowing-
the-fish/

4 Burton, Mark, David Burns, and Ron Kermisch. November
22, 2019. "Choosing the Right Pricing Model for Equipment
as a Service." Bain & Company. https://www.bain.com/
insights/choosing-the-right-pricing-model-for-equipment-
as-a-service/

5 Luna, Jennie. December 3, 2018. "Netflix, Prime, Blue
Apron: How Subscription Businesses Are Taking Over."
Fast Company. https://www.fastcompany.com/90272720/
netflix-prime-blue-apron-how-subscription-businesses-
are-taking-over

6　Tobak, Steve. June 14, 2012. "The 10 Worst Corporate Boards in the World." Moneywatch.cbsnews.com. https://www.cbsnews.com/news/the-10-worst-corporate-boards-in-the-world/

7　Lah, Thomas. November 2020. "From Technology as an Asset to Technology as a Service: The Four Phases of Swallowing the Fish." TSIA. https://www.tsia.com/resources/from_technology_as_an_asset_to_technology_as_a_service_the_four_phases_of_swallowing_the_fish

8　Lah, Thomas. June 2018. "Update: Swallowing the Fish." TSIA. https://www.tsia.com/resources/update-swallowing-the-fish

9　Lah, Thomas and Laura Fay. September 2020. "Swallowing Half the Fish: The Impact of Changing License Models without Changing Deployment or Operational Models." https://www.tsia.com/resources/swallowing-half-the-fish

10　Boland, Mike and Don Hofstrand. "The Role of the Board of Directors." Iowa State University. https://www.extension.iastate.edu/agdm/wholefarm/html/c5-71.html

11　Muck, Susan. February 26, 2020. "Want to Join a Corporate Board? Here's How." Harvard Law School Forum on Corporate Governance. https://corpgov.law.harvard.edu/2020/02/26/want-to-join-a-corporate-board-heres-how/

12　April 20, 2020. "New Relic Announces Appointment of Anne DelSanto and David Henshall to Its Board of Directors; Hope Cochran Named Chair of the Board." New Relic Press Release. https://ir.newrelic.com/press-releases/Press-Release-Details/2020/New-Relic-Announces-Appointment-of-Anne-DelSanto-and-David-Henshall-to-Its-Board-of-Directors-Hope-Cochran-Named-Chair-of-the-Board/

13　Wilhelm, Alex and Ron Miller. May 14, 2021. "New Relic's Business Remodel Will Leave New CEO with Work to Do." TechCrunch. https://techcrunch.com/2021/05/14/new-relics-business-remodel-will-leave-new-ceo-with-work-to-do/

14 New Relic Investor Letter, Third Quarter Fiscal Year 2021.

15 Barton, Dominic and Mark Wiseman. January-February 2015. "Where Boards Fall Short." *Harvard Business Review.* https://hbr.org/2015/01/where-boards-fall-short

Appendix A

1 Wood, J.B. 2009. *Complexity Avalanche: Overcoming the Threat to Technology Adoption.* San Diego, CA: Point B, Inc.

2 Lah, Thomas. June 2018. "Emerging Economic Engines of Technology Providers." TSIA.

3 Lah, Thomas. March 2021. "Update: The XaaS Transformation." TSIA.

4 Hewlett Packard Enterprise website: https://www.hpe.com/us/en/greenlake.html Accessed January 19, 2022.

5 "The Growing 'XaaS' Service Economy Trend." April 4, 2018. Diebold Nixdorf. https://www.dieboldnixdorf.com/en-us/banking/insights/blog/growing-xaas-service-economy-trend Accessed January 19, 2022.

6 Dell Technologies website: https://www.delltechnologies.com/en-us/cloud/platforms/data-center-as-a-service.htm Accessed January 19, 2022.

Appendix B

1 McKenzie, Cameron. October 2021. "Open API (Public API)." TechTarget. https://searchapparchitecture.techtarget.com/definition/open-API-public-API Accessed January 25, 2022.

2 Price, Nicholas. December 16, 2020. "What Is an Open API & Why Have One?" Air Call. https://aircall.io/blog/tech/what-open-api-why-have-one/ Accessed January 25, 2022.

3 Wikipedia website. https://en.wikipedia.org/wiki/Force_
multiplication Accessed January 25, 2022.

4 Liferay website. https://www.liferay.com/solutions/integration-
platforms Accessed January 25, 2022.

Index